# FORTUNES OF FEMINISM

Martial Rose Library
Tel: 01962 827306

D1494365

To be returned on or before the day marked above, subject to recall.

# FORTUNES OF FEMINISM:
## From State-Managed Capitalism to Neoliberal Crisis

Nancy Fraser

## VERSO
London • New York

First published by Verso 2013
© Nancy Fraser 2013

1 3 5 7 9 10 8 6 4 2

**Verso**
UK: 6 Meard Street, London W1F 0EG
US: 20 Jay Street, Suite 1010, Brooklyn, NY 11201
www.versobooks.com

Verso is the imprint of New Left Books

ISBN-13: 978-1-84467-984-3 (PBK)
ISBN-13: 978-1-84467-985-0 (HBK)

**British Library Cataloguing in Publication Data**
A catalogue record for this book is available from the British Library

**Library of Congress Cataloging-in-Publication Data**

Fraser, Nancy.
Fortunes of feminism : from state-managed capitalism
to neoliberal crisis and beyond / Nancy Fraser. — 1st
Edition.
pages cm
Includes bibliographical references and index.
ISBN 978-1-84467-984-3 (pbk. : alk. paper) — ISBN
978-1-84467-985-0 (hbk. : alk. paper)
1. Feminist theory. 2. Distributive justice. 3. Culture
conflict. I. Title.
HQ1190.F73 2013
305.4201—dc23
2012050039

Typeset in Bembo by Hewer Text UK Ltd, Edinburgh
Printed in the US by Maple Vail

For

Natasha Zaretsky
Kathleen Engst
Gina Engst

Three paths to a feminist future

Grateful recognition of institutional support and intellectual inspiration appears in the initial starred note of each chapter. Here I thank Tomer Zeigerman and Mine Yildirim for expert assistance in preparing the manuscript, and I acknowledge support from the New School for Social Research, the Stellenbosch Institute for Advanced Studies, the Einstein Foundation of the City of Berlin, and the Centre for Advanced Studies "Justitia Amplificata."

I am grateful as well for permission to reprint the following chapters:

Chapter 1 was originally published in *New German Critique* 35, 1985. An earlier version of Chapter 2 appeared as "Talking About Needs: Interpretive Contests as Political Conflicts in Welfare-State Societies," in *Ethics* 99:2, 1989. The version reprinted here appeared in Nancy Fraser, *Justice Interruptus: Critical Reflections on the "Postsocialist" Condition*, New York: Routledge, 1997. Chapter 3 was originally published in *Signs: Journal of Women in Culture and Society* 19:2, 1994. An earlier version of Chapter 4 appeared in *Political Theory* 22:4, 1994. The version reprinted here was subsequently published in Nancy Fraser, *Justice Interruptus*. An Earlier version of Chapter 5 appeared in *Boundary 2* 17:2, 1990. The version reprinted here was subsequently published in Nancy Fraser *Justice Interruptus*. Chapter 6 first appeared in French translation in *Actuel Marx* 30, 2001. Chapter 7 was originally published in *New Left Review*, I/228, 1998. Chapter 8 was originally published in *New Left Review* 36, 2005. Chapter 9 was originally published in *New Left Review* 56, 2009. Chapter 10 was originally published in French translation in *Revue de l'OFCE* 114, 2010.

# Contents

# Prologue to a Drama in Three Acts

From today's vantage point, the history of second-wave feminism appears as a drama in three acts. Emerging from the ferment surrounding the New Left, the "movement for women's liberation" began life as an insurrectionary force, which challenged male domination in state-organized capitalist societies of the postwar era. In Act One, feminists joined with other currents of radicalism to explode a social-democratic imaginary that had occulted gender injustice and technicized politics. Insisting that "the personal is political," this movement exposed capitalism's deep androcentrism and sought to transform society root and branch. Later, however, as utopian energies began to decline, second-wave feminism was drawn into the orbit of identity politics. In Act Two, its transformative impulses were channeled into a new political imaginary that foregrounded "difference." Turning "from redistribution to recognition," the movement shifted its attention to cultural politics, just as a rising neoliberalism declared war on social equality. More recently, however, as neoliberalism has entered its current crisis, the urge to reinvent feminist radicalism may be reviving. In an Act Three that is still unfolding, we *could* see a reinvigorated feminism join other emancipatory forces aiming to subject runaway markets to democratic control. In that case, the movement would retrieve its insurrectionary spirit, while deepening its signature insights: its structural critique of capitalism's androcentrism, its systemic analysis of male domination, and its gender-sensitive revisions of democracy and justice.

Historians will eventually explain how neoliberalizing forces succeeded, for a time at least, in defusing the more radical currents of second-wave feminism—and how (one hopes) a new insurrectionary upsurge managed to reanimate them. For critical theorists, however, there remains a prior task: to analyze alternative grammars of the feminist imaginary in order to assess their emancipatory potential. Here the goal is to ascertain which understandings of androcentrism and male domination, which interpretations of gender justice and sexual democracy, which conceptions of equality and difference are likely to be most fruitful for future engagements. Above all, which modes of feminist theorizing should be incorporated into the new political imaginaries now being invented by new generations for Act Three?

Though not written with this aim in mind, the essays collected here can nevertheless be read today as preliminary attempts at such a reckoning. Composed over the past twenty-five-plus years as interventions in theoretical debates, they document major shifts in the feminist imaginary since the 1970s. For this volume, I have grouped them in three parts, which correspond to the three acts of the drama I have just sketched. In Part I, I have included pieces that seek to marry a feminist sensibility to a New Left critique of the welfare state. Targeting not only the latter's androcentrism, but also its bureaucratic organization and near-exclusive focus on distribution, these essays situate second-wave feminism in a broader field of democratizing, anti-capitalist struggles. Reflecting the historical shift from mainstream social democracy to the new social movements, they defend the latter's expanded understanding of politics, even as they also criticize some influential ways of theorizing it. Part II charts subsequent alterations in the feminist imaginary. Noting the broader cultural shift from the politics of equality to the politics of identity, these chapters diagnose dilemmas facing feminist movements in a period of ascendant neoliberalism. Troubled by the relative neglect of political economy at the fin de siècle, they criticize the eclipse of "struggles for redistribution" by "struggles for recognition," even as they also defend a non-identitarian version of the latter. Part III contemplates prospects for a revival of feminist radicalism in a time of neoliberal crisis. Advocating a "post-Westphalian" turn, the essays comprising this section situate struggles for women's emancipation in relation to two other sets of social forces: those bent on extending the sway of markets, on the one hand, and those seeking to "defend society" from them, on the other. Diagnosing a "dangerous liaison" between feminism and marketization, these essays urge feminists to break that unholy alliance and forge a principled new one, between "emancipation" and "social protection."

In general, then, the concerns shaping the volume's organization are both systematic and historical. A record of one theorist's ongoing efforts to track the movement's trajectory, the book assesses feminism's current prospects and future possibilities. Let me elaborate.

*       *       *

When second-wave feminism first erupted on the world stage, the advanced capitalist states of Western Europe and North America were still enjoying the unprecedented wave of prosperity that followed

World War II. Utilizing new tools of Keynesian economic steering, they had apparently learned to counteract business downturns and to guide national economic development so as to secure near full employment for men. Incorporating once unruly labor movements, the advanced capitalist countries had built more or less extensive welfare states and institutionalized national cross-class solidarity. To be sure, this historic class compromise rested on a series of gender and racial-ethnic exclusions, not to mention external neocolonial exploitation. But those potential fault lines tended to remain latent in a social-democratic imaginary that foregrounded class redistribution. The result was a prosperous North Atlantic belt of mass-consumption societies, which had apparently tamed social conflict.

In the 1960s, however, the relative calm of this "Golden Age of capitalism" was suddenly shattered.[1] In an extraordinary international explosion, radical youth took to the streets—at first to oppose the Vietnam War and racial segregation in the US. Soon they began to question core features of capitalist modernity that social democracy had heretofore naturalized: materialism, consumerism, and "the achievement ethic"; bureaucracy, corporate culture, and "social control"; sexual repression, sexism, and heteronormativity. Breaking through the normalized political routines of the previous era, new social actors formed new social movements, with second-wave feminism among the most visionary.

Along with their comrades in other movements, the feminists of this era recast the radical imaginary. Transgressing a political culture that had privileged actors who cast themselves as nationally bounded and politically tamed classes, they challenged the gender exclusions of social democracy. Problematizing welfare paternalism and the bourgeois family, they exposed the deep androcentrism of capitalist society. Politicizing "the personal," they expanded the boundaries of contestation beyond socioeconomic distribution—to include housework, sexuality, and reproduction.

In fact, the initial wave of postwar feminism had an ambivalent relationship to social democracy. On the one hand, much of the early second wave rejected the latter's *étatism* and its tendency to marginalize class and social injustices other than "maldistribution." On the other hand, many feminists presupposed key features of the socialist imaginary as a basis for more radical designs. Taking for granted the welfare state's solidaristic ethos and prosperity-securing steering capacities, they too were committed to taming markets and promoting equality. Acting from a critique that was at once radical and immanent, early second-wave feminists sought less to dismantle the

---

1  The phrase "Golden Age of capitalism" comes from Eric Hobsbawm, *The Age of Extremes: The Short Twentieth Century, 1914–1991*, New York: Vintage, 1996.

welfare state than to transform it into a force that could help to over-come male domination.

By the 1980s, however, history seemed to have bypassed that political project. A decade of conservative rule in much of Western Europe and North America, capped by the fall of Communism in the East, miracu-lously breathed new life into free-market ideologies previously given up for dead. Rescued from the historical dustbin, "neoliberalism" author-ized a sustained assault on the very idea of egalitarian redistribution. The effect, amplified by accelerating globalization, was to cast doubt on the legitimacy and viability of the use of public power to tame market forces. With social democracy on the defensive, efforts to broaden and deepen its promise naturally fell by the wayside. Feminist movements that had earlier taken the welfare state as their point of departure, seeking to extend its egalitarian ethos from class to gender, now found the ground cut out from under their feet. No longer able to assume a social-democratic base-line for radicalization, they gravitated to newer grammars of political claims-making, more attuned to the "post-socialist" zeitgeist.

Enter the politics of recognition. If the initial thrust of postwar femi-nism was to "engender" the socialist imaginary, the later tendency was to redefine gender justice as a project aimed at "recognizing difference." "Recognition," accordingly, became the chief grammar of feminist claims-making at the fin de siècle. A venerable category of Hegelian philosophy, resuscitated by political theorists, this notion captured the distinctive character of "post-socialist" struggles, which often took the form of identity politics, aimed more at valorizing cultural difference than at promoting economic equality. Whether the question was care work, sexual violence, or gender disparities in political representation, feminists increasingly resorted to the grammar of recognition to press their claims. Unable to transform the deep gender structures of the capi-talist economy, they preferred to target harms rooted in androcentric patterns of cultural value or status hierarchies. The result was a major shift in the feminist imaginary: whereas the previous generation had sought to remake political economy, this one focused more on transforming culture.

The results were decidedly mixed. On the one hand, the new femi-nist struggles for recognition continued the earlier project of expanding the political agenda beyond the confines of class redistribution; in prin-ciple they served to broaden, and to radicalize, the concept of justice. On the other hand, however, the figure of the struggle for recognition so thoroughly captured the feminist imagination that it served more to displace than to deepen the socialist imaginary. The effect was to subor-dinate social struggles to cultural struggles, the politics of redistribution to the politics of recognition. That was not, to be sure, the original intention. It was assumed, rather, by proponents of the cultural turn that a feminist politics of identity and difference would synergize with struggles for gender equality. But that assumption fell prey to the larger zeitgeist. In the fin de siècle context, the turn to recognition dovetailed all too neatly with a rising neoliberalism that wanted nothing more than to repress all memory of social egalitarianism. The result was a tragic historical irony. Instead of arriving at a broader, richer paradigm that could encompass both redistribution and recognition, feminists effectively traded one truncated paradigm for another—a truncated economism for a truncated culturalism.

Today, however, perspectives centered on recognition alone lack all credibility. In the context of escalating capitalist crisis, the critique of political economy is regaining its central place in theory and practice. No serious social movement, least of all feminism, can ignore the evisceration of democracy and the assault on social reproduction now being waged by finance capital. Under these conditions, a feminist theory worth its salt must revive the "economic" concerns of Act One—without, however, neglecting the "cultural" insights of Act Two. But that is not all. It must integrate these not only with one another but also with a new set of "political" concerns made salient by globalization: How might emancipatory struggles serve to secure democratic legitimacy and to expand and equalize political influence in a time when the powers that govern our lives increasingly overrun the borders of territorial states? How might feminist movements foster equal participation transnationally, across entrenched power asymmetries and divergent worldviews? Struggling simultaneously on three fronts—call them redistribution, recognition, and representation—the feminism of Act Three must join with other anti-capitalist forces, even while exposing their continued failure to absorb the insights of decades of feminist activism.

Today's feminism must, moreover, be sensitive to the historical context in which we operate. Situating ourselves vis-à-vis the broader constellation of political forces, we need to keep our distance both from market-besotted neoliberals and from those who seek to "defend society" (replete with hierarchy and exclusion) from the market. Charting a third path between that Scylla and Charybdis, a feminism worthy of Act Three must join other emancipatory movements in integrating our fundamental interest in non-domination with protectionists' legitimate concerns for social security, without neglecting the importance of negative liberty, which is usually associated with liberalism.

Such, at least, is the reading of recent history that emerges from the essays collected here. The chapters comprising Part I document the shift from postwar social democracy to early second-wave feminism, seen as a current of New Left radicalism. Exuding the heady spirit of the 1960s and '70s, these essays reflect the successes of the new social movements in breaking through the confines of welfare-state politics as usual. Expanding the political meant exposing neglected axes of domination other than class—above all, but not only, gender. Equally important, it meant exposing illegitimate power beyond the usual precincts of the state and economy—in sexuality and subjectivity, in domesticity and social services, in academia and commodified leisure, in the social practices of everyday life.

No one better captured these "post-Marxian" impulses than Jürgen Habermas, the subject of Chapter 1. A radical critic of postwar social democracy, Habermas sought to scrutinize aspects of the Keynesian welfare state that escaped standard liberal analyses. Eschewing the "labor monism" of his Frankfurt School predecessors, while seeking to continue the critique of reification by other means, he proposed a "communications-theoretic" reconstruction of Critical Theory. The upshot was a new diagnosis of late-capitalist ills: the "internal colonization of the lifeworld by systems." Endemic to postwar social democracy, colonization occurred when "systems rationality" was illegitimately extended beyond its proper purview (the market economy and state administration) to the "core domains of the lifeworld" (the family and political public sphere). In that case, as administrative coordination replaced communicative interaction in domains that required the latter, the welfare state spawned "social pathologies." Equally important, this development sparked new forms of social conflict, centered less on distribution than on the "grammar of forms of life."[2] Resonating with New Left antipathy to bureaucratic paternalism, Habermas's diagnosis validated the "post-materialist" concerns of the new social movements. Exceeding liberal criticisms of distributive injustice, it promised to broaden our sense of what could be subject to political challenge—and emancipatory change.

Nevertheless, as I argue in "What's Critical About Critical Theory?" (1985), Habermas failed to actualize the full radical potential of his own critique. Substantializing analytical distinctions between public and private, symbolic reproduction and material reproduction, system integration and social integration, he missed their gender subtext and naturalized androcentic features of the social order. Lacking the resources to adequately conceptualize male domination, he ended up suggesting that "juridification" in familial matters led necessarily to colonization—hence that feminist struggles to expand women's and children's rights were problematic. The effect was to jeopardize the analytical insights and practical gains of second-wave feminism.

In general, then, this volume's first chapter develops a critique of an

---

2　Jürgen Habermas, *The Theory of Communicative Action*, esp. Chapter VIII, "Marx and the Thesis of Internal Colonization," in Volume Two: *Lifeworld and System: A Critique of Functionalist Reason*, trans. Thomas McCarthy, Boston: Beacon Press, 1989.

important left-wing critic of social democracy. Chapter 2, in contrast, marks a shift to constructive feminist theorizing. Aiming to put to work the lessons of the previous chapter, I sketch a gender-sensitive critique of the structural dynamics and conflict tendencies of late-capitalist societies. "Struggle over Needs" (1989) reconceptualizes the welfare state by resituating distribution within discourse. Building on Habermas's insights, it employs a version of the linguistic turn to underwrite the expanded understanding of politics associated with second-wave feminism. The key move here is a shift from the usual social-democratic focus on conflicts over need satisfaction to a new, democratic-feminist focus on the "politics of need interpretation." The effect is to replace the distributive paradigm, which posits a monological objectivism of basic needs, with a gender-sensitive communicative paradigm, which construes the interpretation of needs as a political stake. This approach differs from Habermas's in a crucial respect. Instead of naturalizing hegemonic notions of public and private, I treat those categories, too, as discursively constructed, gender- and power-saturated objects of political struggle; and I link the politicization of needs to feminist struggles over where and how to draw the boundaries between "the political," "the economic," and "the domestic." The aim is to repoliticize a range of gender issues that Habermas unwittingly took off the table.

"Struggle over Needs" also borrows from, and revises, another great New Left–inspired critic of the democratic welfare state: Michel Foucault. Like Foucault, I maintain that needs politics is implicated in the constitution of subject positions, on the one hand, and of new bodies of disciplinary expertise, on the other. But unlike him, I do not assume that welfare professionals monopolize the interpretation of needs. Rather, situating "expert discourses" alongside both the "oppositional discourses" of democratizing movements and the "reprivatization discourses" of neoconservatives, I map conflicts among these three types of "needs-talk." Thus, where Foucault assumed a single, disciplinary logic, my approach discerns a plurality of competing logics—including some with emancipatory potential, capable of challenging male domination. Drawing not only on empirical insights but also on normative distinctions, it aims to guide a feminist activism that would transform social reality.

If "Struggle over Needs" maps the contours of welfare-state discourse in the 1980s, the next chapter examines a term that became central in the 1990s. Coauthored with the feminist historian Linda Gordon, "A Genealogy of 'Dependency'" (1994) reads the changing vicissitudes of that "keyword of the welfare state" as a barometer of shifting political winds. Written at the height of the "welfare reform" frenzy in the US, when attacks on "welfare dependency" dominated policy debates, this essay charts the process by which that characteristic neoliberal preoccupation came to supplant the long-standing social-democratic focus on combating poverty.

"A Genealogy of 'Dependency'" excavates buried layers of discursive history that continue to weigh on the present. Mapping changing configurations of political economy and gender dynamics, this chapter analyzes two epochal historical shifts in the meanings of "dependency": first, the shift from a preindustrial patriarchal usage, in which "dependency" was a non-stigmatized majority condition, to a modern industrial male-supremacist usage, which constructed a specifically feminine and highly stigmatized sense of "dependency"; and second, the subsequent shift to a postindustrial usage, in which growing numbers of relatively prosperous women claim the same kind of "independence" that men do, while a more stigmatized but still feminized sense of "dependency" attaches to "deviant" groups who are considered "superfluous." Along the way, Gordon and I demonstrate that racializing practices play a major role in historical reconstructions of "dependency," as do changes in the organization and meaning of labor. Questioning current assumptions about the meaning and desirability of "independence," we conclude by sketching a "transvaluative" feminist critique aimed at overcoming the dependence/independence dichotomy.

If the dependency essay provides a feminist critique of postwar welfare states, the following chapter seeks to envision a feminist alternative. The key, I claim in "After the Family Wage" (1994), is to modernize the obsolete underpinnings of current arrangements—especially the presupposition of long-lasting, male-headed nuclear families, in which well-paid, securely employed husbands support non-employed or low-earning wives. This assumption, which descends from industrial capitalism and still undergirds social policy, is wildly askew of postindustrial realities: the coexistence of diverse family forms, increased divorce and non-marriage, widespread female participation in waged work, and more precarious employment for all. It must give way, in the welfare states of the future, to arrangements that can institutionalize gender justice.

What, accordingly, should a postindustrial welfare state look like? "After the Family Wage" evaluates two alternative scenarios, each of which qualifies as feminist. In the first, the age of the family wage would give way to the age of the "Universal Breadwinner." Presupposed by liberals and "equality feminists," this approach would guarantee social security chiefly by facilitating women's wage-earning—above all, by reforming labor markets and providing employment-enabling services such as day care and elder care. In a second vision of postindustrial society, the era of the family wage would give way to the era of "Caregiver Parity." Favored by conservatives and "difference feminists," this approach would support informal carework in families—especially through caregiver allowances. These approaches assume divergent conceptions of gender justice: whereas the first aims to conform women's lives to the way men's lives are supposed to be now, the second would elevate caregiving to parity with breadwinning in order to "make difference costless." Yet neither approach, I argue here, is wholly satisfactory. Whereas the Universal Breadwinner model penalizes women for not being like men, the Caregiver Parity model relegates them to an inferior "mommy track." I conclude, accordingly, that feminists should develop a third model— "Universal Caregiver"—which would induce men to become more like women are now: people who combine employment with responsibilities for primary caregiving. Treating women's current life patterns as the norm, this model would aim to overcome the separation of breadwinning and carework. Avoiding both the workerism of Universal Breadwinner and the domestic privatism of Caregiver Parity, it aims to provide gender justice and security for all.

In general, then, the chapters comprising Part I advance a radical critique of the welfare state from a feminist perspective. Exuding an optimistic sense of expansive possibility, they assume that feminist movements could help to remake the world, dissolving male-supremacist structures and overturning gender hierarchies. Simultaneously presupposing and radicalizing the socialist imaginary, they validate the efforts of second-wave feminists to expand the political agenda beyond the confines of social democracy. Repudiating welfare paternalism, they shift the focus of critical scrutiny from class distribution to gender injustice broadly conceived. Whether critical or constructive, these chapters seek to render visible, and criticizable, the entire panoply of structures and practices that prevent women from participating on a par with men in social life.

Part II, in contrast, evinces a more sober mood. Written during a period of waning left-wing energies, the chapters included here map the shift from early second-wave feminism to identity politics. Interrogating various currents of feminist theorizing, they document the process by which the cultural turn seemed to swallow up political economy, even as it should have enriched it. In addition, these essays track the growing centrality of claims for recognition within feminist activism. Situating those claims in historical context, they probe the fateful coincidence of the rise of identity politics with the revival of free-market fundamentalism; and they analyze the dilemmas feminists faced as a result. More generally, Part II diagnoses the shrinking of emancipatory vision at the fin de siècle. Seeking to dispel the mystique of cultural feminism, these chapters aim to retrieve the best insights of socialist-feminism and to combine them with a non-identitarian version of the politics of recognition. Only such an approach, I maintain, can meet the intellectual and political challenges facing feminist movements in a period of neoliberal hegemony.

"Against Symbolicism" (1990) scrutinizes one influential current of theorizing that unwittingly helped to divert the feminist imagination into culturalist channels. On its face, of course, nothing could be more opposed to identity politics than Lacanian psychoanalysis, which associates the wish for a stable identity with a devalorized "imaginary register." Nevertheless, as I argue here, feminist efforts to appropriate that theoretical paradigm inadvertently undermined their own professed anti-essentialism by failing to challenge some basic assumptions of Lacanian thought. Moreover, and equally unfortunate, by slighting political economy and avoiding institutional analysis, they ended up colluding with cultural feminists in making language and subjectivity the privileged foci of feminist critique.

"Against Symbolicism" discloses the self-defeating character of Lacanian feminism. Building on my earlier efforts to theorize the discursive dimension of women's subordination, this chapter assesses the relative merits of two ideal-typical approaches to signification: a structuralist approach, which analyzes symbolic systems or codes, and a pragmatics approach, which studies speech as a social practice. If one's goal is to analyze the workings of gender domination in capitalist societies and to clarify the prospects for overcoming it, then the pragmatics approach has more to offer.

"Against Symbolicism" elaborates this claim via critical discussions of Jacques Lacan (as read by feminists) and Julia Kristeva. Although both thinkers are widely viewed as poststructuralists, I contend that both continue the structuralist legacy in important respects. Thus, feminist efforts to appropriate Lacan have foundered on what I call "symbolicism": the homogenizing reification of diverse signifying practices into a monolithic, all-pervasive, and all-determining symbolic order. In Kristeva's case, this problem is complicated but not overcome by the incorporation of an anti-structuralist, "semiotic" moment, intended to historicize "the symbolic." The effect is to establish an unending oscillation between two equally unsatisfactory alternatives: in one moment, Kristeva naturalizes a reified maternal identity; in another, she nullifies women's identities altogether.

The feminist quarrel over essentialism is broached more directly in Chapter 6. Diagnosing the shriveling of the feminist imagination, "Feminist Politics in the Age of Recognition" (2001) charts the progressive uncoupling of recognition from redistribution in feminist theorizing and feminist politics. Troubled by the prevalence of one-sided, culturalist feminisms, this essay proposes to marry the best insights of the cultural turn with the nearly forgotten but still indispensable insights of socialist-feminism. Rejecting sectarian constructions that cast those perspectives as mutually incompatible, I analyze sexism as a two-dimensional mode of subordination, rooted simultaneously in the political economy and status order of capitalist society. Overcoming gender subordination, I argue, requires combining a feminist politics of recognition with a feminist politics of redistribution.

Developing such a politics is not easy, however, as gender cuts across other axes of subordination, and claims for gender justice can conflict with other presumptively legitimate claims, such as claims for minority cultural recognition. It follows that feminists should eschew "single-variable" perspectives, which focus on gender alone, in favor of approaches that can handle hard cases, where injustices intersect and claims collide. To adjudicate such cases, such as the "headscarf affair" in France, I introduce two conceptual innovations. First, at the normative-philosophical level, I introduce the view of justice as *parity of participation*. Designed to identify two different kinds of obstacles (economic and cultural) that prevent some people from participating as peers in social interaction, the principle of participatory parity overarches both dimensions of (in)justice—(mal)distribution *and* (mis)recognition—and allows us to bring them together in a common framework. Second, at the social-theoretical level, I propose to replace the standard "identity" model of recognition with a *status model*. Aimed at avoiding the former's tendency to reify identity and displace struggles for redistribution, the status model posits that what deserves recognition is not group-specific identities or cultural contents, but the equal standing of partners in interaction. Applying these two concepts, the chapter offers a novel reading of the headscarf affair and a sympathetic critique of French feminist understandings of *parité*. More fundamentally, it proposes a way of repositioning feminist politics in the "age of recognition."

Chapter 7 defends this approach against the objections of Judith Butler. In her 1997 essay "Merely Cultural," Butler sought to defend "the cultural Left" against criticisms by me and by unnamed persons she called "neoconservative Marxists."[3] Insisting that heteronormativity is just as fundamental to capitalism as class exploitation, she rejected theorizations that treat sexuality as superstructural. From there, Butler might have gone on to endorse a model that construes "distribution" and "recognition" as two co-fundamental dimensions of capitalist society, corresponding respectively to class and status, and that analyzes heterosexism as a deep-seated form of misrecognition or status subordination. Instead, however, she rejected the very distinction between cultural and economic injustices as a tactic aimed at trivializing heterosexism. Claiming to deconstruct my distinction between maldistribution and

---

3    Judith Butler, "Merely Cultural," *Social Text* 52/53, 1997, 265–77.

misrecognition, she went on to argue that heterosexism is so essential to capitalism that LGBT struggles threaten the latter's existence.

"Heterosexism, Misrecognition, and Capitalism" (1997) rebuts Butler's arguments. Defending my quasi-Weberian dualism of status and class, I maintain that heterosexism can be every bit as serious and material as other harms and yet still be an injustice of misrecognition, grounded in the status order of society as opposed to the political economy. Tracing the economic/cultural differentiation to the rise of capitalism, I contend that, far from deconstructing that distinction, feminist theorists should rather historicize it. Mapping recent shifts in the institutionalization of economy and culture, I conclude that late-capitalist forms of sexual regulation are only indirectly tied to mechanisms for the accumulation of surplus value. Hence, struggles against heterosexist misrecognition do not automatically threaten capitalism, but must be linked to other (anti-capitalist) struggles. The resulting approach discloses gaps in the current order that open space for emancipatory practice. Unlike Butler's framework, mine makes visible the non-isomorphisms of status and class, the multiple contra-dictory interpellations of social subjects, and the many complex moral imperatives that motivate struggles for social justice in the present era.

In general, then, Part II assesses the state of the feminist imagination in a time of rising neoliberalism. Analyzing the shift from early second-wave feminism, which sought to engender the socialist imaginary, to identity politics, which jettisoned the latter in favor of a politics centered on recognition, these essays provide a sober accounting of the losses and gains. Leery of identity politics in a period of neoliberal hegemony, they aim to revive the project of egalitarian gender redistribution in combination with a de-reified politics of recognition. The goal through-out is to develop new conceptual and practical strategies for combating gender injustices of economy and culture simultaneously. Only a perspective that encompasses both of those dimensions of gender in-justice can adequately inform feminist theorizing in capitalist society.

Part III shifts the scene to the present. Today, when neoliberalism is everywhere in crisis, reductive culturalism is widely discredited, and feminist interest in political economy is fast reviving. What is needed now, accordingly, is a gender-sensitive framework that can grasp the fundamental character of the crisis—as well as the prospects for an emancipatory resolution. One imperative is to conceptualize the multilayered nature of the current crisis, which encompasses simulta-neous destabilizations of finance, ecology, and social reproduction. Another is to map the grammar of the social struggles that are respond-ing to the crisis and reshaping the political terrain on which feminists operate. Crucial to both enterprises is the new salience of transnationalizing forces, which are problematizing "the Westphalian frame": that is, the previously unquestioned idea that the bounded territorial state is the appropriate unit for reflecting on, and struggling for, justice. As that doxa recedes in the face of intensified transnational power, feminist struggles are transnationalizing too. Thus, many of the assumptions that undergirded earlier feminist projects are being called into question—revealed to be indefensible expressions of what Ulrich Beck calls "methodological nationalism."[4]

The chapters comprising Part III aim to develop models of feminist theorizing that can clarify this situation. "Reframing Justice in a Global World" (2005) observes that so-called "globalization" is changing the grammar of political claims-making. Contests that used to focus chiefly on the question of *what* is owed as a matter of justice to members of political communities now turn quickly into disputes about *who* should count as a member and *which* is the relevant community. Not only the substance of justice but also the *frame* is in dispute. The result is a major challenge to received understandings, which fail to ponder *who should count* in matters of justice. To meet the challenge, I argue, the theory of justice must become three-dimensional, incorporating the political dimension of *representation* alongside the economic dimension of distribution and the cultural dimension of recognition.

"Reframing Justice in a Global World" constitutes a major revision of the model developed in the previous chapters. Adapting Weber's triad of class, status, and party, it identifies not two but three analytically distinct kinds of obstacles to parity of participation in capitalist societies. Whereas distribution foregrounds impediments rooted in political economy, and recognition discloses obstacles grounded in the status order, representation conceptualizes barriers to participatory parity that are entrenched in the political constitution of society. At issue here are the procedures for staging and resolving conflicts over injustice: How are claims for redistribution and recognition to be adjudicated? And who belongs to the circle of those who are entitled to raise them?

Directed at clarifying struggles over globalization, this third, "political" dimension of justice operates on two different levels. On the one hand, I theorize "ordinary-political injustices," which arise internally, *within* a bounded political community, when skewed decision rules entrench disparities of political voice among fellow citizens. Feminist struggles for gender quotas on electoral lists are a response to this sort of ordinary-political misrepresentation. But that's not all. Equally important, if less familiar, are "meta-political injustices," which arise when the division of political space *into* bounded polities miscasts what are actually

---

4   Ulrich Beck, "Toward a New Critical Theory with a Cosmopolitan Intent," *Constellations: An International Journal of Critical and Democratic Theory* 10:4, 2003, 453–68.

transnational injustices as national matters. In this case, affected non-citizens are wrongly excluded from consideration—as, for example, when the claims of the global poor are shunted into the domestic polit-ical arenas of weak or failed states and diverted from the offshore causes of their dispossession. Naming this second, meta-political injustice "misframing," I argue for a post-Westphalian theory of democratic justice which problematizes unjust frames. The result is a major revision of my theory, aimed at addressing transborder inequities in a globalizing world.

The following chapter applies this revised, three-dimensional frame-work to the historical trajectory of second-wave feminism. Effectively recapitulating the overall argument of this book, "Feminism, Capital-ism, and the Cunning of History" (2009) situates the movement's unfolding in relation to three different moments in the history of capi-talism. First, I locate the movement's beginnings in the context of "state-organized capitalism." Here I chart the emergence of second-wave feminism from out of the anti-imperialist New Left as a radical challenge to the pervasive androcentrism of state-led capitalist societies in the postwar era. And I identify the movement's fundamental eman-cipatory promise with its expanded sense of injustice and its structural critique of capitalist society. Second, I consider the process of femi-nism's evolution in the dramatically changed social context of rising neoliberalism. I explore not only the movement's extraordinary successes but also the disturbing convergence of some of its ideals with the demands of an emerging new form of capitalism—post-fordist, "disor-ganized," transnational. And I suggest that second-wave feminism has unwittingly supplied a key ingredient of what Luc Boltanski and Eve Chiapello call "the new spirit of capitalism."[5] Finally, I contemplate prospects for reorienting feminism in the present context of capitalist crisis, which could mark the beginnings of a shift to a new, post-neolib-eral form of social organization. I examine the prospects for reactivating feminism's emancipatory promise in a world that has been rocked by financial crisis and the surrounding political fallout.

"Feminism, Capitalism, and the Cunning of History" constitutes a provocation of sorts. Contending that feminism has entered a danger-ous liaison with neoliberalism, this chapter identifies four major historical ironies. First, the feminist critique of social-democratic economism, undeniably emancipatory in the era of state-organized capitalism, has assumed a more sinister valence in the subsequent period, as it dovetailed with neoliberalism's interest in diverting polit-ical-economic struggles into culturalist channels. Second, the feminist critique of the "family wage," once the centerpiece of a radical

---

5   Luc Boltanski and Eve Chiapello, *The New Spirit of Capitalism*, trans. Geoffrey Elliott, London: Verso, 2005.

analysis of capitalism's androcentrism, increasingly serves today to legitimate a new mode of capital accumulation, heavily dependent on women's waged labor, as idealized in the "two-earner family." Third, the feminist critique of welfare-state paternalism has converged unwittingly with neoliberalism's critique of the nanny state, and with its increasingly cynical embrace of micro-credit and NGOs. Finally, efforts to expand the scope of gender justice beyond the nation-state are increasingly resignified to cohere with neoliberalism's global governance needs, as "femocrats" have entered the policy apparatuses of the United Nations, the European Union, and the "international community." In every case, an idea that served emancipatory ends in one context became ambiguous, if not worse, in another.

Where does this argument leave feminism today? In the final chapter, I propose a framework aimed at disrupting our dangerous liaison with neoliberalism and liberating our radical energies. Revisiting a landmark study of capitalist crisis, "Between Marketization and Social Protection" (2010) offers a feminist reading of Karl Polanyi's 1944 classic *The Great Transformation*.[6] Eschewing economism, this book analyzed a previous crisis of capitalism as a crisis of social reproduction, as earlier efforts to create a "free market society" undermined the shared understandings and solidary relations that underpin social life. In Polanyi's view, such efforts proved so destructive of livelihoods, communities, and habitats as to trigger a century-long struggle between free-marketeers and proponents of "social protection," who sought to defend "society" from the ravages of the market. The end result of this struggle, which he called a "double movement," was fascism and World War II.

Without question, Polanyi's diagnosis is relevant today. Our crisis, too, can be fruitfully analyzed as a "great transformation" in which a new round of efforts to free markets from political regulation is threatening social reproduction and sparking a new wave of protectionist protest. Nevertheless, I argue here, Polanyi's framework harbors a major blindspot. Focused single-mindedly on harms emanating from marketization, his account overlooks harms originating elsewhere, in the surrounding "society." As a result, it neglects the fact that social protections are often vehicles of domination, aimed at entrenching hierarchies and at excluding "outsiders." Preoccupied overwhelmingly with struggles over marketization, Polanyi occults struggles over injustices rooted in "society" and encoded in social protections.

"Between Marketization and Social Protection" aims to correct this blindspot. Seeking to develop a broader critique, I propose to transform Polanyi's double movement into a *triple movement*. The key move

---

6  Karl Polanyi, *The Great Transformation*, 2nd ed., Boston: Beacon Press, 1944 [2001].

here is to introduce a third pole of social struggle, which I call "emancipation." Crosscutting his central conflict between marketization and social protection, emancipation aims to overcome forms of domination rooted in "society," as well as those based in "economy." Opposing oppressive protections without thereby becoming free-marketeers, emancipation's ranks have included feminists as well as the billions of people—peasants, serfs, and slaves; racialized, colonized, and indigenous peoples—for whom access to a wage promised liberation from traditional authority. By thematizing emancipation as colliding with marketization and social protection, the triple movement clarifies the political terrain on which feminism operates today. On the one hand (contra Polanyi), this figure discloses the ambivalence of social protection, which often entrenches domination even while counteracting the disintegrative effects of marketization. On the other hand, however, (contra mainstream liberal feminism), the triple movement reveals the ambivalence of emancipation, which may dissolve the solidary ethical basis of social protection and can thereby foster marketization even as it dismantles domination. Probing these ambivalences, I conclude that feminists should end our dangerous liaison with marketization and forge a principled new alliance with social protection. In so doing, we could reactivate and extend the insurrectionary, anti-capitalist spirit of the second wave.

A compilation of essays written over a period of more than twenty-five years, this volume's orientation is at once retrospective and prospective. Charting shifts in the feminist imaginary since the 1970s, it offers an interpretation of the recent history of feminist thought. At the same time, however, it looks forward, to the feminism of the future now being invented by new generations of feminist activists. Schooled in digital media and comfortable in transnational space, yet formed in the crucible of capitalist crisis, this generation promises to reinvent the feminist imagination yet again. Emerging from the long slog through identity politics, the young feminists of this generation seem poised to conjure up a new synthesis of radical democracy and social justice. Combining redistribution, recognition, and representation, they are seeking to transform a world that no longer resembles the Westphalian international system of sovereign states. Faced with the gravest crisis of capitalism since the 1930s, they have every incentive to devise new, systematic critiques that combine the enduring insights of socialist-feminism with those of newer paradigms, such as postcolonialism and ecology. Whatever helpful lessons they can glean from this volume will pale in comparison with those its author expects to learn from them.

# PART I

Feminism Insurgent:
Radicalizing Critique in the Era of Social Democracy

# What's Critical About Critical Theory?
# The Case of Habermas and Gender*

To my mind, no one has yet improved on Marx's 1843 definition of Critical Theory as "the self-clarification of the struggles and wishes of the age."[1] What is so appealing about this definition is its straightforwardly political character. It makes no claim to any special epistemological status but, rather, supposes that with respect to justification, there is no philosophically interesting difference between a critical theory of society and an uncritical one. But there is, according to this definition, an important political difference. A critical social theory frames its research program and its conceptual framework with an eye to the aims and activities of those oppositional social movements with which it has a partisan—though not uncritical—identification. The questions it asks and the models it designs are informed by that identification and interest. So, for example, if struggles contesting the subordination of women figured among the most significant of a given age, then a critical social theory for that time would aim, among other things, to shed light on the character and bases of such subordination. It would employ categories and explanatory models that reveal rather than occlude relations of male dominance and female subordination. And it would demystify as ideological rival approaches that obfuscate or rationalize those relations. In this situation, then, one of the standards for assessing a critical theory, once it had been subjected to all the usual tests of empirical adequacy, would be: How well does it theorize the situation and prospects of the

---

\*  I am grateful to John Brenkman, Thomas McCarthy, Carole Pateman and Martin Schwab for helpful comments and criticism; to Dee Marquez and Marina Rosiene for crackerjack word processing; and to the Stanford Humanities Center for research support.

1  Karl Marx, "Letter to A. Ruge, September 1843," in *Karl Marx: Early Writings*, trans. Rodney Livingstone and Gregor Benton, New York: Vintage Books, 1975, 209.

feminist movement? To what extent does it serve the self-clarification of the struggles and wishes of contemporary women?

In what follows, I will presuppose the conception of Critical Theory I have just outlined. In addition, I will take as the actual situation of our age the scenario I just sketched as hypothetical. On the basis of these presuppositions, I want to examine the critical social theory of Jürgen Habermas as elaborated in *The Theory of Communicative Action* and related recent writings.[2] I want to read this work from the standpoint of the following questions: In what proportions and in what respects does Habermas's theory clarify and/or mystify the bases of male dominance and female subordination in modern societies? In what proportions and in what respects does it challenge and/or replicate prevalent ideological rationalizations of such dominance and subordination? To what extent does it or can it be made to serve the self-clarification of the struggles and wishes of feminist movements? In short, with respect to gender, what is critical and what is not in Habermas's social theory?

This would be a fairly straightforward enterprise were it not for one thing. Apart from a brief discussion of feminism as a "new social movement" (a discussion I shall consider anon), Habermas says virtually nothing about gender in *The Theory of Communicative Action*. Given my view of Critical Theory, this is a serious deficiency. But it need not stand in the way of the sort of inquiry I am proposing. It only necessitates that one read the work from the standpoint of an absence; that one extrapolate from things Habermas does say to things he does not; that one reconstruct how various matters of concern to feminists would appear from his perspective had they been thematized.

Here, then, are the steps I shall follow. In the first section of this essay, I shall examine some elements of Habermas's social-theoretical framework in order to see how it tends to cast childrearing and

---

2  Jürgen Habermas, *The Theory of Communicative Action, Vol. I: Reason and the Rationalization of Society*, trans. Thomas McCarthy, Boston: Beacon Press, 1984. Hereafter, TCA I. Jürgen Habermas, *Theorie des kommunikativen Handelns, Vol. II: Zur Kritik der funktionalistischen Vernunft*, Frankfurt am Main: Suhrkamp Verlag, 1981. Hereafter TCA II. I shall also draw on some other writings by Habermas, especially *Legitimation Crisis*, trans. Thomas McCarthy, Boston: Beacon Press, 1975; "Introduction," in *Observations on "The Spiritual Situation of the Age": Contemporary German Perspectives*, ed. Jürgen Habermas, trans. Andrew Buchwalter, Cambridge, MA: MIT Press, 1984; and "A Reply to my Critics," in *Habermas: Critical Debates*, ed. David Held and John B. Thompson, Cambridge, MA: MIT Press, 1982. I shall draw likewise on two helpful overviews of this material: Thomas McCarthy, "Translator's Introduction," in Habermas, TCA I, v–xxxvii; and John B. Thompson, "Rationality and Social Rationalisation: An Assessment of Habermas's Theory of Communicative Action," *Sociology* 17:2, 1983, 278–94.

the male-headed, modern, restricted, nuclear family. In the second section, I shall consider his account of the relations between the public and private spheres of life in classical capitalist societies and reconstruct its unthematized gender subtext. In section three, finally, I shall examine Habermas's account of the dynamics, crisis tendencies, and conflict potentials specific to contemporary, Western, welfare-state capitalism, so as to see in what light it casts contemporary feminist struggles.

## 1. THE SOCIAL-THEORETICAL FRAMEWORK: A FEMINIST INTERROGATION

Let me begin by considering two distinctions central to Habermas's social-theoretical categorial framework. The first is the distinction between the symbolic and the material reproduction of societies. On the one hand, claims Habermas, societies must reproduce themselves materially: they must successfully regulate the metabolic exchange of groups of biological individuals with a nonhuman, physical environment and with other social systems. On the other hand, societies must reproduce themselves symbolically: they must maintain and transmit to new members the linguistically elaborated norms and patterns of interpretation which are constitutive of social identities. For Habermas, material reproduction is secured by means of "social labor." Symbolic reproduction, on the other hand, comprises the socialization of the young, the cementing of group solidarity, and the transmission and extension of cultural traditions.[3]

This distinction between symbolic and material reproduction is in the first instance a functional one. It distinguishes two different functions that must be fulfilled more or less successfully if a society is to survive and persist. At the same time, however, the distinction is used by Habermas to classify actual social practices and activities. These are distinguished according to which one of the two functions they are held to serve exclusively or primarily. Thus, according to Habermas, in capitalist societies, the activities and practices which make up the sphere of paid work count as material reproduction activities since, in his view, they are "social labor" and serve the function of material reproduction. By contrast, the childrearing activities and practices which in our society are performed without pay by women in the domestic sphere—let us call them "women's unpaid childrearing work"—count as symbolic reproduction activities since, in

---

3   TCA II, 214, 217, 348–9; *Legitimation Crisis*, 8–9; "A Reply to my Critics," 268, 278–9. McCarthy, "Translator's Introduction," xxv–xxvii; Thompson, "Rationality," 285.

Habermas's view, they serve socialization and the function of symbolic reproduction.[4]

It is worth noting that Habermas's distinction between symbolic and material reproduction is open to two different interpretations. The first takes the two functions as two objectively distinct natural kinds to which both actual social practices and the actual organization of activities in any given society may correspond more or less faithfully. On this view, childrearing practices simply are, in and of themselves, oriented to symbolic reproduction, whereas the practices that produce food and objects are, by their essential nature, concerned with material reproduction. And modern capitalist social organization—unlike, say, that of archaic societies—would be a faithful mirror of the distinction between the two natural kinds, since it separates these practices institutionally. This "natural kinds" interpretation, as I shall call it, is at odds with another possible interpretation, which I shall call the "pragmatic-contextual" interpretation. The latter would not cast childrearing practices as inherently oriented to symbolic reproduction. Yet it would allow for the possibility that, under certain circumstances and given certain purposes, they could be usefully considered from that standpoint—if, for example, one wished to contest the dominant view, in a sexist political culture, according to which this traditionally female occupation is merely instinctual, natural, and ahistorical.

Now I want to argue that the natural kinds interpretation is conceptually inadequate and potentially ideological. It is not the case that childrearing practices serve symbolic as opposed to material reproduction. Granted, they comprise language-teaching and initiation into social mores, but also feeding, bathing, and protection from physical harm. Granted, they regulate children's interactions with other people, but also their interactions with physical nature (in the form, for example, of milk, germs, dirt, excrement, weather, and animals). In short, not just the construction of children's social identities but also their biological survival is at stake. And so, therefore, is the biological survival of the societies they belong to. Thus, childrearing is not *per se* symbolic reproduction activity; it is equally and at the same time material reproduction activity. It is what we might call a "dual-aspect" activity.[5]

But the same is true of the activities institutionalized in modern capitalist paid work. Granted, the production of food and objects contributes to the biological survival of members of society. But such production also and at the same time reproduces social identities. Not

---

4   TCA II, 208; "A Reply to my Critics," 223–5; McCarthy, "Translator's Introduction," xxiv–xxv.

5   I am indebted to Martin Schwab for the expression "dual-aspect activity."

just nourishment and shelter *simpliciter* are produced, but culturally elaborated forms of nourishment and shelter that have symbolically mediated social meanings. Moreover, such production occurs via culturally elaborated social relations and symbolically mediated, norm-governed social practices. The contents of these practices as well as the results serve to form, maintain, and modify the social identities of persons directly involved and indirectly affected. One need only think of an activity like computer programming for a wage in the US pharmaceutical industry to appreciate the thoroughly symbolic character of "social labor." Thus, such labor, like unpaid childrearing work, is a "dual-aspect" activity.[6]

It follows that the distinction between women's unpaid childrearing work and other forms of work from the standpoint of reproduction cannot be a distinction of natural kinds. If it is to be drawn at all, it must be drawn as a pragmatic-contextual distinction for the sake of focusing on what is in each case only one aspect of a dual-aspect phenomenon. And this, in turn, must find its warrant relative to

---

6   It might be argued that Habermas's categorial distinction between "social labor" and "socialization" helps overcome the androcentrism of orthodox Marxism. Orthodox Marxism allowed for only one kind of historically significant activity: "production," or "social labor." Moreover, it understood that category androcentrically and thereby excluded women's unpaid childrearing from history. By contrast, Habermas allows for two kinds of historically significant activity: "social labor" and the "symbolic" activities that include, among other things, childrearing. Thus, he manages to include women's unpaid activity in history. While this is an improvement, it does not suffice to remedy matters. At best, it leads to what has come to be known as "dual systems theory," an approach which posits two distinct "systems" of human activity and, correspondingly, two distinct "systems" of oppression: capitalism and male dominance. But this is misleading. These are not, in fact, two distinct systems but, rather, two thoroughly interfused dimensions of a single social formation. In order to understand that social formation, a critical theory requires a single set of categories and concepts which integrate internally both gender and political economy (perhaps also race). For a classic statement of dual systems theory, see Heidi Hartmann, "The Unhappy Marriage of Marxism and Feminism: Toward a More Progressive Union," in *Women and Revolution*, ed. Lydia Sargent, Boston: South End Press, 1981. For a critique of dual systems theory, see Iris Young, "Beyond the Unhappy Marriage: A Critique of Dual Systems Theory," in *Women and Revolution*, ed. Sargent; and "Socialist Feminism and the Limits of Dual Systems Theory," *Socialist Review* 50–51, 1980, 169–80. In sections two and three of this essay, I develop arguments and lines of analysis that rely on concepts and categories that internally integrate gender and political economy (see note 30 below). This might be considered a "single system" approach. However, I find that label misleading because I do not consider my approach primarily or exclusively a "systems" approach in the first place. Rather, like Habermas, I am trying to link structural (in the sense of objectivating) and interpretive approaches to the study of societies. Unlike him, however, I do not do this by dividing society into two components, "system" and "lifeworld." See this section below and especially note 14.

specific purposes of analysis and description, purposes which are themselves susceptible to analysis and evaluation and which need, therefore, to be justified via argument.

But if this is so, then the natural kinds classification of childrearing as symbolic reproduction and of other work as material reproduction is potentially ideological. It could be used, for example, to legitimize the institutional separation, in capitalist societies, of childrearing from waged work, a separation which many feminists, including myself, consider a mainstay of modern forms of women's subordination. It could be used, in combination with other assumptions, to legitimate the confinement of women to a "separate sphere." Whether Habermas uses it this way will be considered shortly.

The second component of Habermas's categorial framework I want to examine is his distinction between "socially integrated" and "system integrated action contexts." Socially integrated action contexts are those in which different agents coordinate their actions with one another by reference to some form of explicit or implicit intersubjective consensus about norms, values and ends, consensus predicated on linguistic speech and interpretation. By contrast, system-integrated action contexts are those in which the actions of different agents are coordinated with one another by the functional interlacing of unintended consequences, while each individual action is determined by self-interested, utility-maximizing calculations typically entertained in the idioms—or, as Habermas says, in the "media"—of money and power.[7] Habermas considers the capitalist economic system to be the

---

7    TCA I, 85, 87–8, 101, 342, 357–60; TCA II, 179; *Legitimation Crisis*, 4–5; "A Reply to my Critics," 234, 237, 264–5; McCarthy, "Translator's Introduction," ix, xvix–xxx. In presenting the distinction between system-integrated and socially-integrated action contexts, I am relying on the terminology of *Legitimation Crisis* and modifying the terminology of *The Theory of Communicative Action*. Or, rather, I am selecting one of the several various usages deployed in the latter work. There, Habermas often speaks of what I have called "socially integrated action" as "communicative action." But this gives rise to confusion. For he also uses this latter expression in another, stronger sense, namely, for actions in which coordination occurs by explicit, dialogically achieved consensus only (see below, this section). In order to avoid repeating Habermas's equivocation on "communicative action," I adopt the following terminology: I reserve the expression "communicatively achieved action" for actions coordinated by explicit, reflective, dialogically achieved consensus. I contrast such action, in the first instance, with "normatively secured action," or actions coordinated by tacit, pre-reflective, pre-given consensus (see below, this section). I take "communicatively achieved" and "normatively secured" actions, so defined, to be subspecies of what I here call "socially integrated action," or actions coordinated by any form of normed consensus whatsoever. This last category, in turn, contrasts with "system integrated action" or actions coordinated by the functional interlacing of unintended consequences, determined by egocentric calculations in the media of money and power, and involving little or no normed

paradigm case of a system-integrated action context. By contrast, he takes the modern, restricted, nuclear family to be a case of a socially integrated action context.[8]

This distinction is a rather complex one, comprising what I take to be six analytically distinct conceptual elements: functionality, intentionality, linguisticality, consensuality, normativity, and strategicality. However, three of them—functionality, intentionality, and linguisticality—are patently operative in virtually every major context of social action and so can be set aside. Certainly, in both the capitalist workplace and the modern, restricted, nuclear family, the consequences of actions may be functionally interlaced in ways unintended by agents. Likewise, in both contexts, agents coordinate their actions with one another consciously and intentionally. Finally, in both contexts, agents coordinate their actions with one another in and through language.[9] I assume, therefore, that Habermas's distinction effectively turns on the elements of consensuality, normativity, and strategicality.

Once again, I shall distinguish two possible interpretations of Habermas's position. The first takes the contrast between the two kinds of action contexts as an absolute difference. On this view, system-integrated contexts would involve absolutely no consensuality or reference to moral norms and values, while socially integrated contexts would involve absolutely no strategic calculations in the media of money and power. This "absolute differences" interpretation is at odds with a second possibility, which takes the contrast rather as a difference in degree. According to this second interpretation, system-integrated contexts would involve some consensuality and reference to moral norms and values, but less than socially integrated contexts; in the same way, socially integrated contexts would involve some strategic calculations in the media of money and power, but less than system-integrated contexts.

I want to argue that the absolute differences interpretation is too extreme to be useful for social theory and that, in addition, it is

---

consensus of any sort. These terminological commitments do not so much represent a departure from Habermas's usage—he does in fact frequently use these terms in the senses I have specified. They represent, rather, a stabilization or rendering consistent of his usage.

8　TCA I, 341, 357–59; TCA II, 256, 266; McCarthy, "Translator's Introduction," xxx.

9　Here I follow the arguments of Thomas McCarthy. He contended, in "Complexity and Democracy, or the Seducements of Systems Theory," *New German Critique* 35, Spring/Summer 1985, 27–55, that state administrative bureaucracies cannot be distinguished from participatory democratic political associations on the basis of functionality, intentionality, and linguisticality since all three of these features are found in both contexts. For McCarthy, functionality, intentionality, and linguisticality are not mutually exclusive. I find these arguments persuasive. I see no reason why they do not hold also for the capitalist workplace and the modern, restricted, nuclear family.

potentially ideological. In few, if any, human action contexts are actions coordinated absolutely non-consensually and absolutely non-normatively. However morally dubious the consensus, and however problematic the content and status of the norms, virtually every human action context involves some form of both of them. In the capitalist marketplace, for example, strategic, utility-maximizing exchanges occur against a horizon of intersubjectively shared meanings and norms; agents normally subscribe at least tacitly to some commonly held notions of reciprocity and to some shared conceptions about the social meanings of objects, including about what sorts of things are exchangeable. Similarly, in the capitalist workplace, managers and subordinates, as well as coworkers, normally coordinate their actions to some extent consensually and with some explicit or implicit reference to normative assumptions, though the consensus may be arrived at unfairly and the norms may be incapable of withstanding critical scrutiny.[10] Thus, the capitalist economic system has a moral-cultural dimension.

Similarly, few if any human action contexts are wholly devoid of strategic calculation. Gift rituals in noncapitalist societies, for example, once seen as veritable crucibles of solidarity, are now widely understood to have a significant strategic, calculative dimension, one enacted in the medium of power, if not in that of money.[11] And, as I shall argue in more detail later, the modern, restricted, nuclear family is not devoid of individual, self-interested, strategic calculations in either medium. These action contexts, then, while not officially counted as economic, have a strategic, economic dimension.

Thus, the absolute differences interpretation is not of much use in social theory. It fails to distinguish the capitalist economy—let us call it "the official economy"—from the modern, restricted, nuclear family. In reality, both of these institutions are mélanges of consensuality, normativity, and strategicality. If they are to be distinguished with respect to mode of action-integration, the distinction must be

---

10    Here, too, I follow McCarthy, ibid. He argues that in modern, state administrative bureaucracies, managers must often deal consensually with their subordinates. I contend that this is also the case for business firms and corporations.

11    See, for example, the brilliant and influential discussion of gifting by Pierre Bourdieu in *Outline of a Theory of Practice*, trans. Richard Nice, New York: Cambridge University Press, 1977. By recovering the dimension of time, Bourdieu substantially revises the classical account by Marcel Mauss in *The Gift: Forms and Functions of Exchange in Archaic Societies*, trans. Ian Cunnison, New York: W.W. Norton & Company, 1967. For a discussion of some recent revisionist work in cultural economic anthropology, see Arjun Appadurai, *The Social Life of Things: Commodities in Cultural Perspective*, Cambridge: Cambridge University Press, 1986, especially the chapter titled "Commodities and the Politics of Value."

drawn as a difference of degree. It must turn on the place, proportions, and interactions of the three elements within each.

But if this is so, then the absolute differences classification of the
official economy as a system-integrated action context and of the
modern family as a socially integrated action context is potentially
ideological. It could be used, for example, to exaggerate the differences and occlude the similarities between the two institutions. It
could be used to construct an ideological opposition which posits the
family as the "negative," the complementary "other," of the (official)
economic sphere, a "haven in a heartless world."

Which of these possible interpretations of the two distinctions are
the operative ones in Habermas's social theory? He asserts that he
understands the reproduction distinction according to the pragmatic-
contextual interpretation and not the natural kinds one.[12] Likewise, he
asserts that he takes the action-context distinction to mark a difference in degree, not an absolute difference.[13] However, I propose to
bracket these assertions and to examine what Habermas actually does
with these distinctions.

Habermas maps the distinction between action contexts onto the
distinction between reproduction functions in order to arrive at a
definition of societal modernization and at a picture of the institutional structure of modern societies. He holds that modern societies
differ from premodern societies in that they split off some material
reproduction functions from symbolic ones and hand over the former
to two specialized institutions—the (official) economy and the administrative state—which are system-integrated. At the same time,
modern societies situate these "subsystems" in the larger social environment by developing two other institutions that specialize in
symbolic reproduction and are socially integrated: the modern,
restricted, nuclear family or "private sphere," and the space of political
participation, debate, and opinion formation or "public sphere,"
which together constitute the two "institutional orders of the modern
lifeworld." Thus, modern societies "uncouple" or separate what
Habermas takes to be two distinct but previously undifferentiated
aspects of society: "system" and "lifeworld." And so, in his view, the
institutional structure of modern societies is dualistic. On one side
stand the institutional orders of the modern lifeworld: the socially
integrated domains specializing in symbolic reproduction (that is, in

---

12   TCA II, 348–9; McCarthy, "Translator's Introduction," xxvi–xxvii. The
expressions "pragmatic-contextual" and "natural kinds" are mine, not Habermas's.

13   TCA I, 94–5, 101; TCAII, 348–9; "A Reply to My Critics," 227, 237, 266–8;
*Legitimation Crisis*, 10; McCarthy, "Translator's Introduction," xxvi–xxvii. The
expressions "absolute differences" and "difference of degree" are mine, not Habermas's.

socialization, solidarity formation, and cultural transmission). On the other side stand the systems: the system-integrated domains specializing in material reproduction. On one side, the nuclear family and the public sphere. On the other side, the (official) capitalist economy and the modern administrative state.[14]

What are the critical insights and blind spots of this model? Attending first to the question of its empirical adequacy, let us focus, for now, on the contrast between "the private sphere of the lifeworld" and the (official) economic system. Consider that this aspect of Habermas's categorial divide between system and lifeworld institutions faithfully mirrors the institutional separation of family and official economy, household and paid workplace, in male-dominated, capitalist societies. It thus has some *prima facie* purchase on empirical social reality. But consider, too, that the characterization of the family as a socially integrated, symbolic reproduction domain and of the paid workplace as a system-integrated, material reproduction domain tends to exaggerate the differences and occlude the similarities between them. Among other things, it directs attention away from the fact that the household, like the paid workplace, is a site of labor, albeit of unremunerated and often unrecognized labor. Likewise, it occults the fact that in the paid workplace, as in the household, women are assigned to, indeed ghettoized in, distinctively feminine, service-oriented, and often sexualized occupations. Finally, it fails to focus on the fact that in both spheres women are subordinated to men.

Moreover, this characterization presents the male-headed, nuclear

---

14    TCA I, 72, 341–2, 359–60; TCA II, 179; "A Reply to my Critics," 268, 279–80; *Legitimation Crisis*, 20–1; McCarthy, "Translator's Introduction," xxviii–xxix. Thompson, "Rationality," 285, 287. It should be noted that in TCA, Habermas draws the contrast between system and lifeworld in two distinct senses. On the one hand, he contrasts them as two different methodological perspectives on the study of societies. The system perspective is objectivating and "externalist," while the lifeworld perspective is hermeneutical and "internalist." In principle, either can be applied to the study of any given set of societal phenomena. Habermas argues that neither alone is adequate. So he seeks to develop a methodology that combines both. On the other hand, Habermas also contrasts system and lifeworld in another way, namely, as two different kinds of institutions. It is this second system lifeworld contrast that I am concerned with here. I do not explicitly treat the first one in this essay. I am sympathetic to Habermas's general methodological intention of combining or linking structural (in the sense of objectivating) and interpretive approaches to the study of societies. I do not, however, believe that this can be done by assigning structural properties to one set of institutions (the official economy and the state) and interpretive ones to another set (the family and the "public sphere"). I maintain, rather, that all of these institutions have both structural and interpretive dimensions and that all should be studied both structurally and hermeneutically. I have tried to develop an approach that meets these desiderata in Chapter 2 of the present volume, "Struggle over Needs."

family, qua socially integrated institutional order of the modern life-world, as having only an extrinsic and incidental relation to money and power. These "media" are taken as definitive of interactions in the official economy and state administration but as only incidental to intrafamilial ones. But this assumption is counterfactual. Feminists have shown via empirical analyses of contemporary familial decision-making, handling of finances, and wife-battering that families are thoroughly permeated by money and power. Sites of egocentric, strategic, and instrumental calculation, households are also loci of (usually exploitative) exchanges of services, labor, cash, and sex, as well as of coercion and violence.[15] But Habermas's way of contrasting the modern family with the official capitalist economy tends to occlude all this. It overstates the differences between these institutions and blocks the possibility of analyzing families as economic systems—that is, as sites of labor, exchange, calculation, distribution, and exploitation. Or, to the degree that Habermas would acknowledge that families can be seen as economic systems, his framework implies that this is due to the intrusion or invasion of alien forces—to the "colonization" of the family by the (official) economy and the state. This, too, however, is a dubious proposition, which I shall discuss in detail in section three below.

In general, then, Habermas's model has some empirical deficiencies. It fails to focus on some dimensions of male dominance in modern societies. However, his framework does offer a conceptual resource suitable for understanding other aspects of modern male dominance. Consider that Habermas subdivides the category of socially integrated action-contexts into two further subcategories. One pole comprises "normatively secured" forms of socially integrated action. Such action is coordinated on the basis of a conventional, pre-reflective, taken-for-granted consensus about values and ends, consensus rooted in the pre-critical internalization of socialization and cultural tradition. The other pole of the contrast concerns "communicatively achieved" forms of socially integrated action. Such action is coordinated on the basis of explicit, reflectively achieved understandings, agreement reached by unconstrained discussion under conditions of freedom, equality, and fairness.[16] This distinction, which is a subdistinction within the category of socially integrated action, provides Habermas with some critical resources for analyzing the

---

15   See, for example, *Rethinking the Family: Some Feminist Questions*, ed. Barrie Thorne and Marilyn Yalom, New York and London: Longman, 1982, and Michele Barrett and Mary McIntosh, *The Anti-Social Family*, London: Verso, 1982.

16   TCA I, 85–6, 88–90, 101, 104–5; TCA II, 179; McCarthy, "Translator's Introduction," ix, xxx. In presenting the distinction between normatively secured and communicatively achieved action, I am again modifying, or rather stabilizing, the variable usage in *Theory of Communicative Action*. See note 7 above.

modern, restricted, male-headed, nuclear family. Such families can be understood as normatively secured rather than communicatively achieved action contexts—that is, as contexts where actions are (sometimes) mediated by consensus and shared values, but where such consensus is suspect because it is pre-reflective or because it is achieved through dialogue vitiated by unfairness, coercion, or inequality.

To what extent does the distinction between normatively secured and communicatively achieved action contexts succeed in overcoming the problems discussed earlier? Only partially, I think. On the one hand, this distinction is a morally significant and empirically useful one. The notion of a normatively secured action context fits nicely with recent research on patterns of communication between husbands and wives. This research shows that men tend to control conversations, determining what topics are pursued, while women do more "interaction work," like asking questions and providing verbal support.[17] Research also reveals differences in men's and women's uses of the bodily and gestural dimensions of speech, differences which confirm men's dominance and women's subordination.[18] Thus, Habermas's distinction enables us to capture something important about intrafamilial dynamics. What is insufficiently stressed, however, is that actions coordinated by normatively secured consensus in the male-headed nuclear family are actions regulated by power. It seems to me a grave mistake to restrict the use of the term "power" to bureaucratic contexts. Critical theorists would do better to distinguish different kinds of power, for example, domestic-patriarchal power, on the one hand, and bureaucratic-patriarchal power, on the other.

But even that distinction does not by itself suffice to make Habermas's framework fully adequate to all the empirical forms of male dominance in modern societies. For normative-domestic-patriarchal power is only one of the elements which enforce women's subordination in the domestic sphere. To capture the others would require a social-theoretical framework capable of analyzing families also as economic systems involving the appropriation of women's unpaid labor and interlocking in complex ways with other economic systems involving paid work. Because Habermas's framework draws the major categorial divide between system and lifeworld institutions, and hence between (among other things) official economy and family, it is not very well suited to that task.

Let me turn now from the question of the empirical adequacy of Habermas's model to the question of its normative political implications.

---

17   Pamela Fishman, "Interaction: The Work Women Do," *Social Problems* 25:4, 1978, 397–406.

18   Nancy Henley, *Body Politics*, Englewood Cliffs, NJ: Prentice-Hall, 1977.

What sorts of social arrangements and transformations does his modernization conception tend to legitimate? And what sorts does it tend to rule out? Here it will be necessary to reconstruct some implications of the model which are not explicitly thematized by Habermas.

Consider that the conception of modernization as the uncoupling of system and lifeworld institutions tends to legitimate the modern institutional separation of family and official economy, childrearing and paid work. For Habermas claims that there is an asymmetry between symbolic and material reproduction with respect to system-integration. Symbolic reproduction activities, he claims, are unlike material reproduction activities in that they cannot be turned over to specialized, system-integrated institutions set apart from the lifeworld. Their inherently symbolic character requires that they be socially integrated.[19] It follows that women's unpaid childrearing work could not be incorporated into the (official) economic system without "pathological" results. At the same time, Habermas also holds that it is a mark of societal rationalization that system-integrated institutions be differentiated to handle material reproduction functions. The separation of a specialized (official) economic system enhances a society's capacity to deal with its natural and social environment. "System complexity," then, constitutes a "developmental advance."[20] It follows that the (official) economic system of paid work could not be dedifferentiated with respect to, say, childrearing, without societal "regression." But if childrearing could not be non-pathologically incorporated into the (official) economic system, and if the (official) economic system could not be non-regressively dedifferentiated, then the continued separation of childrearing from paid work would be required.

Effectively, then, Habermas's framework is primed to defend at least one aspect of what feminists call "the separation of public and private," namely, the separation of the official economic sphere from the domestic sphere and the enclaving of childrearing from the rest of social labor. It defends, therefore, an institutional arrangement that is widely held to be one, if not *the*, linchpin of modern women's subordination. And it should be noted that the fact that Habermas is a socialist does not alter the matter. Even were he to endorse the elimination of private ownership, profit-orientation, and hierarchical command in paid work, this would not of itself affect the official-economic/domestic separation.

19   TCA II, 523–4, 547; "A Reply to my Critics," 237; Thompson, "Rationality," 288, 292.

20   McCarthy pursues some of the normative implications of this for the differentiation of the administrative state system from the public sphere in "Complexity and Democracy."

Now I want to challenge several premises of the reasoning I have just reconstructed. First, this reasoning assumes the natural kinds interpretation of the symbolic versus material reproduction distinction. But since, as I have argued, childrearing is a dual-aspect activity, and since it is not categorially different in this respect from other work, there is no warrant for the claim of an asymmetry vis-à-vis system integration. That is, there is no warrant for assuming that the system-integrated organization of childrearing would be any more (or less) pathological than that of other work. Second, this reasoning assumes the absolute differences interpretation of the social versus system integration distinction. But since, as I have argued, the modern, male-headed, nuclear family is a mélange of (normatively secured) consensuality, normativity, and strategicality, and since it is in this respect not categorially different from the paid workplace, then privatized childrearing is already, to a not insignificant extent, permeated by the media of money and power. Moreover, there is no empirical evidence that children raised in commercial day-care centers (even profit-based or corporate ones) turn out any more "pathological" than those raised, say, in suburban homes by full-time mothers. Third, the reasoning just sketched elevates system complexity to the status of an overriding consideration with effective veto-power over proposed social transformations aimed at overcoming women's subordination. But this is at odds with Habermas's professions that system complexity is only one measure of "progress" among others.[21] More importantly, it is at odds with any reasonable standard of justice.

What, then, should we conclude about the normative, political implications of Habermas's model? If the conception of modernization as the uncoupling of system and lifeworld does indeed have the implications I have just drawn from it, then it is in important respects androcentric and ideological.

## 2. PUBLIC AND PRIVATE IN CLASSICAL CAPITALISM: THEMATIZING THE GENDER SUBTEXT

The foregoing difficulties notwithstanding, Habermas offers an account of the inter-institutional relations among various spheres of public and private life in classical capitalism which has some genuine critical potential. But in order to realize this potential fully, we need to reconstruct the unthematized gender subtext of his material.

Let me return to his conception of the way in which the (official) economic and state systems are situated with respect to the lifeworld.

---

21   McCarthy makes this point with respect to the dedifferentiation of the state administrative system and the public sphere. Ibid.

Habermas holds that, with modernization, the (official) economic and state systems are not simply disengaged or detached from the lifeworld; they must also be related to and embedded in it. Concomitant with the beginnings of classical capitalism, then, is the development within the lifeworld of "institutional orders" that situate the systems in a context of everyday meanings and norms. The lifeworld, as we saw, gets differentiated into two spheres that provide appropriate complementary environments for the two systems. The "private sphere" or modern, restricted, nuclear family is linked to the (official) economic system. The "public sphere" or space of political participation, debate, and opinion-formation is linked to the state-administrative system. The family is linked to the (official) economy by means of a series of exchanges conducted in the medium of money; it supplies the (official) economy with appropriately socialized labor power in exchange for wages; and it provides appropriate, monetarily measured demand for commodified goods and services. Exchanges between family and (official) economy, then, are channeled through the "roles" of worker and consumer. Parallel exchange processes link the public sphere and the state system. These, however, are conducted chiefly in the medium of power. Loyalty, obedience, and tax revenues are exchanged for "organizational results" and "political decisions." Exchanges between public sphere and state, then, are channeled through the "role" of citizen and, in late welfare-state capitalism, that of client.[22]

This account of inter-institutional relations in classical capitalism has a number of important advantages. First, it treats the modern, restricted, nuclear family as a historically emergent institution with its own positive, determinate features. And it specifies that this type of family emerges concomitantly with and in relation to the emerging capitalist economy, administrative state, and (eventually) the political public sphere. Moreover, this account charts some of the dynamics of exchange among these institutions, while also indicating some of the ways in which they are fitted to the needs of one another so as to accommodate the exchanges among them.

Finally, Habermas's account offers an important corrective to the standard dualistic approaches to the separation of public and private in capitalist societies. He conceptualizes the problem as a relation among four terms: family, (official) economy, state, and "public sphere." His view suggests that in classical capitalism there are actually two distinct but interrelated public-private separations. There is one public-private separation at the level of "systems," namely, the separation of the state or public system from the (official) capitalist economy or private system.

----

22   TCA I, 341–2, 359–60; TCA II, 256, 473; "A Reply to my Critics," 280; McCarthy, "Translator's Introduction," xxxii; Thompson, "Rationality," 286–8.

There is another public-private separation at the level of the "lifeworld," namely, the separation of the family, or private lifeworld sphere, from the space of political opinion formation and participation, or public lifeworld sphere. Moreover, each of these public-private separations is coordinated with the other. One axis of exchange runs between private system and private lifeworld sphere—that is, between (official) capitalist economy and modern, restricted, nuclear family. Another axis of exchange runs between public system and public lifeworld sphere, or between state administration and the organs of public opinion and will formation. In both cases, the exchanges can occur because of the institutionalization of specific roles that connect the domains in question. Thus, the roles of worker and consumer link the (official) private economy and the private family, while the roles of citizen and (later) client link the public state and the public opinion institutions.

Thus, Habermas provides an extremely sophisticated account of the relations between public and private institutions in classical capitalist societies. At the same time, however, his account has some weaknesses. Many of these stem from his failure to thematize the gender subtext of the relations and arrangements he describes. Consider, first, the relations between (official) private economy and private family as mediated by the roles of worker and consumer. These roles, I submit, are gendered roles. And the links they forge between family and (official) economy are adumbrated as much in the medium of gender identity as in the medium of money.

Take the role of the worker.[23] In male-dominated, classical capitalist societies, this role is a masculine role, and not just in the relatively superficial statistical sense. There is rather a very deep sense in which masculine identity in these societies is bound up with the breadwinner role. Masculinity is in large part a matter of leaving home each day for a place of paid work and returning with a wage that provides for one's dependents. It is this internal relation between being a man and being a provider that explains why in capitalist societies unemployment can be so psychologically, as well as economically, devastating for men. It also sheds light on the centrality of the struggle for a family wage in the history of the workers' and trade union movements of the nineteenth and twentieth centuries. This was a struggle for a wage conceived not as a payment to a genderless individual for the use of labor power, but rather as a payment to a man for the support of his economically

---

23   The following account of the masculine gender subtext of the worker role draws on Carole Pateman, "The Personal and the Political: Can Citizenship Be Democratic?," Lecture 3 of her "Women and Democratic Citizenship" series, The Jefferson Memorial Lectures, delivered at the University of California, Berkeley, February 1985.

dependent wife and children. This conception, of course, legitimized the practice of paying women less for equal or comparable work.

The masculine subtext of the worker role is confirmed by the vexed and strained character of women's relation to paid work in male-dominated classical capitalism. As Carole Pateman puts it, it is not that women are absent from the paid workplace; it's rather that they are present differently[24]—for example, as feminized and sometimes sexualized "service" workers (secretaries, domestic workers, salespersons, prostitutes, and flight attendants); as members of the "helping professions" utilizing mothering skills (nurses, social workers, childcare workers, primary school teachers); as targets of sexual harassment; as low-waged, low-skilled, low-status workers in sex-segregated occupations; as part-time workers; as workers who work a double shift (both unpaid domestic labor and paid labor); as "working wives" and "working mothers," i.e., as primarily wives and mothers who happen, secondarily, to "go out to work"; as "supplemental earners." These differences in the quality of women's presence in the paid workplace testify to the conceptual dissonance between femininity and the worker role in classical capitalism. And this in turn confirms the masculine subtext of that role. It confirms that the role of the worker, which links the private (official) economy and the private family in male-dominated capitalist societies, is a masculine role. Pace Habermas, the link it forges is elaborated as much in the medium of masculine gender identity as in the medium of gender-neutral money.

Conversely, the other role linking official economy and family in Habermas's scheme has a feminine subtext. The consumer, after all, is the worker's companion and helpmeet in classical capitalism. For the sexual division of domestic labor assigns to women the work—and it is indeed work, though unpaid and usually unrecognized work—of purchasing and preparing goods and services for domestic consumption. You can confirm this even today by visiting any supermarket or department store. Or by looking at the history of consumer goods advertising. Such advertising has nearly always interpellated its subject, the consumer, as feminine. In fact, it has elaborated an entire phantasmatics of desire premised on the femininity of the subject of consumption. It is only relatively recently, and with some difficulty, that advertisers have devised ways of interpellating a masculine subject of consumption. The trick was to find means of positioning a male consumer that did not feminize, emasculate, or sissify him. In *The Hearts of Men*, Barbara Ehrenreich quite shrewdly credits Playboy magazine with pioneering such means.[25] But the difficulty and lateness of the

---

24  Ibid., 5.
25  Barbara Ehrenreich, *The Hearts of Men: American Dreams and the Flight from*

project confirm the gendered character of the consumer role in classical capitalism. Men occupy it with conceptual strain and cognitive dissonance, much as women occupy the role of worker. So the role of consumer linking family and official economy is a feminine role. *Pace* Habermas, it forges the link in the medium of feminine gender identity as much as in the apparently gender-neutral medium of money.

Moreover, Habermas's account of the roles linking family and (official) economy suffers from a significant omission. There is no mention in his schema of any childrearer role, although the material clearly requires one. For who else is performing the unpaid work of overseeing the production of the "appropriately socialized labor power" which the family exchanges for wages? Of course, the childrearer role in classical capitalism (as elsewhere) is patently a feminine role. Its omission here is a mark of androcentrism and entails some significant consequences. A consideration of the childrearer role in this context might well have pointed to the central relevance of gender to the institutional structure of classical capitalism. And this in turn could have led to the disclosure of the gender subtext of the other roles and of the importance of gender identity as an "exchange medium."

What, then, of the other set of roles and linkages identified by Habermas? What of the citizen role, which he claims connects the public system of the administrative state with the public lifeworld sphere of political opinion and will formation? This role, too, is a gendered role in classical capitalism, indeed, a masculine role.[26] And not simply in the sense that women did not win the vote in, for example, the US and Britain until the twentieth century. Rather, the lateness and difficulty of those victories are symptomatic of deeper strains. As Habermas understands it, the citizen is centrally a participant in political debate and public opinion formation. This means that citizenship, in his view, depends crucially on the capacities for consent and speech, the ability to participate on a par with others in dialogue. But these are capacities that are connected with masculinity in male-dominated classical capitalism. They are capacities that are in myriad ways denied to women and deemed at odds with femininity. I have already cited studies about the effects of male dominance and female subordination on the dynamics of dialogue. Now consider that even today in most jurisdictions there is no such thing as marital rape. That is, a wife is legally subject to her husband; she is not an individual who can give or withhold consent to his demands for sexual access. Consider also that even outside of marriage the legal test of

---

*Commitment*, Garden City, NY: Anchor Books, 1984.

26   The following account of the masculine gender subtext of the citizen role draws on Carole Pateman, "The Personal and the Political."

rape often boils down to whether a "reasonable man" would have assumed that the woman had consented. Consider what that means when both popular and legal opinion widely holds that when a woman says "no" she means "yes." It means, says Carole Pateman, that "women find their speech . . . persistently and systematically invalidated in the crucial matter of consent, a matter that is fundamental to democracy. [But] if women's words about consent are consistently reinterpreted, how can they participate in the debate among citizens?"[27]

Generally, then, there is a conceptual dissonance between femininity and the dialogical capacities central to Habermas's conception of citizenship. And there is another aspect of citizenship not discussed by him that is even more obviously bound up with masculinity. I mean the soldiering aspect of citizenship, the conception of the citizen as the defender of the polity and protector of those—women, children, the elderly—who allegedly cannot protect themselves. As Judith Stiehm has argued, this division between male protectors and female protected introduces further dissonance into women's relation to citizenship.[28] It confirms the gender subtext of the citizen role. And the view of women as needing men's protection "underlies access not just to the means of destruction, but also [to] the means of production—witness all the 'protective' legislation that has surrounded women's access to the workplace—and [to] the means of reproduction . . . [witness] women's status as wives and sexual partners."[29]

Thus, the citizen role in male-dominated classical capitalism is a masculine role. It links the state and the public sphere, as Habermas claims. But it also links these to the official economy and the family. In every case, the links are forged in the medium of masculine gender identity rather than, as Habermas has it, in the medium of a gender-neutral power. Or, if the medium of exchange here is power, then the power in question is gender power, the power of male domination.

Thus, there are some major lacunae in Habermas's otherwise powerful and sophisticated model of the relations between public and private institutions in classical capitalism. The gender-blindness of the model occludes important features of the arrangements he wants to understand. By omitting any mention of the childrearer role, and by failing to thematize the gender subtext underlying the roles of worker and consumer, Habermas fails to understand precisely how the capitalist workplace is linked to the modern, restricted, male-headed, nuclear family. Similarly, by failing to thematize the masculine subtext of the

27 Ibid., 8.
28 Judith Hicks Stiehm, "The Protected, the Protector, the Defender," in *Women and Men's Wars*, ed. Judith Hicks Stiehm, New York: Pergamon Press, 1983.
29 Pateman, "The Personal and the Political," 10.

citizen role, he misses the full meaning of the way the state is linked to the public sphere of political speech. Moreover, Habermas misses important cross-connections among the four elements of his two public-private schemata. He misses, for example, the way the masculine citizen-soldier-protector role links the state and public sphere not only to one another but also to the family and to the paid workplace—that is, the way the assumptions of man's capacity to protect and woman's need of man's protection run through all of them. He misses, too, the way the masculine citizen-speaker role links the state and public sphere not only to one another but also to the family and official economy— that is, the way the assumptions of man's capacity to speak and consent and woman's incapacity therein run through all of them. He misses, also, the way the masculine worker-breadwinner role links the family and official economy not only to one another but also to the state and the political public sphere—that is, the way the assumptions of man's provider status and of woman's dependent status run through all of them, so that even the coin in which classical capitalist wages and taxes are paid is not gender-neutral. And he misses, finally, the way the feminine childrearer role links all four institutions to one another by overseeing the construction of the masculine and feminine gendered subjects needed to fill every role in classical capitalism.

Once the gender-blindness of Habermas's model is overcome, however, all these connections come into view. It then becomes clear that feminine and masculine gender identity run like pink and blue threads through the areas of paid work, state administration, and citizenship, as well as through the domain of familial and sexual relations. Lived out in all arenas of life, gender identity is one (if not the) "medium of exchange" among all of them, a basic element of the social glue that binds them to one another.

Moreover, a gender-sensitive reading of these connections has some important theoretical implications. It reveals that male dominance is intrinsic rather than accidental to classical capitalism. For the institutional structure of this social formation is actualized by means of gendered roles. It follows that the forms of male dominance at issue here are not properly understood as lingering forms of premodern status inequality. They are, rather, intrinsically modern in Habermas's sense, because they are premised on the separation of waged labor and the state from female childrearing and the household. It also follows that a critical social theory of capitalist societies needs gender-sensitive categories. The foregoing analysis shows that, contrary to the usual androcentric understanding, the relevant concepts of worker, consumer, and wage are not, in fact, strictly economic concepts. Rather, they have an implicit gender subtext and thus are "gender-economic" concepts. Likewise, the relevant concept of citizenship is not strictly a political concept; it has an implicit gender subtext and so, rather, is a "gender-political" concept. Thus, this analysis reveals the inadequacy of those critical theories that treat gender as incidental to politics and political economy. It highlights the need for a critical-theoretical categorial framework in which gender, politics, and political economy are internally integrated.[30]

In addition, a gender-sensitive reading of these arrangements reveals the thoroughly multidirectional character of social motion and causal influence in classical capitalism. It reveals, that is, the inadequacy of the orthodox Marxist assumption that all or most significant causal influence runs from the (official) economy to the family and not vice versa. It shows that gender identity structures paid work, state administration, and political participation. Thus, it vindicates Habermas's claim that in classical capitalism the (official) economy is not all-powerful but is, rather, in some significant measure inscribed within and subject to the norms and meanings of everyday life. Of course, Habermas assumed that in making this claim he was saying something more or less positive. The norms and meanings he had in mind were not the ones I have been discussing. Still, the point is a valid one. It remains to be seen, though, whether it holds also for late welfare-state capitalism, as I believe; or whether it ceases to hold, as Habermas claims.

Finally, this reconstruction of the gender subtext of Habermas's model has normative political implications. It suggests that an emancipatory transformation of male-dominated capitalist societies, early and late, requires a transformation of these gendered roles and of the institutions they mediate. As long as the worker and childrearer roles are such as to be fundamentally incompatible with one another, it will not be possible to universalize either of them to include both genders. Thus, some form of dedifferentiation of unpaid childrearing and other work is required. Similarly, as long as the citizen role is defined to encompass death-dealing soldiering but not life-fostering childrearing, as long as it is tied to male-dominated modes of dialogue, then it, too, will remain incapable of including women fully. Thus, changes in the very concepts of citizenship, childrearing, and paid work are necessary, as are changes in the relationships among the domestic, official economic, state, and political public spheres.

---

30 Insofar as the foregoing analysis of the gender subtext of Habermas's role theory deploys categories in which gender and political economy are internally integrated, it represents a contribution to the overcoming of "dual systems theory" (see note 6 above). It is also a contribution to the development of a more satisfactory way of linking structural (in the sense of objectivating) and interpretive approaches to the study of societies than that proposed by Habermas. For I am suggesting here that the domestic sphere has a structural as well as an interpretive dimension and that the official economic and state spheres have an interpretive as well as a structural dimension.

## 3. DYNAMICS OF WELFARE-STATE CAPITALISM: A FEMINIST CRITIQUE

Let me turn, then, to Habermas's account of late welfare-state capitalism. Unlike his account of classical capitalism, its critical potential cannot be released simply by reconstructing the unthematized gender subtext. Here, the problematical features of his social-theoretical framework tend to inflect the analysis as a whole and diminish its capacity to illuminate the struggles and wishes of contemporary women. In order to show how this is the case, I shall present Habermas's view in the form of six theses.

1) Welfare-state capitalism emerges as a result of and in response to instabilities or crisis tendencies inherent in classical capitalism. It realigns the relations between the (official) economy and state, that is, between the private and public systems. These become more deeply intertwined with one another as the state actively assumes the task of crisis management. It tries to avert or manage economic crises by Keynesian market-replacing strategies which create a "public sector." And it tries to avert or manage social and political crises by market-compensating measures, including welfare concessions to trade unions and social movements. Thus, welfare-state capitalism partially overcomes the separation of public and private at the level of systems.[31]

2) The realignment of (official) economy-state relations is accompanied by a change in the relations of those systems to the private and public spheres of the lifeworld. First, with respect to the private sphere, there is a major increase in the importance of the consumer role as dissatisfactions related to paid work are compensated by enhanced commodity consumption. Second, with respect to the public sphere, there is a major decline in the importance of the citizen role as journalism becomes mass media, political parties are bureaucratized, and participation is reduced to occasional voting. Instead, the relation to the state is increasingly channeled through a new role: the social-welfare client.[32]

3) These developments are "ambivalent." On the one hand, there are gains in freedom with the institution of new social rights limiting the heretofore unrestrained power of capital in the (paid) workplace and of the paterfamilias in the bourgeois family; and social insurance programs represent a clear advance over the paternalism of poor relief. On the other hand, the means employed to realize these new social rights tend perversely to endanger freedom. These means are

---

31 TCA II, 505ff; *Legitimation Crisis*, 33–6, 53–5; McCarthy, "Translator's Introduction," xxxiii.

32 TCA II, 522–4; *Legitimation Crisis*, 36–7, McCarthy, "Translator's Introduction," xxxiii.

bureaucratic procedure and the money form, which structure the entitlements, benefits, and social services of the welfare system. In the process, they disempower clients, rendering them dependent on bureaucracies and therapeutocracies, and preempting their capacities to interpret their own needs, experiences, and life-problems.[33]

4) The most ambivalent welfare measures are those concerned with things like health care, care of the elderly, education, and family law. For when bureaucratic and monetary media structure these things, they intrude upon "core domains" of the lifeworld. They turn over symbolic reproduction functions like socialization and solidarity formation to system-integration mechanisms that position people as strategically acting, self-interested monads. But given the inherently symbolic character of these functions, and given their internal relation to social integration, the results, necessarily, are "pathological." Thus, these measures are more ambivalent than, say, reforms of the paid workplace. The latter bear on a domain that is already system integrated via money and power and which serves material as opposed to symbolic reproduction functions. So paid workplace reforms, unlike, say, family law reforms, do not necessarily generate "pathological" side-effects.[34]

5) Welfare-state capitalism thus gives rise to an "inner colonization of the lifeworld." Money and power cease to be mere media of exchange between system and lifeworld. Instead, they tend increasingly to penetrate the lifeworld's internal dynamics. The private and public spheres cease to subordinate (official) economic and administrative systems to the norms, values, and interpretations of everyday life. Rather, the latter are increasingly subordinated to the imperatives of the (official) economy and administration. The roles of worker and citizen cease to channel the influence of the lifeworld to the systems. Instead, the newly inflated roles of consumer and client channel the influence of the system to the lifeworld. Moreover, the intrusion of system-integration mechanisms into domains inherently requiring social integration gives rise to "reification phenomena." The affected domains are detached not merely from traditional, normatively secured consensus, but from "value-orientations per se." The result is the "desiccation of communicative contexts" and the "depletion of the nonrenewable cultural resources" needed to maintain personal and collective identity. Thus, symbolic reproduction is destabilized, identities are threatened, and social crisis tendencies develop.[35]

---

33   TCA II, 530–40; McCarthy, "Translator's Introduction," xxxiii–xxxiv.

34   TCA II, 540–7; McCarthy, "Translator's Introduction," xxxi.

35   TCA II, 275–7, 452, 480, 522–4; "A Reply to my Critics," 226, 280–1; *Observations*, 11–12, 16–20; McCarthy, "Translator's Introduction," xxxi–xxxii; Thompson, "Rationality," 286, 288.

6) The colonization of the lifeworld sparks new forms of social conflict specific to welfare-state capitalism. "New social movements" emerge in a "new conflict zone" at the "seam of system and lifeworld." They respond to system-induced identity threats by contesting the roles that transmit these. They contest the instrumentalization of professional labor and the performatization of education transmitted via the worker role; the monetarization of relations and lifestyles transmitted by the inflated consumer role; the bureaucratization of services and life-problems transmitted via the client role; and the rules and routines of interest politics transmitted via the impoverished citizen role. Thus, the conflicts at the cutting edge of developments in welfare capitalism differ both from class struggles and from bourgeois liberation struggles. They respond to crisis tendencies in symbolic as opposed to material reproduction, and they contest reification and "the grammar of forms of life" as opposed to distributive injustice or status inequality.[36]

The various new social movements can be classified with respect to their emancipatory potential. The criterion is the extent to which they advance a genuinely emancipatory resolution of welfare capitalist crisis, namely, the "decolonization of the lifeworld." Decolonization encompasses three things: first, the removal of system-integration mechanisms from symbolic reproduction spheres; second, the replacement of (some) normatively secured contexts by communicatively achieved ones; and third, the development of new, democratic institutions capable of asserting lifeworld control over state and (official) economic systems. Thus, those movements, like religious fundamentalism, which seek to defend traditional lifeworld norms against system intrusions are not genuinely emancipatory; they actively oppose the second element of decolonization and do not take up the third. Movements like peace and ecology are better; they aim both to resist system intrusions and also to instate new, reformed, communicatively achieved zones of interaction. But even these are "ambiguous" inasmuch as they tend to "retreat" into alternative communities and "particularistic" identities, thereby effectively renouncing the third element of decolonization and leaving the (official) economic and state systems unchecked. In this respect, they are more symptomatic than emancipatory, as they express the identity disturbances caused by colonization. The feminist movement, on the other hand, represents something of an anomaly. For it alone is "offensive," aiming to "conquer new territory"; and it alone retains links to historic liberation movements. In principle, then, feminism remains rooted in "universalist morality." Yet it is linked to resistance movements by an element of "particularism." And it tends,

36   TCA II, 581–3; *Observations*, 18–19, 27–8.

at times, to "retreat" into identities and communities organized around the natural category of biological sex.[37]

What are the critical insights and blind spots of this account of the dynamics of welfare-state capitalism? To what extent does it serve the self-clarification of the struggles and wishes of contemporary women? I shall take up the six theses one by one.

1) Habermas's first thesis is straightforward and unobjectionable. Clearly, the welfare state does engage in crisis management and does partially overcome the separation of public and private at the level of systems.

2) Habermas's second thesis contains some important insights. Clearly, welfare-state capitalism does inflate the consumer role and deflate the citizen role, reducing the latter essentially to voting—and, we should add, to soldiering. Moreover, the welfare state does indeed increasingly position its subjects as clients. However, Habermas again fails to see the gender subtext of these developments. He fails to see that the new client role has a gender, that it is a paradigmatically feminine role. He overlooks the reality that it is overwhelmingly women who are the clients of the welfare state: especially older women, poor women, and single women with children. He overlooks, in addition, the fact that many welfare systems are internally dualized and gendered. They include two basic kinds of programs: "masculine" ones tied to primary labor-force participation and designed to benefit principal breadwinners; and "feminine" ones oriented to what are understood as domestic "failures," that is, to families without a male breadwinner. Not surprisingly, these two welfare subsystems are separate and unequal. Clients of feminine programs—almost exclusively women and their children—are positioned in a distinctive, feminizing fashion as the "negatives of possessive individuals": they are largely excluded from the market both as workers and as consumers and are familialized, that is, made to claim benefits not as individuals but as members of "defective" households. They are also stigmatized, denied rights, subjected to surveillance and administrative harassment, and generally made into abject dependents of state bureaucracies.[38] But this means

---

37 TCA II, 581–3; *Observations*, 16–17, 27–8.

38 For the US social-welfare system, see the analysis of male vs. female participation rates and the account of the gendered character of the two subsystems in Fraser, "Women, Welfare and the Politics of Need Interpretation," *Hypatia: A Journal of Feminist Philosophy* 2:1, 1987, 103–21. Also, Barbara J. Nelson, "Women's Poverty and Women's Citizenship: Some Political Consequences of Economic Marginality," *Signs: Journal of Women in Culture and Society*, 10:2, 1985; Steven P. Erie, Martin Rein, and Barbara Wiget, "Women and the Reagan Revolution: Thermidor for the Social Welfare Economy," in *Families, Politics and Public Policies: A Feminist Dialogue on Women and the State*, ed. Irene Diamond, New York: Longman, 1983; Diana Pearce, "Women,

that the rise of the client role in welfare-state capitalism has a more complex meaning than Habermas allows. It is not only a change in the link between system and lifeworld institutions. It is also a change in the character of male dominance, a shift, in Carol Brown's phrase, "from private patriarchy to public patriarchy."[39]

3) This gives a rather different twist to the meaning of Habermas's third thesis. It suggests that he is right about the "ambivalence" of welfare-state capitalism, but not quite and not only in the way he thought. It suggests that welfare measures do have a positive side insofar as they reduce women's dependence on an individual male breadwinner. But they also have a negative side insofar as they substitute dependence on a patriarchal and androcentric state bureaucracy. The benefits provided are, as Habermas says, "system-conforming" ones. But the system they conform to is not adequately characterized as the system of the official, state-regulated capitalist economy. It is also the system of male dominance that extends even to the socio-cultural lifeworld. In other words, the ambivalence here does not only stem, as Habermas implies, from the fact that the role of client carries effects of "reification." It stems also from the fact that this role, qua feminine role, perpetuates in a new, let us say modernized and rationalized form, women's subordination. Or so Habermas's third thesis might be rewritten in a feminist critical theory—without, of course, abandoning his insights into the ways in which welfare bureaucracies and therapeutocracies disempower clients by preempting their capacities to interpret their own needs, experiences, and life-problems.

4) Habermas's fourth thesis, by contrast, is not so easily rewritten. This thesis states that welfare reforms of, for example, the domestic

---

Work and Welfare: The Feminization of Poverty," in *Working Women and Families*, ed. Karen Wolk Feinstein, Beverly Hills, CA: Sage Publications, 1979, and "Toil and Trouble: Women Workers and Unemployment Compensation," *Signs: Journal of Women in Culture and Society*, 10:3, 1985, 439–59; and Barbara Ehrenreich and Frances Fox Piven, "The Feminization of Poverty," *Dissent*, Spring 1984, 162–70. For an analysis of the gendered character of the British social-welfare system, see Hilary Land, "Who Cares for the Family?," *Journal of Social Policy* 7:3, 1978, 257–84. For Norway, see *Patriarchy in a Welfare Society*, ed. Harriet Holter, Oslo: Universitetsforlaget, 1984. See also two comparative studies: Mary Ruggie, *The State and Working Women: A Comparative Study of Britain and Sweden*, Princeton, NJ: Princeton University Press, 1984; and Birte Siim, "Women and the Welfare State: Between Private and Public Dependence" (unpublished typescript).

39   Carol Brown, "Mothers, Fathers and Children: From Private to Public Patriarchy," in Sargent, ed., *Women and Revolution*. Actually, I believe Brown's formulation is theoretically inadequate, since it presupposes a simple, dualistic conception of public and private. Nonetheless, the phrase "from private to public patriarchy" evokes in a rough but suggestive way the phenomena for which a socialist-feminist critical theory of the welfare state would need to account.

sphere are more ambivalent than reforms of the paid workplace. This is true empirically in the sense I have just described. But it is due to the patriarchal character of welfare systems, not to the inherently symbolic character of lifeworld institutions, as Habermas claims. His claim depends on two assumptions I have already challenged. First, it depends on the natural kinds interpretation of the distinction between symbolic and material reproduction activities, i.e., on the false assumption that childrearing is inherently more symbolic and less material than other work. And second, it depends upon the absolute differences interpretation of the system vs. socially integrated contexts distinction, i.e., on the false assumption that money and power are not already entrenched in the internal dynamics of the family. But once we repudiate these assumptions, then there is no categorial, as opposed to empirical, basis for differentially evaluating the two kinds of reforms. If it is basically progressive that paid workers acquire the means to confront their employers strategically and match power against power, right against right, then it must be just as basically progressive in principle that women acquire similar means to similar ends in the politics of familial and personal life. And if it is "pathological" that, in the course of achieving a better balance of power in familial and personal life, women become clients of state bureaucracies, then it must be just as "pathological" in principle that, in the course of achieving a similar end at paid work, paid workers, too, become clients, which does not alter the fact that in actuality they become two different sorts of clients. But of course the real point is that the term "pathological" is misused here insofar as it supposes the untenable assumption that childrearing and other work are asymmetrical with respect to system integration.

5) This also sheds new light on Habermas's fifth thesis, which states that welfare-state capitalism inaugurates an inner colonization of the lifeworld by systems. This claim depends on three assumptions. The first two of these are the two just rejected, namely, the natural kinds interpretation of the distinction between symbolic and material reproduction activities and the assumed virginity of the domestic sphere with respect to money and power. The third assumption is that the basic vector of motion in late capitalist society is from state-regulated economy to lifeworld and not vice versa. But the feminine gender subtext of the client role contradicts this assumption. It suggests that even in late capitalism the norms and meanings of gender identity continue to channel the influence of the lifeworld onto systems. These norms continue to structure the state-regulated economy, as the persistence, indeed exacerbation, of labor-force segmentation according to sex shows.[40] And these norms also structure state

---

40  At the time this essay was written, US data indicated that sex segmentation

administration, as the gender segmentation of US and European social-welfare systems shows.[41] Thus, it is not the case that in late capitalism "system intrusions" detach life contexts from "value-orientations per se." On the contrary, welfare capitalism simply uses other means to uphold the familiar "normatively secured consensus" concerning male dominance and female subordination. But Habermas's theory overlooks this countermotion from lifeworld to system. Thus, it posits the evil of welfare-state capitalism as a general and indiscriminate reification. So it fails to account for the fact that it is disproportionately women who suffer the effects of bureaucratization and monetarization—and for the fact that, viewed structurally, bureaucratization and monetarization are, among other things, instruments of women's subordination.

6) This entails the revision, as well, of Habermas's sixth thesis, concerning the causes, character, and emancipatory potential of social movements, including feminism, in late capitalist societies. Since these issues are so central to the concerns of this paper, they warrant a more extended discussion.

Habermas explains the existence and character of new social movements, including feminism, in terms of colonization—that is, in terms of the intrusion of system-integration mechanisms into symbolic reproduction spheres and the consequent erosion and desiccation of contexts of interpretation and communication. But given the multi-directionality of causal influence in welfare capitalism, the terms "colonization," "intrusion," "erosion," and "desiccation" are too negative and one-sided to account for the identity shifts manifested in social movements. Let me attempt an alternative explanation, at least for women, by returning to Habermas's important insight that much contemporary contestation surrounds the institution-mediating roles

---

in paid work was increasing, despite the entry of women into professions like law and medicine. Even when the gains won by those women were taken into account, there was no overall improvement in the aggregated comparative economic position of paid women workers vis-à-vis male workers. Women's wages remained less than 60 percent of men's wages. Nor was there any overall improvement in occupational distribution by sex. Rather, the ghettoization of women in low-paying, low-status "pink collar" occupations was increasing. For example, in the US in 1973, women held 96 percent of all paid childcare jobs, 81 percent of all primary school teaching jobs, 72 percent of all health technician jobs, 98 percent of all Registered Nurse jobs, 83 percent of all librarian jobs, 99 percent of all secretarial jobs, and 92 percent of all waitperson jobs. The figures for 1983 were, respectively, 97 percent, 83 percent, 84 percent, 96 percent, 87 percent, 99 percent, and 88 percent (Bureau of Labor Statistics figures cited by Drew Christie, "Comparable Worth and Distributive Justice," paper read at meetings of the American Philosophical Association, Western Division, April 1985).

41   See note 38 above.

of worker, consumer, citizen, and client. Let me add to these the child-rearer role and the fact that all of them are gendered roles. Now consider in this light the meaning of the experience of millions of women, especially married women and women with children, who have in the postwar period become paid workers and/or social-welfare clients. I have already indicated that this has been an experience of new, acute forms of domination. But it has also been an experience in which women could, often for the first time, taste the possibilities of a measure of relative economic independence, an identity outside the domestic sphere and expanded political participation. Above all, it has been an experience of conflict and contradiction as women try to do the impossible, namely, to juggle simultaneously the existing roles of childrearer and worker, client and citizen. The cross-pulls of these mutually incompatible roles have been painful and identity-threatening, but not simply negative.[42] Interpellated simultaneously in contradictory ways, women have become split subjects; and, as a result, the roles themselves, previously shielded in their separate spheres, have suddenly been opened to contestation. Should we, like Habermas, speak here of a "crisis in symbolic reproduction"? Surely not, if this means the desiccation of meaning and values wrought by the intrusion of money and organizational power into women's lives. Emphatically yes, if it means, rather, the emergence into visibility and contestability of problems and possibilities that cannot be solved or realized within the established framework of gendered roles and institutions.

If colonization is not an adequate explanation of contemporary feminism (and other new social movements), then decolonization cannot be an adequate conception of an emancipatory solution. From the perspective I have been sketching, the first element of decolonization, namely, the removal of system-integration mechanisms from symbolic reproduction spheres, is conceptually and empirically askew of the real issues. If the real point is the moral superiority of cooperative and egalitarian interactions over strategic and hierarchical ones, then it mystifies matters to single out lifeworld institutions—the point should hold for paid work and political administration as well as for domestic life. Similarly, the third element of decolonization, namely, the reversal of the direction of influence and control from system to lifeworld, needs modification. Since the social meanings of gender still structure late-capitalist official economic and state systems, the question is not whether lifeworld norms will be decisive but, rather, which lifeworld norms will.

---

42  Cf. Zillah Eisenstein, *The Radical Future of Liberal Feminism*, Boston: Northeastern University Press, 1981, especially Chapter 9. What follows has some affinities with the perspective of Ernesto Laclau and Chantal Mouffe in *Hegemony and Socialist Strategy*, New York: Verso, 1985.

This implies that the key to an emancipatory outcome lies in the second element of Habermas's conception of decolonization, namely, the replacement of normatively secured contexts of interaction by communicatively achieved ones. The centrality of this element is evident when we consider that this process occurs simultaneously on two fronts. First, in the struggles of social movements with the state and official economic system institutions; these struggles are not waged over systems media alone, they are also waged over the meanings and norms embedded and enacted in government and corporate policy. Second, this process occurs in a phenomenon not thematized by Habermas: in the struggles between opposing social movements with conflicting interpretations of social needs. Both kinds of struggles involve confrontations between normatively secured and communicatively achieved action. Both involve contestation for hegemony over the socio-cultural "means of interpretation and communication." For example, in many late-capitalist societies, women's contradictory, self-dividing experience of trying to be both workers and mothers, clients and citizens, has given rise to not one but two women's movements, a feminist one and an anti-feminist one. These movements, along with their respective allies, are engaged in struggles with one another and with state and corporate institutions over the social meanings of "woman" and "man," "femininity" and "masculinity," over the interpretation of women's needs, over the interpretation and social construction of women's bodies, and over the gender norms that shape the major institution-mediating social roles. Of course, the means of interpretation and communication in terms of which the social meanings of these things are elaborated have always been controlled by men. Thus feminist women are struggling in effect to redistribute and democratize access to and control over the means of interpretation and communication. We are, therefore, struggling for women's autonomy in the following special sense: a measure of collective control over the means of interpretation and communication sufficient to permit us to participate on a par with men in all types of social interaction, including political deliberation and decision-making.[43]

The foregoing suggests that a caution is in order concerning the use of the terms "particularism" and "universalism." Recall that Habermas's sixth thesis emphasized feminism's links to historic liberation movements and its roots in universalist morality. Recall that he was critical of those tendencies within feminism, and in resistance movements in general, which try to resolve the identity problematic by recourse to

---

43   I develop this notion of the "socio-cultural means of interpretation and communication" and the associated conception of autonomy in "Toward a Discourse Ethic of Solidarity," *Praxis International*, 5:4, 1986, 425–9. Both notions are extensions and modifications of Habermas's conception of "communicative ethics."

particularism, that is, by retreating from arenas of political struggle into alternative communities delimited on the basis of natural categories like biological sex. I want to suggest that there are really three issues here and that they need to be disaggregated from one another. One is the issue of political engagement vs. apolitical countercultural activity. Insofar as Habermas's point is a criticism of cultural feminism, it is well taken in principle, although it needs the following qualifications: cultural separatism, while inadequate as long-term political strategy, is in many cases a shorter-term necessity for women's physical, psychological, and moral survival; and separatist communities have been the source of numerous reinterpretations of women's experience which have proved politically fruitful in contestation over the means of interpretation and communication. The second issue is the status of women's biology in the elaboration of new social identities. Insofar as Habermas's point is a criticism of reductive biologism, it is well taken. But this does not mean that one can ignore the fact that women's biology has nearly always been interpreted by men, and that women's struggle for autonomy necessarily and properly involves, among other things, the reinterpretation of the social meanings of our bodies. The third issue is the difficult and complex one of universalism vs. particularism. Insofar as Habermas's endorsement of universalism pertains to the meta-level of access to and control over the means of interpretation and communication, it is well taken. At this level, women's struggle for autonomy can be understood in terms of a universalist conception of distributive justice. But it does not follow that the substantive content which is the fruit of this struggle, namely, the new social meanings we give our needs and our bodies, our new social identities and conceptions of femininity, can be dismissed as particularistic lapses from universalism. For these are no more particular than the sexist and androcentric meanings and norms they are meant to replace. More generally, at the level of substantive content, as opposed to dialogical form, the contrast between universalism and particularism is out of place. Substantive social meanings and norms are always necessarily culturally and historically specific; they always express distinctive shared, but non-universal, forms of life. Feminist meanings and norms will be no exception. But they will not, on that account, be particularistic in any pejorative sense. Let us simply say that they will be different.

I have been arguing that struggles of social movements over the means of interpretation and communication are central to an emancipatory resolution of crisis tendencies in welfare-state capitalism. Now let me clarify their relation to institutional change. Such struggles, I claim, implicitly and explicitly raise the following sorts of questions. Should the roles of worker, childrearer, citizen, and client be fully degendered? Can they be? Or do we, rather, require arrangements that permit women to be workers and citizens *as women*, just as men have always been workers and citizens as men? And what might that mean? In any case, does not an emancipatory outcome require a profound transformation of the current gender roles at the base of contemporary social organization? And does not this, in turn, require a fundamental transformation of the content, character, boundaries, and relations of the spheres of life which these roles mediate? How should the character and position of paid work, childrearing, and citizenship be defined vis-à-vis one another? Should democratic-socialist-feminist, self-managed, paid work encompass childrearing? Or should childrearing, rather, replace soldiering as a component of transformed, democratic-socialist-feminist, participatory citizenship? What other possibilities are conceivable?

Let me conclude this discussion of the six theses by restating the most important critical points. First, Habermas's account fails to theorize the patriarchal, norm-mediated character of late-capitalist official-economic and administrative systems. Likewise, it fails to theorize the systemic, money- and power-mediated character of male dominance in the domestic sphere of the late-capitalist lifeworld. Consequently, his colonization thesis fails to grasp that the channels of influence between system and lifeworld institutions are multidirectional. And it tends to replicate, rather than to problematize, a major institutional support of women's subordination in late capitalism, namely, the gender-based separation of the state-regulated economy of sex-segmented paid work and social welfare, and the male-dominated public sphere, from privatized female childrearing. Thus, while Habermas wants to be critical of male dominance, his diagnostic categories deflect attention elsewhere, to the allegedly overriding problem of gender-neutral reification. As a result, his programmatic conception of decolonization bypasses key feminist questions; it fails to address the issue of how to restructure the relation of childrearing to paid work and citizenship. Finally, Habermas's categories tend to misrepresent the causes and underestimate the scope of the feminist challenge to welfare-state capitalism. In short, the struggles and wishes of contemporary women are not adequately clarified by a theory that draws the basic battle line between system and lifeworld institutions. From a feminist perspective, there is a more basic battle line between the forms of male dominance linking "system" to "lifeworld" and us.

## CONCLUSION

In general, then, the principal blind spots of Habermas's theory with respect to gender are traceable to his categorial opposition between system and lifeworld institutions, and to the two more elementary

oppositions from which it is compounded: the one concerning reproduction functions and the one concerning types of action integration.
Or, rather, the blind spots are traceable to the way in which these
oppositions, ideologically and androcentrically interpreted, tend to
override and eclipse other, potentially more critical elements of
Habermas's framework—elements like the distinction between normatively secured and communicatively achieved action contexts, and
like the four-term model of public-private relations.

Habermas's blind spots are instructive, I think. They permit us to
conclude something about what the categorial framework of a socialist-feminist critical theory of welfare-state capitalism should look like.
One crucial requirement is that this framework not be such as to put
the male-headed, nuclear family and the state-regulated official economy on two opposite sides of the major categorial divide. We require,
rather, a framework sensitive to the similarities between them, one
which puts them on the same side of the line as institutions which,
albeit in different ways, enforce women's subordination, since both
family and official economy appropriate our labor, short-circuit our
participation in the interpretation of our needs, and shield normatively secured need interpretations from political contestation. A
second crucial requirement is that this framework contain no a priori
assumptions about the unidirectionality of social motion and causal
influence, that it be sensitive to the ways in which allegedly disappearing institutions and norms persist in structuring social reality. A third
crucial requirement, and the last I shall mention here, is that this
framework not be such as to posit the evil of welfare-state capitalism
exclusively or primarily as the evil of reification. It must also be capable of foregrounding the evil of dominance and subordination.[44]

---

44 My own recent work attempts to construct a conceptual framework for a
socialist-feminist critical theory of the welfare state that meets these requirements.
See "Women, Welfare and the Politics of Need Interpretation," "Toward a Discourse
Ethic of Solidarity," and, especially, "Struggle over Needs" (Chapter 2 in this
volume). Each of these essays draws heavily on those aspects of Habermas's thought
which I take to be unambiguously positive and useful, especially his conception of
the irreducibly socio-cultural, interpretive character of human needs, and his
contrast between dialogical and monological processes of need interpretation. The
present chapter, on the other hand, focuses mainly on those aspects of Habermas's
thought which I find problematical or unhelpful, and so does not convey the full
range either of his work or of my views about it. Readers are warned, therefore,
against drawing the conclusion that Habermas has little or nothing positive to
contribute to a socialist-feminist critical theory of the welfare state. They are urged,
rather, to consult the essays cited above for the other side of the story.

# 2

# Struggle over Needs: Outline of a Socialist-Feminist Critical Theory of Late-Capitalist Political Culture*

*Need is also a political instrument, meticulously prepared, calculated and used.*
—*Michel Foucault*[1]

In late-capitalist, welfare-state societies, talk about people's needs is an important species of political discourse. In the US we argue, for example, about whether the government should provide for citizens' needs. Thus, feminists claim that the state should provide for parents' day-care needs, while social conservatives insist that children need their mothers' care, and economic conservatives claim that the market, not the government, is the best institution for meeting needs. Americans also argue about whether existing social-welfare programs really do meet the needs they purport to satisfy, or whether these programs misconstrue the latter. For example, right-wing critics claim that unconditional income support programs destroy the incentive to work and undermine the family. Left critics, in contrast, oppose workfare proposals as coercive and punitive, while many poor women with young children say they want to work at good-paying jobs. All these cases involve disputes about what exactly various groups of people really do need and about who should have the last word in such matters. In all these cases, moreover, needs-talk is a medium for the making and contesting of political claims, an idiom in which

* I am grateful for helpful comments from Sandra Bartky, Linda Gordon, Paul Mattick, Jr., Frank Michelman, Martha Minow, Linda Nicholson, and Iris Young. The Mary Ingraham Bunting Institute of Radcliffe College provided generous research support and a utopian working situation.

1 Foucault, *Discipline and Punish: The Birth of the Prison*, trans. Alan Sheridan, New York: Vintage, 1979, 26.

political conflict is played out and inequalities are symbolically elaborated and challenged.

Talk about needs has not always been central to Western political
culture; it has often been considered antithetical to politics and relegated to the margins of political life. However, in welfare-state
societies, needs-talk has been institutionalized as a major idiom of
political discourse. It coexists, albeit often uneasily, with talk about
rights and interests at the very center of political life. Indeed, this
peculiar juxtaposition of a discourse about needs with discourses
about rights and interests is one of the distinctive marks of late-capitalist political culture.

Feminists (and others) who aim to intervene in this culture could
benefit from posing the following questions: Why has needs-talk
become so prominent in the political culture of welfare-state societies? What is the relation between this development and changes in
late-capitalist social structure? What does the emergence of the needs
idiom imply about shifts in the boundaries between "political,"
"economic," and "domestic" spheres of life? Does it betoken an extension of the political sphere or, rather, a colonization of that domain by
newer modes of power and social control? What are the major varieties of needs-talk and how do they interact polemically with one
another? What opportunities and/or obstacles does the needs idiom
pose for movements, like feminism, that seek far-reaching social transformation?

In what follows, I outline an approach for thinking about such
questions rather than proposing definitive answers to them. What I
have to say falls into five parts. In the first section, I break with standard theoretical approaches by shifting the focus of inquiry from needs
to discourses about needs, from the distribution of need satisfactions
to "the politics of need interpretation." I also propose a model of
social discourse designed to bring into relief the contested character
of needs-talk in welfare-state societies. In the second section, I relate
this discourse model to social-structural considerations, especially to
shifts in the boundaries between "political," "economic," and "domestic" spheres of life. In the third section, I identify three major strands
of needs-talk in late-capitalist political culture, and I map some of the
ways in which they compete for potential adherents. In the fourth
section, I apply the model to some concrete cases of contemporary
needs politics in the US. Finally, in the concluding section, I consider
some moral and epistemological issues raised by the phenomenon of
needs-talk.

## 1. POLITICS OF NEED INTERPRETATION:
## A DISCOURSE MODEL

Let me begin by explaining some of the peculiarities of the approach I am proposing. In my approach, the focus of inquiry is not needs but rather *discourses* about needs. The point is to shift our angle of vision on the politics of needs. Usually, the politics of needs is understood to concern the distribution of satisfactions. In my approach, by contrast, the focus is *the politics of need interpretation.*

I focus on discourses and interpretation in order to bring into view the contextual and contested character of needs claims. As many theorists have noted, needs claims have a relational structure; implicitly or explicitly, they have the form "A needs X in order to Y." This "in-order-to" structure, as I shall call it, poses no special problems when we consider very thin, general needs, such as food or shelter *simpliciter.* Thus, we can uncontroversially say that homeless people, like everyone else in non-tropical climates, need shelter in order to live. And many people will infer that governments, as guarantors of life and liberty, have a responsibility to provide for this need in the last resort. However, as soon as we descend to lesser levels of generality, needs claims become far more controversial. What, more "thickly," do homeless people need *in order to* be sheltered from the elements? What specific forms of provision are implied once we acknowledge their very general, thin need? Do homeless people need society's willingness to allow them to sleep undisturbed next to a hot air vent on a street corner? A space in a subway tunnel or a bus terminal? A bed in a temporary shelter? A permanent home? Suppose we say the latter. What kind of permanent housing do homeless people need? High-rise rental units in city centers that are remote from good schools, discount shopping, and job opportunities? Single family homes designed for single-earner, two-parent families? And what else do homeless people need in order to have permanent homes? Rent subsidies? Income support? Jobs? Job training and education? Day care? Finally, what is needed, at the level of housing policy, in order to insure an adequate stock of affordable housing? Tax incentives to encourage private investment in low-income housing? Concentrated or scattered public housing projects within a generally commodified housing environment? Rent control? Decommodification of urban housing?[2]

We could continue proliferating such questions indefinitely. And we would, at the same time, be proliferating controversy. That is precisely

---

2  Decommodification of housing could mean socialized ownership or, alternatively, occupant ownership combined with a non-market mechanism for determining values during transfers (e.g., price controls).

the point about needs claims. These claims tend to be nested, connected to one another in ramified chains of in-order-to relations: not only does A need X in order to Y; she also needs P in order to X, Q in order to P, and so on. Moreover, when such in-order-to chains are unraveled in the course of political disputes, disagreements usually deepen rather than abate. Precisely how such chains are unraveled depends on what the interlocutors share in the way of background assumptions. Does it go without saying that policy designed to deal with homelessness must not challenge the basic ownership and investment structure of urban real estate? Or is that a point at which people's assumptions and commitments diverge?

It is such networks of contested in-order-to relations that I aim to highlight when I propose to focus on the politics of need interpretation. Thin theories of needs that do not undertake to explore such networks cannot shed much light on the politics of needs in contemporary societies. Such theories assume that the politics of needs concerns only whether various predefined needs will or will not be provided for. As a result, they deflect attention from a number of important political questions.[3] First, they take the *interpretation* of people's needs as simply given and unproblematic; they thus occlude the interpretive dimension of needs politics, the fact that not just satisfactions but *need interpretations* are politically contested. They assume, second, that it does not matter who interprets the needs in question and from what perspective and in the light of what interests; they thus overlook the fact that *who* gets to establish authoritative, thick definitions of people's needs is itself a political stake. They take for granted, third, that the socially authorized forms of public discourse available for interpreting people's needs are adequate and fair; they thus neglect the question whether these forms of public discourse are skewed in favor of the self-interpretations and interests of dominant social groups and, so, work to the disadvantage of subordinate or oppositional groups—in other words, they occlude the fact that the means of public discourse themselves may be at issue in needs politics. Fourth, such theories fail to problematize the social and institutional logic of processes of need interpretation; they thus neglect such important political questions as: Where in society, in what institutions, are authoritative need interpretations developed? And what sorts of social relations are in force among the interlocutors or co-interpreters?

---

3   An example of the kind of theory I have in mind is David Braybrooke, *Meeting Needs*, Princeton, NJ: Princeton University Press, 1987. Braybrooke claims that a thin concept of need "can make a substantial contribution to settling upon policies without having to descend into the melee" (68). Thus, he does not take up any of the issues I am about to enumerate.

In order to remedy these blind spots, I propose a more politically critical, discourse-oriented alternative. I take the politics of need interpretation to comprise three analytically distinct but practically interrelated moments. The first is the struggle to establish or deny the political status of a given need, the struggle to validate the need as a matter of legitimate political concern or to enclave it as a nonpolitical matter. The second is the struggle over the interpretation of the need, the struggle for the power to define it and, so, to determine what would satisfy it. The third moment is the struggle over the satisfaction of the need, the struggle to secure or withhold provision.

A focus on the politics of need interpretation requires a model of social discourse. The model I propose foregrounds the multivalent and contested character of needs-talk, the fact that in welfare-state societies we encounter a plurality of competing ways of talking about people's needs. The model theorizes what I call "the socio-cultural means of interpretation and communication" (MIC). By this I mean the historically and culturally specific ensemble of discursive resources available to members of a given social collectivity in pressing claims against one another. Such resources include:

1. The officially recognized idioms in which one can press claims; for example, needs-talk, rights-talk, interests-talk.

2. The concrete vocabularies available for making claims in these recognized idioms: in the case of needs-talk, for example, therapeutic vocabularies, administrative vocabularies, religious vocabularies, feminist vocabularies, socialist vocabularies.

3. The paradigms of argumentation accepted as authoritative in adjudicating conflicting claims: Are conflicts over the interpretation of needs resolved, for example, by appeal to scientific experts? By brokered compromises? By voting according to majority rule? By privileging the interpretations of those whose needs are in question?

4. The narrative conventions available for constructing the individual and collective stories which are constitutive of people's social identities.

5. The modes of subjectification: the ways in which discourses position interlocutors as specific sorts of subjects endowed with specific sorts of capacities for action—for example, as "normal" or "deviant," as causally conditioned or freely self-determining, as victims or as potential activists, as unique individuals or as members of social groups.[4]

---

4  The expression "mode of subjectification" is inspired by Foucault, although his term is "mode of subjection" and his usage differs somewhat from mine. Cf. Michel Foucault, "On the Genealogy of Ethics: An Overview of Work in Progress," in Paul Rabinow, ed., *The Foucault Reader*, New York: Pantheon, 1984, 340–73. For

All these elements comprise the MIC in late-capitalist, welfare-state societies. To grasp their function, one must recall that such societies harbor a plurality of forms of association, roles, groups, institutions, and discourses. Thus, the means of interpretation and communication are not all of a piece. Far from constituting a coherent, monolithic web, they form a heterogeneous field of polyglot possibilities and diverse alternatives. In welfare-state societies, moreover, discourses about needs typically make at least implicit reference to alternative interpretations. Particular claims about needs are "internally dialogized," resonating implicitly or explicitly with competing need interpretations.[5] They allude, in other words, to a conflict of interpretations. For example, groups seeking to restrict or outlaw abortion counterpose "the sanctity of life" to the mere "convenience" of "career women"; thus, they cast their claims in terms that refer, however disparagingly, to feminist inter-pretations of reproductive needs.[6]

On the other hand, late-capitalist societies are not simply pluralist. Rather, they are stratified, differentiated into social groups with unequal status, power, and access to resources, traversed by pervasive axes of inequality along lines of class, gender, race, ethnicity, and age. The MIC in these societies are also stratified, organized in ways that are congruent with societal patterns of dominance and subordination.

It follows that we must distinguish those elements of the MIC that

---

another account of this idea of the socio-cultural means of interpretation and communication, see Nancy Fraser, "Toward a Discourse Ethic of Solidarity," *Praxis International* 5:4, January 1986, 425–9.

5    The expression "internally dialogized" comes from Mikhail Bakhtin. I consider his notion of a "dialogic heteroglossia" (or a cross-referential, multivoiced field of significations) more apt for characterizing the MIC in late-capitalist, welfare-state societies than the more monolithic Lacanian idea of the symbolic. In this respect, however, I part company with Bakhtin's own view that these conceptions found their most robust expression in the "carnivalesque" culture of late-medieval Europe and that the subsequent history of Western societies brought a flattening out of language and a restriction of dialogic heteroglossia to the specialized, esoteric domain of "the literary." This seems wrong to me, given that the dialogic, polemical character of speech is related to the availability in a culture of a plurality of competing discourses and of subject positions from which to articulate them. Thus, conceptually, one would expect what, I take it, is in fact the case: that speech in complex, differentiated societies would be especially suitable for analysis in terms of these Bakhtinian categories. For the Bakhtinian conceptions of heteroglossia and internal dialogization, see Bakhtin, "Discourse in the Novel," in *The Dialogic Imagination: Four Essays*, trans. Caryl Emerson and Michael Holquist, Austin: University of Texas Press, 1981, 259–422. For an argument for the superiority of the Bakhtinian conception of discourse to the Lacanian for theorizing matters of feminist concern, see Chapter 5 of this volume, "Against Symbolicism."

6    On anti-abortion discourse, see Kristin Luker, *Abortion and the Politics of Motherhood*, Berkeley: University of California Press, 1984.

are hegemonic, authorized, and officially sanctioned, on the one hand, from those that are non-hegemonic, disqualified, and discounted, on the other hand. Some ways of talking about needs are institutionalized in the central discursive arenas of late-capitalist societies: parliaments, academies, courts, and mass circulation media. Other ways of talking about needs are enclaved as socially marked subdialects and normally excluded from the central discursive arenas.[7] Until recently, for example, moralistic and scientific discourses about the needs of people with AIDS, and of people at risk of contracting AIDS, were well represented on government commissions, while gay and lesbian rights activists' interpretations were largely excluded. To change that distribution of discursive power, it was necessary to wage a political struggle.

From this perspective, needs-talk appears as a site of struggle where groups with unequal discursive (and extra-discursive) resources compete to establish as hegemonic their respective interpretations of legitimate social needs. Dominant groups articulate need interpretations intended to exclude, defuse, and/or co-opt counter-interpretations. Subordinate or oppositional groups, in contrast, articulate need interpretations intended to challenge, displace, and/or modify dominant ones. In neither case are the interpretations simply "representations." In both cases, rather, they are acts and interventions.[8]

## 2. ENCLAVED AND RUNAWAY NEEDS: ON THE "POLITICAL," "ECONOMIC," AND "DOMESTIC"

Let me now situate the discourse model I have just sketched with respect to some social-structural features of late-capitalist societies. Here, I seek to relate the rise of politicized needs-talk to shifts in the boundaries separating "political," "economic," and "domestic" dimensions of life. However, unlike many social theorists, I shall treat the terms "political," "economic," and "domestic" as cultural classifications and ideological labels rather than as designations of structures, spheres, or things.[9]

---

7 If the previous point was Bakhtinian, this one could be considered Bourdieusian. There is probably no contemporary social theorist who has worked more fruitfully than Bourdieu at understanding cultural contestation in relation to societal inequality. See his *Outline of a Theory of Practice*, trans. Richard Nice, Cambridge: Cambridge University Press, 1977, and *Distinction: A Social Critique of the Judgment of Pure Taste*, Cambridge, Mass.: Harvard University Press, 1979. For an account of Bourdieu's enduring relevance, see Nancy Fraser, "Bourdieu: Une réflexion pour l'ère postindustrielle," *Le monde*, January 24, 2012. Accessible at lemonde.fr.

8 Here the model aims to marry Bakhtin with Bourdieu.

9 I owe this formulation to Paul Mattick, Jr. For a thoughtful discussion of the

I begin by noting that the terms "politics" and "political" are highly contested and have a number of different senses.[10] In the present context, the two most important senses are the following. There is, first, an institutional sense, in which a matter is deemed "political" if it is handled directly in the institutions of the official governmental system, including parliaments, administrative apparatuses, and the like. In this sense, what is political—call it "official-political"— contrasts with what is handled in institutions like "the family" and "the economy," which are defined as being outside the official-political system, even though they are in actuality underpinned and regulated by it. In addition, there is, second, a discursive sense of the term "political" in which something is "political" if it is contested across a broad range of different discursive arenas and among a wide range of different publics. In this sense, what is political—call it "discursive-political" or "politicized"—contrasts both with what is not contested in public at all and also with what is contested only by and within relatively specialized, enclaved, and/or segmented publics. These two senses are not unrelated. In democratic theory, if not always in practice, a matter becomes subject to legitimate state intervention only after it has been debated across a wide range of discourse publics.

In general, there are no a priori constraints dictating that some matters are intrinsically political and others are intrinsically not. As a matter of fact, these boundaries are drawn differently from culture to culture and from historical period to historical period. For example, reproduction became an intensely political matter in the 1890s in the US amid a panic about "race suicide." By the 1940s, however, it was widely assumed that birth control was a "private" matter. Finally, with the emergence of the women's movement in the 1960s, reproduction was repoliticized.[11]

Yet it would be misleading to suggest that, for any society in any period, the boundary between what is political and what is not is simply fixed. On the contrary, this boundary may itself be an object of conflict. For example, struggles over Poor Law "reform" in nine-teenth-century England were also conflicts about the scope of the political. And as I shall argue shortly, one of the primary stakes of social conflict in late-capitalist societies is precisely where the limits of the political will be drawn.

---

advantages of this sort of approach, see his "On *Feminism as Critique*" (unpublished manuscript).

10   Included among the senses I shall not discuss are (1) the pejorative colloquial sense according to which a decision is political when personal jockeying for power overrides germane substantive considerations; and (2) the radical political-theoretical sense according to which all interactions traversed by relations of power and inequality are political.

11   Linda Gordon, *Woman's Body, Woman's Right*, New York: Viking, 1976.

Let me spell out some of the presuppositions and implications of the discursive sense of "politics." Recall that this sense stipulates that a matter is "political" if it is contested across a range of different discursive arenas and among a range of different discourse publics. Note, therefore, that it depends upon the idea of discursive publicity. However, in this conception, publicity is not understood in a simple unitary way as the undifferentiated opposite of discursive privacy. Rather, publicity is understood to be differentiated on the assumption that it is possible to identify a plurality of distinct discourse publics and to theorize the relations among them.

Clearly, publics can be distinguished along a number of different axes, for example: by ideology (the readership of *The Nation* versus the readership of *The Public Interest*), by stratification axes such as gender (the viewers of "Cagney and Lacey" versus the viewers of "Monday Night Football") or class (the readership of *The New York Times* versus that of *The New York Post*), by profession (the membership of the Chamber of Commerce versus that of the American Medical Association), by central mobilizing issue (the nuclear freeze movement versus the pro-life movement).

Publics can also be distinguished in terms of relative power. Some are large, authoritative, and able to set the terms of debate for many of the rest. Others, by contrast, are small, self-enclosed, and enclaved, unable to make much of a mark beyond their own borders. Publics of the former sort are often able to take the lead in the formation of hegemonic blocs: concatenations of different publics, which together construct "the common sense" of the day. As a result, such leading publics usually have a heavy hand in defining what is "political" in the discursive sense. They can politicize an issue simply by entertaining contestation concerning it, since such contestation will be transmitted as a matter of course to and through other allied and opposing publics. Smaller, counter-hegemonic publics, by contrast, generally lack the power to politicize issues in this way. When they succeed in fomenting widespread contestation over what was previously "nonpolitical," it is usually by far slower and more laborious means. In general, it is the relative power of various publics that determines the outcome of struggles over the boundaries of the political.

How, then, should we conceptualize the politicization of needs in late-capitalist societies? What must be grasped here are the processes by which some matters break out of zones of discursive privacy and out of specialized or enclaved publics so as to become foci of generalized contestation. When this happens, previously taken-for-granted interpretations of these matters are called into question, and naturalized chains of in-order-to relations become subject to dispute.

What, then, are the zones of privacy and the specialized publics that previously enveloped newly politicized needs in late-capitalist societies? Which institutions sheltered these needs from contestation, naturalizing their interpretations in taken-for-granted networks of in-order-to relations? In male-dominated, capitalist societies, what is "political" is normally defined in contrast to what is "economic" and "domestic" or "personal." Here, accordingly, we encounter two principal sets of institutions that depoliticize social needs: first, domestic institutions, especially the normative domestic form, namely, the modern, male-headed, nuclear family; and, second, official-economic capitalist system institutions, especially paid workplaces, markets, credit mechanisms, and "private" enterprises and corporations.[12] Domestic institutions depoliticize certain matters by personalizing and/or familializing them; they cast these as private-domestic or personal-familial matters in contradistinction to public, political matters. Official-economic capitalist system institutions depoliticize certain matters by economizing them; the issues in question here are cast as impersonal market imperatives or as "private" ownership prerogatives or as technical problems for managers and planners, all in contradistinction to political matters. In both cases, the result is a foreshortening of chains of in-order-to relations for interpreting people's needs; interpretive chains are truncated and prevented from spilling across the boundaries separating "the domestic" and "the economic" from "the political."

Clearly, domestic and official-economic system institutions differ in many important respects. However, in *these* respects they are exactly on a par with one another: both enclave certain matters into specialized discursive arenas; both thereby shield such matters from generalized contestation and from widely disseminated conflicts of interpretation. As a result, both entrench as authoritative certain specific interpretations of needs by embedding them in certain specific, but largely unquestioned, chains of in-order-to relations.

Since both domestic and official-economic system institutions support relations of dominance and subordination, the specific interpretations they naturalize usually tend to advantage dominant groups and individuals and to disadvantage their subordinates. If wife battering, for example, is enclaved as a "personal" or "domestic" matter within male-headed, nuclear families; and if public discourse about this phenomenon is canalized into specialized publics associated with, say, family law, social work, and the sociology and psychology of

---

12    Throughout this chapter, I refer to paid workplaces, markets, credit systems, etc., as "*official*-economic system institutions" so as to avoid the androcentric implication that domestic institutions are not also "economic." For a discussion of this issue, see Chapter 1 of this volume, "What's Critical About Critical Theory?

"deviancy"; then this serves to reproduce women's subordination to men. Similarly, if questions of workplace democracy are enclaved as "economic" or "managerial" problems in profit-oriented, hierarchically managed, paid workplaces; and if discourse about these questions is shunted into specialized publics associated with, say, "industrial relations" sociology, labor law, and "management science"; then this serves to perpetuate class (and usually also gendered and raced) exploitation and domination.

As a result of these processes, members of subordinated groups commonly internalize need interpretations that work to their own disadvantage. Sometimes, however, culturally dominant need interpretations are superimposed upon latent or embryonic oppositional interpretations. This is most likely where there persist, however fragmentedly, subculturally transmitted traditions of resistance, as in some sections of the US labor movement and in the collective historical memory of many African Americans. Under special circumstances, moreover, processes of depoliticization are disrupted. At that point, dominant classifications of needs as "economic" or "domestic," as opposed to "political," lose their aura of self-evidence, and alternative, oppositional, and *politicized* interpretations emerge in their stead.[13]

In late-capitalist societies, in any case, family and official-economy are the principal depoliticizing enclaves that needs must exceed in order to become political in the discursive sense. Thus, the emergence of needs-talk as a political idiom in these societies is the other side of the increased permeability of domestic and official-economic institutions, their growing inability to fully depoliticize certain matters. The politicized needs at issue in late-capitalist societies, then, are *leaky* or *runaway* needs, which have broken out of the discursive enclaves constructed in and around domestic and official-economic institutions.

---

13 The difficulty in specifying theoretically the conditions under which processes of depoliticization are disrupted stems from the difficulty of relating what are usually considered "economic" and "cultural" "factors." In my view, rational choice models err in overweighting "economic" at the expense of "cultural" determinants, as in the (not always accurate) prediction that culturally dominant but ultimately disadvantageous need interpretations lose their hold when economic prosperity heralds reduced inequality and promotes "rising expectations." See Jon Elster, "Sour Grapes," in *Utilitarianism and Beyond*, ed. Amartya Sen and Bernard Williams, Cambridge: Cambridge University Press, 1982. An alternative model developed by Jane Jenson emphasizes the cultural-ideological lens through which "economic" effects are filtered. Jenson relates "crises in the mode of regulation" to shifts in cultural "paradigms" that cast into relief previously present but non-emphasized elements of people's social identities. See her "Paradigms and Political Discourse: Labor and Social Policy in the USA and France before 1914," Working Paper Series, Center for European Studies, Harvard University, Winter 1989.

Runaway needs are a species of *excess* with respect to the normative modern domestic and economic institutions. Initially at least, they bear the stamp of those institutions, remaining embedded in conventional chains of in–order–to relations. For example, many runaway needs are colored by the assumption that "the domestic" is supposed to be separated from "the economic" in male-dominated, capitalist societies. Thus, throughout most of US history, child care has been cast as a "domestic" rather than an "economic" need; it has been interpreted as the need of children for the full-time care of their mothers rather than as the need of workers for time away from their children; and its satisfaction has been construed along the lines of "mothers' pensions" rather than of day care.[14] Here, the assumption of separate spheres truncates possible chains of in–order–to relations which would yield alternative interpretations of social needs.

Where, then, do runaway needs run to when they break out of domestic or official-economic enclaves? I propose that runaway needs enter a historically specific and relatively new societal arena. Following Hannah Arendt, I call this arena "the social" in order to mark its noncoincidence with the family, official-economy, or state.[15] As a site of contested discourse about runaway needs, "the social" cuts across these traditional divisions. It is an arena of conflict among rival interpretations of needs embedded in rival chains of in–order–to relations.[16]

As I conceive it, the social is a switch point for the meeting of heterogeneous contestants associated with a wide range of different

------

14   See Sonya Michel, "American Women and the Discourse of the Democratic Family in World War II," in *Behind the Lines: Gender and the Two World Wars*, ed. Margaret Higonnet, Jane Jenson, and Sonya Michel, New Haven: Yale University Press, 1987, and "Children's Interests/Mothers' Rights: A History of Public Child Care in the United States" (unpublished typescript).

15   Hannah Arendt, *The Human Condition*, Chicago: University of Chicago Press, especially Chapter 2, 22–78. However, it should be noted that my view of "the social" differs significantly from Arendt's. Whereas she sees the social as a one-dimensional space wholly under the sway of administration and instrumental reason, I see it as multivalent and contested. Thus, my view incorporates some features of the Gramscian conception of "civil society."

16   In some times and places, the idea of "the social" has been elaborated explicitly as an alternative to "the political." For example, in nineteenth-century England, "the social" was understood as the sphere in which (middle-class) women's supposed distinctive domestic virtues could be diffused for the sake of the larger collective good without suffering the "degradation" of participation in the competitive world of "politics." Thus, "social" work, figured as "municipal motherhood," was heralded as an alternative to suffrage. See Denise Riley, *"Am I That Name?" Feminism and the Category of "Women" in History*, Minneapolis: University of Minnesota Press, 2003. Similarly, the invention of sociology required the conceptualization of an order of "social" interaction distinct from "politics." See Jacques Donzelot, *The Policing of Families*, New York: Pantheon, 1979.

publics. These contestants range from proponents of politicization to defenders of (re)depoliticization, from loosely organized social movements to members of specialized, expert publics in and around the social state. Moreover, they vary greatly in relative power. Some are associated with leading publics capable of setting the terms of political debate; others are linked, by contrast, to enclaved publics and must oscillate between marginalization and co-optation.

The social is also the site where successfully politicized runaway needs get translated into claims for state provision. Here, rival need interpretations are elaborated into rival programmatic conceptions; rival alliances are forged around rival policy proposals; and unequally endowed groups compete to shape the formal policy agenda. For example, in the US in the 1990s, various interest groups, movements, professional associations, and parties scrambled for formulations around which to build alliances sufficiently powerful to dictate the shape of impending "welfare reform."

Eventually, if and when such contests are (at least temporarily) resolved, runaway needs may become objects of state intervention. At that point, they become targets and levers for various strategies of crisis management, while also supplying rationales for the proliferation of new state agencies. Such agencies, which comprise the "social state," are engaged in regulating and/or funding and/or providing the satisfaction of social needs.[17] They do not merely satisfy, but also interpret the needs in question. For example, the US social-welfare system is divided into two unequal subsystems, which are coded by gender and race: an implicitly "masculine" social insurance subsystem tied to "primary" labor-force participation and historically geared to (white male) "breadwinners"; and an implicitly "feminine" relief subsystem tied to household income and geared to homemaker-mothers and their "defective" (female-headed) families, originally restricted to white women, but subsequently racialized. With the underlying (but counterfactual) assumption of "separate spheres," the two subsystems differ markedly in the degree of autonomy, rights, and presumption of desert they accord beneficiaries, as well as in their funding base, mode of administration and character, and level of benefits.[18] Thus, the vari-

17 The social state is not a unitary entity but a multiform, differentiated complex of agencies and apparatuses. In the US it comprises the welter of agencies that make up especially the Departments of Labor and of Health and Human Services.

18 For an analysis of the gendered structure of the US social-welfare system, see Nancy Fraser, "Women, Welfare and the Politics of Need Interpretation," *Hypatia: A Journal of Feminist Philosophy* 2:1, Winter 1987, 103–21; Barbara Nelson, "Women's Poverty and Women's Citizenship: Some Political Consequences of Economic Marginality," *Signs: Journal of Women in Culture and Society* vol. 10, 1984,

ous agencies comprising the social-welfare system provide more than material aid. They also provide clients, and the public at large, with a tacit but powerful interpretive map of normative, differentially valued gender roles and gendered needs. Therefore, the different branches of the social state, too, are players in the politics of need interpretation.[19]

To summarize: in late-capitalist societies, runaway needs that have broken out of domestic or official-economic enclaves enter that hybrid discursive space that Hannah Arendt called "the social." They may then become foci of state intervention geared to crisis management. These needs are thus markers of major social-structural shifts in the boundaries separating what are classified as "political," "economic," and "domestic" or "personal" spheres of life.

### 3. CONFLICTING NEED INTERPRETATIONS: ON OPPOSITIONAL, REPRIVATIZING, AND EXPERT DISCOURSES

Let me now propose a scheme for classifying the many varieties of needs-talk in late-capitalist societies. My aim is to identity some distinct types of discourse and to map the lines along which they compete. The result should be an account of some basic axes of needs politics in welfare-state societies.

I begin by distinguishing three major kinds of needs discourses in late-capitalist societies. The first I shall call "oppositional" forms of needs-talk, which arise when needs are politicized "from below." These contribute to the crystallization of new social identities on the part of subordinated social groups. The second type I call "reprivatization" discourses, which emerge in response to the first. These articulate entrenched need interpretations that could previously go without saying. Finally, there are what I shall call "expert" needs discourses, which link popular movements to the state. They can best be understood in the context of "social problem-solving," institution-building, and professional class formation. In general, it is the contestatory interaction of these three strands of needs-talk that structures the politics of needs in late-capitalist societies.[20]

---

209–31; and Diana Pearce, "Women, Work and Welfare: The Feminization of Poverty," in Karen Wolk Feinstein, ed., *Working Women and Families*, Beverly Hills, CA: Sage Publications, 1979.

19   For an analysis of US social-welfare agencies as purveyors and enforcers of need interpretations, see Nancy Fraser, "Women, Welfare and the Politics of Need Interpretation."

20   This picture is at odds with the one implicit in the writings of Foucault. From my perspective, Foucault focuses too single-mindedly on expert discourses at the expense of oppositional and reprivatization discourses. Thus, he misses

Let us look first at the politicization of runaway needs via *oppositional discourses*. Here, needs become politicized when, for example, women, workers, and/or peoples of color come to contest the subordinate identities and roles, the traditional, reified, and disadvantageous need interpretations previously assigned to and/or embraced by them. By insisting on speaking publicly of heretofore depoliticized needs, by claiming for these needs the status of legitimate political issues, such persons and groups do several things simultaneously. First, they contest the established boundaries separating "politics" from "economics" and "domestics." Second, they offer alternative interpretations of their needs embedded in alternative chains of in-order-to relations. Third, they create new discourse publics from which they try to disseminate their interpretations of their needs throughout a wide range of different discourse publics. Finally, they challenge, modify, and/or displace hegemonic elements of the means of interpretation and communication, as they invent new forms of discourse for interpreting their needs.

In oppositional discourses, needs-talk is a moment in the self-constitution of new collective agents or social movements. For example, in the current wave of feminist ferment, groups of women have politicized and reinterpreted various needs, have instituted new vocabularies and forms of address, and, so, have become "women" in a different, though not uncontested or univocal, sense. By speaking publicly the heretofore unspeakable, by coining terms like "sexism," "sexual harassment," "marital, date, and acquaintance rape," "labor force sex-segregation," "the double shift," "wife-battery," etc., feminist women have become "women" in the sense of a discursively self-constituted political collectivity, albeit a very heterogeneous and fractured one.[21]

Of course, the politicization of needs in oppositional discourses does not go uncontested. One type of resistance involves defending the established boundaries separating "political," "economic," and

---

contestation among competing discourses and the fact that any given outcome is a result of such contestation. For all his theoretical talk about power without a subject, then, Foucault's historical practice is surprisingly traditional in treating social service experts as the only historical subjects.

21   The point could be reformulated more skeptically as follows: feminists have shaped discourses embodying a claim to speak for "women." In fact, this question of "speaking for 'women'" has been a burning issue within the feminist movement. For an interesting take on it, see Riley, *"Am I That Name?"* For a thoughtful discussion of the general problem of the constitution and representation (in both senses) of social groups as sociological classes and as collective agents, see Pierre Bourdieu, "The Social Space and the Genesis of Groups," *Social Science Information* 24, 1985, 195–220.

"domestic" spheres by means of *reprivatization discourses*. Institution-ally, reprivatization designates initiatives aimed at dismantling or cutting back social-welfare services, selling off nationalized assets, and/or deregulating "private" enterprise; discursively, it means depo-liticization. Thus, in reprivatization discourses, speakers oppose state provision of runaway needs and they seek to contain forms of needs-talk that threaten to spill across a wide range of discourse publics. Reprivatizers may insist, for example, that domestic battery is not a legitimate subject of political discourse but a familial or religious matter, or, to take a different example, that a factory closing is not a political question but an unimpeachable prerogative of private owner-ship or an unassailable imperative of an impersonal market mechanism. In both cases, the speakers are contesting the breakout of runaway needs and trying to (re)depoliticize them.

Interestingly, reprivatization discourses blend the old and the new. On the one hand, they seem merely to render explicit need interpre-tations which could earlier go without saying. But, on the other hand, by the very act of articulating such interpretations, they simultane-ously modify them. Because reprivatization discourses respond to competing, oppositional interpretations, they are internally dialo-gized, incorporating references to the alternatives they resist, even while rejecting them. For example, although "pro-family" discourses of the social New Right are explicitly anti-feminist, some of them incorporate in a depoliticized form feminist-inspired motifs implying women's right to sexual pleasure and to emotional support from their husbands.[22]

In defending the established social division of discourses, reprivati-zation discourses deny the claims of oppositional movements for the legitimate political status of runaway needs. However, in so doing, they tend further to politicize those needs in the sense of increasing their cathectedness as foci of contestation. Moreover, in some cases, reprivatization discourses, too, become vehicles for mobilizing social movements and for reshaping social identities. An example is Thatch-erism in Britain, where a set of reprivatization discourses articulated in the accents of authoritarian populism refashioned the subjectivities of a wide range of disaffected constituencies and united them in a powerful coalition.[23]

---

22   See the chapter on "Fundamentalist Sex: Hitting Below the Bible Belt," in Barbara Ehrenreich, Elizabeth Hess, and Gloria Jacobs, *Re-making Love: The Feminization of Sex*, New York: Anchor Books, 1987. For a fascinating account of "postfeminist" women incorporating feminist motifs into born-again Christianity, see Judith Stacey, "Sexism by a Subtler Name? Postindustrial Conditions and Postfeminist Consciousness in the Silicon Valley," *Socialist Review* no. 96, 1987, 7–28.

23   See Stuart Hall, "Moving Right," *Socialist Review* no. 55, January–February

Together, oppositional discourses and reprivatization discourses define one axis of needs-struggle in late-capitalist societies. But there is also a second, rather different axis of conflict. Here, the focal issue is no longer politicization versus depoliticization but rather the interpreted content of contested needs once their political status has been successfully secured. And the principal contestants are oppositional social movements and organized interests like business, which seek to influence public policy.

Consider an example from the US. As day care has gained some increased legitimacy as a political issue, we have seen a proliferation of competing interpretations and programmatic conceptions. In one view, day care would serve poor children's needs for "enrichment" and/or moral supervision. In a second, it would serve the middle-class taxpayer's need to get welfare recipients off the rolls. A third interpretation would shape day care as a measure for increasing the productivity and competitiveness of American business, while yet a fourth would treat it as part of a package of policies aimed at redistributing income and resources to women. Each of these interpretations carries a distinct programmatic orientation with respect to funding, institutional siting and control, service design, and eligibility. As they collide, we see a struggle to shape the hegemonic understanding of day care, which may eventually make its way onto the formal political agenda. Clearly, not just feminist groups, but also business interests, trade unions, children's rights advocates, and educators are contestants in this struggle. Needless to say, they bring to it vast differentials in power.

The struggle for hegemonic need interpretations usually points to the future involvement of the state. Thus, it anticipates yet a third axis of needs struggle in late-capitalist societies. Here, a major issue is politics versus administration, and the principal contestants are oppositional social movements, on the one hand, and social service "experts," on the other.

Recall that "the social" is a site where runaway needs, which have been politicized in the discursive sense, become candidates for state-organized provision. Consequently, these needs become the object of yet another group of discourses: the complex of *expert discourses* about public policy, which find their institutional base in social service agencies and professional circles.

Expert needs discourses are the vehicles for translating sufficiently politicized runaway needs into objects of potential state intervention.

---

1981, 113–37. For an account of New Right reprivatization discourses in the US, see Barbara Ehrenreich, "The New Right Attack on Social Welfare" in Fred Block, Richard A. Cloward, Barbara Ehrenreich, and Frances Fox Piven, *The Mean Season: The Attack on the Welfare State*, New York: Pantheon Books, 1987, 161–95.

Closely connected with institutions of knowledge production and utilization, they include qualitative and especially quantitative social-scientific discourses generated in universities and "think-tanks"; legal discourses generated in judicial institutions and their satellite schools, journals, and professional associations; administrative discourses circulated in various agencies of the social state; and therapeutic discourses circulated in public and private medical and social service agencies.[24]

As the expression suggests, expert discourses tend to be restricted to specialized publics. Associated with professional class formation, they serve to build institutions and to "solve social problems." But in some cases, such as law and psychotherapy, expert vocabularies and rhetorics are disseminated to a wider spectrum of educated laypersons, some of whom are participants in social movements. Moreover, social movements sometimes manage to co-opt or create critical, oppositional segments of expert discourse publics. For all these reasons, expert discourse publics sometimes acquire a certain porousness. And expert discourses become the *bridge* discourses linking loosely organized social movements with the social state.

Because of this bridge role, the rhetoric of expert needs discourses tends to be administrative. These discourses consist in a series of rewriting operations, procedures for translating politicized needs into administerable needs. Typically, the politicized need is redefined as the correlate of a bureaucratically administerable satisfaction, a "social service." It is specified in terms of an ostensibly general state of affairs which could, in principle, befall anyone—for example, unemployment, disability, death, or desertion of a spouse.[25] As a result, the need is decontextualized and recontextualized: on the one hand, it is represented in abstraction from its class, race, and gender specificity and from whatever oppositional meanings it may have acquired in the course of its politicization; on the other hand, it is cast in terms which tacitly presuppose such entrenched, specific background institutions

---

24   In *Discipline and Punish*, Foucault provides a useful account of some elements of the knowledge production apparatuses that contribute to administrative redefinitions of politicized needs. However, Foucault overlooks the role of social movements in politicizing needs and the conflicts of interpretation that arise between such movements and the social state. His account suggests, incorrectly, that policy discourses emanate unidirectionally from specialized, governmental, or quasi-governmental institutions; thus it misses the contestatory interplay among hegemonic and non-hegemonic, institutionally bound and institutionally unbound, interpretations.

25   Cf. the discussion of the administrative logic of need definition in Jürgen Habermas, *Theorie des kommunikativen Handelns*, Band II, *Zur Kritik der funktionalistischen Vernunft*, Frankfurt am Main: Surhkamp Verlag, 1981, 522–47. And see my critique of Habermas in Chapter 1 of this volume, "What's Critical About Critical Theory?"

as ("primary" versus "secondary") wage labor, privatized childrearing, and their gender-based separation.

As a result of these expert redefinitions, the people whose needs are in question are repositioned. They become individual "cases" rather than members of social groups or participants in political movements. In addition, they are rendered passive, positioned as potential recipients of predefined services rather than as agents involved in interpreting their needs and shaping their life-conditions.

By virtue of this administrative rhetoric, expert needs discourses, too, tend to be depoliticizing. They construe persons simultaneously as rational utility-maximizers and as causally conditioned, predictable, and manipulable objects, thereby screening out those dimensions of human agency that involve the construction and deconstruction of social meanings.

When expert needs discourses are institutionalized in state apparatuses, they tend to become normalizing, aimed at "reforming," if not stigmatizing, "deviancy."[26] This sometimes becomes explicit when services incorporate a therapeutic dimension designed to close the gap between clients' recalcitrant self-interpretations and the interpretations embedded in administrative policy.[27] Now the rational utility-maximizer-cum-causally-conditioned-object becomes, in addition, a deep self to be unraveled therapeutically.[28]

To summarize: when social movements succeed in politicizing previously depoliticized needs, they enter the terrain of the social, where two other kinds of struggles await them. First, they have to contest powerful organized interests bent on shaping hegemonic need interpretations to their own ends. Second, they encounter expert needs discourses in and around the social state. These encounters define two additional axes of needs-struggle in late-capitalist societies. They are highly complex struggles, since social movements typically seek state provision of their runaway needs even while they tend to oppose administrative and therapeutic need interpretations. Thus, these axes, too, involve conflicts among rival interpretations of social needs and among rival constructions of social identity.

---

26 See Foucault, *Discipline and Punish* for an account of the normalizing dimensions of social science and of institutionalized social services.

27 Jürgen Habermas discusses the therapeutic dimension of welfare-state social services in *Theorie des kommunikativen Handelns*, Band II, *Zur Kritik der funktionalistischen Vernunft*, 522–47. But again, see my critique in Chapter 1.

28 In *Discipline and Punish*, Foucault discusses the tendency of social-scientifically informed administrative procedures to posit a deep self. In his *The History of Sexuality, Vol. I: An Introduction*, trans. Robert Hurley, New York: Vintage, 1990, Foucault discusses the positing of a deep self by therapeutic psychiatric discourses.

## 4. EXEMPLARY STRUGGLES OVER NEEDS: FROM POLITICS TO ADMINISTRATION AND BACK

Let me now apply the model I have been developing to some concrete cases of conflicts of need interpretation. The first example I want to discuss serves to identify the tendency in welfare-state societies to transform the politics of need interpretation into the management of need satisfactions. A second group of examples serves to chart a counter-movement from administration to resistance and potentially back to politics.[29]

Consider, first, the politics of needs surrounding wife-battering. Until the 1970s, the expression "wife-battering" did not exist. When spoken of publicly at all, this phenomenon was called "wife-beating" and was often treated comically, as in "Have you stopped beating your wife?" Classed linguistically with the disciplining of children and servants, it was cast as a "domestic," as opposed to a "political," matter. Then, feminist activists renamed the practice with a term drawn from criminal law and created a new kind of public discourse. They claimed that battery was not a personal, domestic problem but a systemic, political one; its etiology was not to be traced to individual women's or men's emotional problems but, rather, to the ways these problems refracted pervasive social relations of male dominance and female subordination.

In this case, as in so many others, feminist activists contested established discursive boundaries and politicized what had previously been a depoliticized phenomenon. In addition, they reinterpreted the experience of battery and posited a set of associated needs. Here, they situated battered women's needs in a long chain of in-order-to relations which spilled across conventional separations of "spheres"; they claimed that, in order to be free from dependence on batterers, battered women needed not just temporary shelter but also jobs paying a "family wage," day care, and affordable permanent housing. Further, feminists created new discourse publics, new spaces and institutions in which such oppositional need interpretations could be developed and from which they could be spread to wider publics. Finally, feminists modified elements of the authorized means of interpretation and communication; they coined new terms of description and analysis and devised new ways of addressing female subjects. In their discourse, battered women were not addressed as individualized

---

29   For the sake of simplicity, I shall restrict the examples treated to cases of contestation between two forces only, where one of the contestants is an agency of the social state. Thus, I shall not consider examples of three-sided contestation, nor examples of two-sided contestation between competing social movements.

victims but as potential feminist activists, members of a politically constituted collectivity.

This discursive intervention was accompanied by feminist efforts to provide for some of the needs they had politicized and reinterpreted. Activists organized battered women's shelters, places of refuge and of consciousness-raising. The organization of these shelters was non-hierarchical; there were no clear lines between staff and users. Many of the counselors and organizers had themselves been battered, and a high percentage of the women who used the shelters went on to counsel other battered women and to become movement activists. Concomitantly, these women came to adopt new self-descriptions. Whereas most had originally blamed themselves and defended their batterers, many came to reject that interpretation in favor of a politicized view that offered them new models of agency. In addition, these women modified their affiliations and social identifications. Whereas most had earlier felt identified with their batterers, many came instead to affiliate with other women.

This organizing eventually had an impact on wider discursive publics. By the late 1970s, feminists had largely succeeded in establishing domestic violence against women as a bona fide political issue. They managed in some cases to change attitudes and policies of police and the courts, and they won for this issue a place on the informal political agenda. Now the needs of battered women were sufficiently politicized to become candidates for publicly organized satisfaction. Finally, in several municipalities and localities, movement shelters began receiving local government funding.

From the feminist perspective, this represented a significant victory, but it was not without cost. Municipal funding brought with it a variety of new administrative constraints ranging from accounting procedures to regulation, accreditation, and professionalization requirements. As a consequence, publicly funded shelters underwent a transformation. Increasingly, they came to be staffed by professional social workers, many of whom had not themselves experienced battery. Thus, a division between professional and client supplanted the more fluid continuum of relations that characterized the earlier shelters. Moreover, since many social-work staffs have been trained to frame problems in a quasi-psychiatric perspective, this perspective structures the practices of many publicly funded shelters even despite the intentions of individual staff, many of whom are politically committed feminists. Consequently, the practices of such shelters have become more individualizing and less politicized. Battered women tend now to be positioned as clients. They are increasingly psychiatrized, addressed as victims with deep, complicated selves. They are only rarely addressed as potential feminist activists.

Increasingly, the language-game of therapy has supplanted that of consciousness-raising. And the neutral scientific language of "spousal abuse" has supplanted more political talk of "male violence against women." Finally, the needs of battered women have been substantially reinterpreted. The far-reaching earlier claims for the social and economic prerequisites of independence have tended to give way to a narrower focus on the individual woman's problems of "low self-esteem."[30]

The battered women's shelter case exemplifies one tendency of needs politics in late-capitalist societies: the tendency for the politics of need interpretation to devolve into the administration of need satisfaction. However, there is also a countertendency which runs from administration to client resistance and potentially back to politics. I would like now to document this countertendency by discussing four examples of client resistance, examples ranging from the individual, cultural, and informal to the collective, political, and formally organized.

First, individuals may locate some space for maneuver within the administrative framework of a government agency. They may displace and/or modify an agency's official interpretations of their needs, even without mounting an overt challenge. Historian Linda Gordon has uncovered examples of this sort of resistance in the records of child-protection agencies during the Progressive Era.[31] Gordon cites cases in which women who had been beaten by their husbands filed complaints alleging child abuse. Having involved case workers in their situations by invoking an interpreted need that was recognized as legitimate and as falling within the agency's jurisdiction, they managed to interest the case workers in a need that was not so recognized. In some cases, these women succeeded in securing intervention under the child abuse rubric that provided them some measure of relief from domestic battery. Thus, they informally broadened the agency's jurisdiction to include, indirectly, a hitherto excluded need. While citing the social state's official definition of their need, they simultaneously displaced that definition and brought it closer in line with their own interpretations.

Second, informally organized groups may develop practices and affiliations that are at odds with the social state's way of positioning them as clients. In so doing, they may alter the uses and meanings of

30   For an account of the history of battered women's shelters, see Susan Schechter, *Women and Male Violence: The Visions and Struggles of the Battered Women's Movement*, Boston: South End Press, 1982.

31   Linda Gordon, *Heroes of Their Own Lives: The Politics and History of Family Violence, Boston 1880–1960*, New York: Viking Press, 1988.

benefits provided by government agencies, even without explicitly calling these into question. Anthropologist Carol Stack has documented examples of this sort of resistance in her study of "domestic kin networks" among poor black AFDC recipients in a Midwestern city in the late 1960s.[32] Stack describes elaborate kinship arrangements that organize delayed exchanges or "gifts" of prepared meals, food stamps, cooking, shopping, groceries, sleeping space, cash (including wages and AFDC allowances), transportation, clothing, child care, even children. It is significant that these domestic kin networks span several physically distinct households. This means that AFDC recipients use their benefits beyond the confines of the principal administrative category of government relief programs, namely, "the household." Consequently, these clients circumvent the nuclear-familializing procedures of welfare administration. By utilizing benefits beyond the confines of a "household," they alter the state-defined meanings of those benefits and, thus, of the needs they purport to satisfy. At the same time, they indirectly contest the state's way of positioning them as subjects. Whereas AFDC addresses them as biological mothers who belong to deviant nuclear families which lack male breadwinners, they double that subject-position with another one, namely, members of socially, as opposed to biologically, constituted kin networks who cooperate in coping with dire poverty.

Third, individuals and/or groups may resist therapeutic initiatives of the social state while accepting material aid. They may reject state-sponsored therapeutic constructions of their life-stories and capacities for agency and insist instead on alternative narratives and conceptions of identity. Sociologist Prudence Rains has documented an example of this kind of resistance in her comparative study of the "moral careers" of black and white pregnant teenagers in the late 1960's.[33]

Rains contrasts the ways the two groups of young women related to therapeutic constructions of their experience in two different institutional settings. The young middle-class white women were in an expensive, private, residential facility. This facility combined traditional services, such as seclusion and a cover for "good girls who had made a mistake," with newer therapeutic services, including required individual and group counseling sessions with psychiatric social workers. In these sessions, the young women were addressed as deep, complicated selves. They were encouraged to regard their pregnancies

32  Carol B. Stack, *All Our Kin: Strategies for Survival in a Black Community*, New York: Harper & Row, 1974.

33  Prudence Mors Rains, *Becoming an Unwed Mother: A Sociological Account*, Chicago: Aldine Atherton, Inc., 1971. In what follows, all citations are to this edition, and page numbers appear in the text following quotations. I am indebted to Kathryn Pyne Addelson for bringing Rains's work to my attention.

not as simple "mistakes," but as unconsciously motivated, meaningful acts expressive of latent emotional problems. This meant that a girl was to interpret her pregnancy (and the sex which was its superficial cause) as a form of acting out—say, a refusal of parental authority or a demand for parental love. She was warned that, unless she came to understand and acknowledge these deep, hidden motives, she would likely not succeed in avoiding future "mistakes."

Rains documents the process by which most of the young white women at this facility came to internalize this perspective and to rewrite themselves in the psychiatric idiom. She records the narratives they devised in the course of rewriting their "moral careers." For example:

> When I first came here I had it all figured out in my mind that Tom . . . had kind of talked me into it and I gave in. I kind of put it all on him. I didn't really accept my own part it it . . . [H]ere they stressed a lot that if you don't realize why you're here or why you ended up here and the emotional reasons behind it, that it will happen again . . . I feel now that I have a pretty full understanding of why I did end up here and that there was an emotional reason for it. And I accept my part in it more. It wasn't just him. (93)

This narrative is interesting in several respects. As Rains notes, the exchange of a "mistake" view of the past for a psychiatric view provided certain comforts: the new interpretation "did not merely set aside the past but accounted for it, and accounted for it in ways which allowed girls to believe they would act differently in the future" (94). Thus, the psychiatric view offers the pregnant teenager a model of agency that seems to enhance her capacity for individual self-determination. On the other hand, the narrative is highly selective, avowing some aspects of the past while disavowing others. It plays down the narrator's sexuality, treating her sexual behavior and desires as epiphenomenal "manifestation[s] of other, deeper, and nonsexual emotional needs and problems" (93). In addition, it defuses the potentially explosive issue of consent versus coercion in the teenage heterosexual milieu by excusing Tom and by revising the girl's earlier sense that their intercourse was not fully consensual. Moreover, the narrative forecloses any question as to the legitimacy of "premarital sex," assuming that for a woman, at least, such sex is morally wrong. Finally, in light of the girls' declarations that they will not need contraceptives when they return home and resume dating, the narrative has yet another meaning. Encapsulating a new awareness of deep emotional problems, it becomes a shield against future pregnancies, a prophylactic. Given these elisions in the story, a skeptic might well conclude that the psychiatric promise of enhanced self-determination is largely illusory.

The relative ease with which Rains's white teenagers internalized the therapeutic interpretation of their situation stands in stark contrast with the resistance offered by her black subjects. The young black women in her study were clients in a nonresidential municipal facility providing prenatal care, schooling, and counseling sessions with a psychiatric social worker. The counseling sessions were similar in intent and design to those at the private residential facility; the young women were encouraged to talk about their feelings and to probe the putative deep, emotional causes of their pregnancies. However, this therapeutic approach was much less successful at the public facility. These young women resisted the terms of the psychiatric discourse and the language-game of question and answer employed in the counseling sessions. They disliked the social worker's stance of nondirectiveness and moral neutrality—her unwillingness to say what *she* thought—and they resented what they considered her intrusive, overly personal questions. These girls did not acknowledge her right to question them in this fashion, given that they could not ask "personal" questions of her in turn. Rather, they construed "personal questioning" as a privilege reserved to close friends and intimates under conditions of reciprocity.

Rains documents several dimensions of the young black women's resistance to the "mental health" aspects of the program. In some instances, they openly challenged the rules of the therapeutic language-game. In others, they resisted indirectly by humor, quasi-deliberately misunderstanding the social worker's vague, nondirective, yet "personal" questions. For example, one girl construed "How did you get pregnant?" as a "stupid" question and replied, "Shouldn't you know?" (136).

Some others subjected the constant therapeutic "How did it feel?" to an operation that can only be called "carnivalesque." The occasion was a group counseling session for which the case worker was late. The young women assembled for the meeting began speculating as to her whereabouts. One mentioned that Mrs. Eckerd had gone to see a doctor. The conversation continued:

"To see if she's pregnant."
   "She probably thinks that's where you get babies."
   "Maybe the doctor's going to give her a baby" . . .
   Bernice then started doing an imitation interview pretending she was a social worker asking questions of a pretend-pregnant Mrs. Eckerd, "Tell me, how did it feel? Did you like it?"
   This brought a storm of laughter, and everybody started mimicking questions they supposedly had had put to them. Someone said,

"She asked me did I want to put my baby for adoption, and how
did it feel?"

When Mrs. Eckerd finally arrived, May said, "Why do social
workers ask so many questions?"

Mrs. Eckerd said, "What kind of questions do you mean, May?"
Bernice . . . said, "Like 'How did it feel?'"
There was an uproar over this . . . (137)

In general, then, Rains's black subjects devised a varied repertoire of
strategies for resisting expert, therapeutic constructions of their life-
stories and capacities for agency. They were keenly aware of the power
subtext underlying their interactions with the social worker and of the
normalization dimension of the therapeutic initiative. In effect, these
young women parried efforts to inculcate in them white, middle-class
norms of individuality and affectivity. They refused the case worker's
inducements to rewrite themselves as psychologized selves, while
availing themselves of the health services at the facility. Thus, they
made use of those aspects of the agency's program that they considered appropriate to their self-interpreted needs and ignored or
sidestepped the others.

Fourth, in addition to informal, ad hoc, strategic, and/or cultural
forms of resistance, there are also more formally organized, explicitly
political, organized kinds. Clients of social-welfare programs may join
together *as clients* to challenge administrative interpretations of their
needs. They may take hold of the passive, normalized, and individualized or familialized identities fashioned for them in expert discourses
and transform them into a basis for collective political action. Frances
Fox Piven and Richard A. Cloward have documented an example of
this kind of resistance in their account of the process by which AFDC
recipients organized the welfare-rights movement of the 1960s.[34]
Notwithstanding the atomizing and depoliticizing dimensions of
AFDC administration, these women were brought together in welfare
waiting rooms. It was as a result of their participation as clients, then,
that they came to articulate common grievances and to act together.
Thus, the same welfare practices that gave rise to these grievances
created the enabling conditions for collective organizing to combat

---

34   Frances Fox Piven and Richard A. Cloward, *Regulating the Poor: The
Functions of Public Welfare*, New York: Vintage Books, 1971, 285–340, and *Poor
People's Movements*, New York: Vintage Books, 1979. Unfortunately, Piven and
Cloward's account is gender-blind and, as a consequence, androcentric. For a
feminist critique, see Linda Gordon, "What Does Welfare Regulate?" *Social Research*
55:4, Winter 1988, 609–30. For a more gender-sensitive account of the history of
the NWRO, see Guida West, *The National Welfare Rights Movement: The Social
Protest of Poor Women*, New York: Praeger Publishers, 1981.

them. As Piven put it, "The structure of the welfare state itself has helped to create new solidarities and generate the political issues that continue to cement and galvanize them."[35]

## 5. CONCLUSION: NEEDS, RIGHTS, AND JUSTIFICATION

Let me conclude by flagging some issues that are central to this project but that I have not yet discussed here. In this essay, I have concentrated on social-theoretical issues at the expense of moral and epistemological issues. However, the latter are very important for a project, like mine, that aspires to be a *critical* social theory.

My analysis of needs-talk raises two very obvious and pressing philosophical issues. One is the question of whether and how it is possible to distinguish better from worse interpretations of people's needs. The other is the question of the relationship between needs claims and rights. Although I cannot offer full answers to these questions here, I would like to indicate something about how I would approach them. I want also to situate my views in relation to contemporary debates among feminist theorists.

Feminist scholars have demonstrated again and again that authoritative views purporting to be neutral and disinterested actually express the partial and interested perspectives of dominant social groups. In addition, many feminist theorists have made use of poststructuralist approaches that deny the possibility of distinguishing warranted claims from power plays. As a result, there is now a significant strand of relativist sentiment within feminist ranks. At the same time, many other feminists worry that relativism undermines the possibility of political commitment. How, after all, can one argue against the possibility of warranted claims while oneself making such claims like "sexism exists and is unjust"?[36]

This relativism problem surfaces here in the form of a question: Can we distinguish better from worse interpretations of people's

---

35   Frances Fox Piven, "Women and the State: Ideology, Power and the Welfare State," *Socialist Review*, no. 74, Mar–Apr 1984, 11–19.

36   For the view that objectivity is just the mask of domination, see Catharine A. MacKinnon, "Feminism, Marxism, Method, and the State: An Agenda for Theory," *Signs: Journal of Women in Culture and Society* 7:3, Spring 1982, 515–44. For the view that relativism undermines feminism, see Nancy Hartsock, "Rethinking Modernism: Minority vs. Majority Theories," *Cultural Critique* 7, Fall 1987, 187–206. For a good discussion of the tensions among feminist theorists on this issue (which does not, however, offer a persuasive resolution), see Sandra Harding, "The Instability of the Analytical Categories of Feminist Theory," *Signs: Journal of Women in Culture and Society* 11:4, 1986, 645–64. For a discussion of related issues raised by the phenomenon of postmodernism, see Nancy Fraser and Linda Nicholson, "Social Criticism without Philosophy: An Encounter between Feminism and Postmodernism," *Theory, Culture & Society* 5, 1988, 373–94.

needs? Or, since all need interpretations emanate from specific, inter-ested locations in society, are all of them equally compromised?

I claim that we *can* distinguish better from worse interpretations of people's needs. To say that needs are culturally constructed and discur-sively interpreted is not to say that any need interpretation is as good as any other. On the contrary, it is to underline the importance of an account of interpretive justification. However, I do not think that justification can be understood in traditional objectivist terms as correspondence, as if it were a matter of finding the interpretation that matches the true nature of the need as it really is in itself, inde-pendent of any interpretation.[37] Nor do I think that justification can be premised on a pre-established point of epistemic superiority, as if it were a matter of finding the one group in society with the privileged "standpoint."[38]

Then what *should* an account of interpretive justification consist in? In my view, there are at least two distinct kinds of considerations such an account would have to encompass and to balance. First, there are procedural considerations concerning the social processes by which various competing need interpretations are generated. For example, how exclusive or inclusive are various rival needs discourses? How hierarchical or egalitarian are the relations among the interlocutors? In general, procedural considerations dictate that, all other things being equal, the best need interpretations are those reached by means of communicative processes that most closely approximate ideals of democracy, equality, and fairness.[39]

In addition, considerations of consequences are relevant in justify-ing need interpretations. This means comparing alternative distributive outcomes of rival interpretations. For example, would widespread acceptance of some given interpretation of a social need disadvantage

37    For a critique of the correspondence model of truth, see Richard Rorty, *Philosophy and the Mirror of Nature*, Princeton: Princeton University Press, 1979.

38    The "standpoint" approach has been developed by Nancy Hartsock. See her *Money, Sex and Power: Toward a Feminist Historical Materialism*, New York: Longman, 1983. For a critique of Hartsock's position, see Harding, "The Instability of the Analytical Categories of Feminist Theory."

39    In its first-order normative content, this formulation is Habermassian. However, I do not wish to follow Habermas in giving it a transcendental or quasi-transcendental meta-interpretation. Thus, while Habermas purports to ground "communicative ethics" in the conditions of possibility of speech understood universalistically and ahistorically, I consider it a contingently evolved, historically specific possibility. See Jürgen Habermas, *The Theory of Communicative Action, Volume One, Reason and the Rationalization of Society*, trans. Thomas McCarthy, Boston: Beacon Press, 1984; *Communication and the Evolution of Society*, trans. Thomas McCarthy, Boston: Beacon Press, 1979; and *Moralbewusstsein und kommunikatives Handeln*, Frankfurt: Suhrkamp Verlag, 1983.

some groups of people vis-à-vis others? Does the interpretation conform to rather than challenge societal patterns of dominance and subordination? Are the rival chains of in-order-to relations to which competing need interpretations belong more or less respectful, as opposed to transgressive, of ideological boundaries that delimit "separate spheres" and thereby rationalize inequality? In general, consequentialist considerations dictate that, all other things being equal, the best need interpretations are those that do not disadvantage some groups of people vis-à-vis others.

In sum, justifying some interpretations of social needs as better than others involves balancing procedural and consequentialist considerations. More simply, it involves balancing democracy and equality.

What, then, of the relationship between needs and rights? This, too, is a controversial issue in contemporary theory. Critical legal theorists have argued that rights claims work against radical social transformation by enshrining tenets of bourgeois individualism.[40] Meanwhile, some feminist moral theorists suggest that an orientation toward responsibilities is preferable to an orientation toward rights.[41] Together, these views might lead some to want to think of needs-talk as an alternative to rights-talk. On the other hand, many feminists worry that left-wing critiques of rights play into the hands of our political opponents. After all, conservatives traditionally prefer to distribute aid as matter of need *instead* of right precisely in order to avoid assumptions of entitlement that could carry egalitarian implications. For these reasons, some feminist activists and legal scholars have sought to develop and defend alternative understandings of rights.[42] Their approach might imply that suitably reconstructed rights claims and needs claims could be mutually compatible, even inter-translatable.[43]

Very briefly, I align myself with those who favor translating justified needs claims into social rights. Like many radical critics of existing social-welfare programs, I am committed to opposing the forms of paternalism that arise when needs claims are divorced from rights claims. And unlike some communitarian, socialist, and feminist

---

40    Elizabeth M. Schneider, "The Dialectic of Rights and Politics: Perspectives from the Women's Movement," in *Women, the State, and Welfare*, ed. Linda Gordon, Madison: University of Wisconsin Press, 1990.

41    For arguments for and against this view, see the essays in *Women and Moral Theory*, eds. E. F. Kittay and Diana T. Meyers, Totowa, NJ: Rowman and Littlefield, 1987.

42    In addition to Schneider, "The Dialectic of Rights and Politics," see Martha Minow, "Interpreting Rights: An Essay for Robert Cover," *The Yale Law Journal* 96:8, July 1987, 860–915; and Patricia J. Williams, "Alchemical Notes: Reconstructed Ideals from Deconstructed Rights," *Harvard Civil Rights-Civil Liberties Law Review* 22:2, Spring 1987, 401–33.

43    I owe this formulation to Martha Minow (personal communication).

critics, I do not believe that rights-talk is inherently individualistic, bourgeois-liberal, and androcentric; it only becomes so where societies establish the *wrong* rights, as, for example, when the (putative) right to private property is permitted to trump *other* rights, including social rights.

Moreover, to treat justified needs claims as the bases for new social rights is to begin to overcome obstacles to the effective exercise of some existing rights. It is true, as Marxists and others have claimed, that classical liberal rights to free expression, assembly, and the like are "merely formal." But this says more about the social context in which they are currently embedded than about their "intrinsic" character, for, in a context devoid of poverty, inequality, and oppression, formal liberal rights could be broadened and transformed into substantive rights, say, to collective self-determination.

Finally, I should stress that this work is motivated by the conviction that, for the time being, needs-talk is with us for better or worse. For the foreseeable future, political agents, including feminists, will have to operate on a terrain where needs-talk is the discursive coin of the realm. But, as I have tried to show, this idiom is neither inherently emancipatory nor inherently repressive. Rather, it is multivalent and contested. The larger aim of my project is to help clarify the prospects for democratic and egalitarian social change by sorting out the emancipatory from the repressive possibilities of needs-talk.

3

# A Genealogy of "Dependency":
# Tracing a Keyword of the US Welfare State*
### *(coauthored with Linda Gordon)*

*Dependency* has become a keyword of US politics. Politicians of diverse views regularly criticize what they term *welfare dependency*. Supreme Court Justice Clarence Thomas spoke for many conservatives in 1980 when he vilified his sister: "She gets mad when the mailman is late with her welfare check. That's how dependent she is. What's worse is that now her kids feel entitled to the check, too. They have no motivation for doing better or getting out of that situation."[1] Liberals are usually less apt to blame the victim, but they, too, decry welfare dependency. Democratic Senator Daniel P. Moynihan prefigured today's discourse when he began his 1973 book by claiming that

> the issue of welfare is the issue of dependency. It is different from poverty. To be poor is an objective condition; to be dependent, a subjective one as well . . . Being poor is often associated with considerable personal qualities; being dependent rarely so. [Dependency] is an incomplete state in life: normal in the child, abnormal in the adult. In a world where completed men and women stand on

\* Nancy Fraser is grateful for research support from the Center for Urban Affairs, Northwestern University; the Newberry Library/National Endowment for the Humanities; and the American Council of Learned Societies. She also thanks Linda Gordon for permission to reprint this chapter in the present volume. Linda Gordon thanks the University of Wisconsin Graduate School, Vilas Trust, and the Institute for Research on Poverty. We both thank the Rockefeller Foundation Research and Study Center, Bellagio, Italy. We are also grateful for helpful comments from Lisa Brush, Robert Entman, Joel Handler, Dirk Hartog, Barbara Hobson, Allen Hunter, Eva Kittay, Felicia Kornbluh, Jenny Mansbridge, Linda Nicholson, Erik Wright, Eli Zaretsky, and the reviewers and editors of *Signs: Journal of Women in Culture and Society*.
  1  Clarence Thomas, quoted by Karen Tumulty, *Los Angeles Times*, July 5, 1991, A4.

their own feet, persons who are dependent—as the buried imagery of the word denotes—hang.[2]

Today, "policy experts" from both major parties agree "that [welfare] dependency is bad for people, that it undermines their motivation to support themselves, and isolates and stigmatizes welfare recipients in a way that over a long period feeds into and accentuates the underclass mindset and condition."[3]

If we step back from this discourse, however, we can interrogate some of its underlying presuppositions. Why are debates about poverty and inequality in the United States now being framed in terms of welfare dependency? How did the receipt of public assistance become associated with dependency, and why are the connotations of that word in this context so negative? What are the gender and racial subtexts of this discourse, and what tacit assumptions underlie it?

We propose to shed some light on these issues by examining welfare-related meanings of the word *dependency*.[4] We will analyze *dependency* as a keyword of the US welfare state and reconstruct its genealogy.[5] By charting some major historical shifts in the usage of this term, we will excavate some of the tacit assumptions and connotations that it still carries today but that usually go without saying.

Our approach is inspired in part by the English cultural-materialist critic Raymond Williams.[6] Following Williams and others, we assume that the terms used to describe social life are also active forces shaping it.[7] A crucial element of politics, then, is the struggle

---

2  Daniel P. Moynihan, *The Politics of a Guaranteed Income: The Nixon Administration and the Family Assistance Plan*, New York: Random House, 1973, 17.

3  Richard P. Nathan, quoted by William Julius Wilson, "Social Policy and Minority Groups: What Might Have Been and What Might We See in the Future," in *Divided Opportunities: Minorities, Poverty, and Social Policy*, eds. Gary D. Sandefur and Marta Tienda, New York: Plenum Press, 1986, 248.

4  Another part of the story, of course, concerns the word "welfare," but we do not have space to consider it fully here. For a fuller discussion, see Nancy Fraser and Linda Gordon, "Contract Versus Charity: Why Is There No Social Citizenship in the United States?" *Socialist Review* 22:3, 1992, 45–68.

5  Our focus is US political culture and thus North American English usage. Our findings should be of more general interest, however, as some other languages have similar meanings embedded in analogous words. In this essay we have of necessity used British sources for the early stages of our genealogy, which spans the sixteenth and seventeenth centuries. We assume that these meanings of "dependency" were brought to "the New World" and were formative for the early stages of US political culture.

6  Raymond Williams, *Keywords: A Vocabulary of Culture and Society*, Oxford: Oxford University Press, 1976.

7  This stress on the performative, as opposed to the representational, dimension of language is a hallmark of the pragmatics tradition in the philosophy of

to define social reality and to interpret people's inchoate aspirations and needs.[8] Particular words and expressions often become focal in such struggles, functioning as keywords, sites where the meaning of social experience is negotiated and contested.[9] Keywords typically carry unspoken assumptions and connotations that can powerfully influence the discourses they permeate—in part by constituting a body of *doxa,* or taken-for-granted commonsense belief that escapes critical scrutiny.[10]

We seek to dispel the doxa surrounding current US discussions of dependency by reconstructing that term's genealogy. Modifying an approach associated with Michel Foucault,[11] we will excavate broad historical shifts in linguistic usage that can rarely be attributed to specific agents. We do *not* present a causal analysis. Rather, by contrasting present meanings of dependency with past meanings, we aim to defamiliarize taken-for-granted beliefs in order to render them susceptible to critique and to illuminate present-day conflicts.

Our approach differs from Foucault's, however, in two crucial respects: we seek to contextualize discursive shifts in relation to broad institutional and social-structural shifts, and we welcome normative political reflection.[12] Our article is a collaboration between

---

language. It has been fruitfully adapted for socio-cultural analysis by several writers in addition to Williams. See, for example, Pierre Bourdieu, *Outline of a Theory of Practice*, Cambridge: Cambridge University Press, 1977; Judith Butler, *Gender Trouble: Feminism and the Subversion of Identity*, New York: Routledge, 1990; and Joan Wallach Scott, *Gender and the Politics of History*, New York: Columbia University Press, 1988. For a fuller discussion of the advantages of the pragmatics approach, see Chapter 5 of this volume, "Against Symbolism."

8    See Chapter 2 of this volume, "Struggle over Needs."

9    Raymond Williams, *Keywords.*

10   Pierre Bourdieu, *Outline of a Theory of Practice.*

11   Michel Foucault, "Nietzsche, Genealogy, History," in *The Foucault Reader*, ed. Paul Rabinow, New York: Pantheon, 1984, 76–100.

12   The critical literature on Foucault is enormous. For feminist assessments, see Linda Alcoff, "Feminist Politics and Foucault: The Limits to a Collaboration," in *Crisis in Continental Philosophy*, ed. Arlene Dallery and Charles Scott, Albany: SUNY Press, 1990; Judith Butler, "Variations on Sex and Gender: Beauvoir, Wittig and Foucault," in *Feminism as Critique*, eds. Seyla Benhabib and Drucilla Cornell, Minneapolis: University of Minnesota Press, 1987, 128–42; Nancy Hartsock, "Foucault on Power: A Theory for Women?" in *Feminism/Postmodernism*, ed. Linda J. Nicholson, New York: Routledge, 1990, 157–75; Chris Weedon, *Feminist Practice and Poststructuralist Theory*, Oxford: Basil Blackwell, 1987; and the essays in *Foucault and Feminism: Reflections on Resistance*, eds. Irene Diamond and Lee Quinby, Boston: Northeastern University Press, 1988. For balanced discussions of Foucault's strengths and weaknesses, see Nancy Fraser, *Unruly Practices*; Axel Honneth, *The Critique of Power: Reflective Stages in a Critical Social Theory*, Cambridge, MA: MIT Press, 1992; and Thomas McCarthy, *Ideals and Illusions: On Reconstruction and Deconstruction in Contemporary Critical Theory*, Cambridge, MA: MIT Press, 1991.

a philosopher and a historian. We combine historical analysis of linguistic and social-structural changes with conceptual analysis of the discursive construction of social problems, and we leaven the mix with a feminist interest in envisioning emancipatory alternatives.

In what follows, then, we provide a genealogy of *dependency*. We sketch the history of this term and explicate the assumptions and connotations it carries today in US debates about welfare—especially assumptions about human nature, gender roles, the causes of poverty, the nature of citizenship, the sources of entitlement, and what counts as work and as a contribution to society. We contend that unreflective uses of this keyword serve to enshrine certain interpretations of social life as authoritative and to delegitimize or obscure others, generally to the advantage of dominant groups in society and to the disadvantage of subordinate ones. All told, we provide a critique of ideology in the form of a critical political semantics.

*Dependency*, we argue, is an ideological term. In current US policy discourse, it usually refers to the condition of poor women with children who maintain their families with neither a male breadwinner nor an adequate wage and who rely for economic support on a stingy and politically unpopular government program called Aid to Families with Dependent Children (AFDC). Participation in this highly stigmatized program may be demoralizing in many cases, even though it may enable women to leave abusive or unsatisfying relationships without having to give up their children. Still, naming the problems of poor, solo-mother families as *dependency* tends to make them appear to be individual problems, as much moral or psychological as economic. The term carries strong emotive and visual associations and a powerful pejorative charge. In current debates, the expression *welfare dependency* evokes the image of "the welfare mother," often figured as a young, unmarried Black woman (perhaps even a teenager) of uncontrolled sexuality. The power of this image is overdetermined, we contend, since it condenses multiple and often contradictory meanings of dependency. Only by disaggregating those different strands, by unpacking the tacit assumptions and evaluative connotations that underlie them, can we begin to understand, and to dislodge, the force of the stereotype.

## 1. REGISTERS OF MEANING

In its root meaning, the verb "to depend" refers to a physical relationship in which one thing hangs from another. The more abstract meanings—social, economic, psychological, and political—were originally metaphorical. In current usage, we find four registers in which the meanings of dependency reverberate. The first is an economic register, in which one depends on some other person(s) or institution for subsistence. In a second register, the term denotes a socio-legal status, the lack of a separate legal or public identity, as in the status of married women created by coverture. The third register is political: here dependency means subjection to an external ruling power and may be predicated of a colony or of a subject caste of noncitizen residents. The fourth register we call the moral/psychological; dependency in this sense is an individual character trait, like lack of willpower or excessive emotional neediness.

To be sure, not every use of *dependency* fits neatly into one and only one of these registers. Still, by distinguishing them analytically we present a matrix on which to plot the historical adventures of the term. In what follows, we shall trace the shift from a patriarchal preindustrial usage in which women, however subordinate, shared a condition of dependency with many men, to a modern, industrial, male-supremacist usage that constructed a specifically feminine sense of dependency. That usage is now giving way, we contend, to a postindustrial usage in which growing numbers of relatively prosperous women claim the same kind of independence that men do while a more stigmatized but still feminized sense of dependency attaches to groups considered deviant and superfluous. Not just gender but also racializing practices play a major role in these shifts, as do changes in the organization and meaning of labor.

## 2. PREINDUSTRIAL "DEPENDENCY"

In preindustrial English usage, the most common meaning of *dependency* was subordination. The economic, socio-legal, and political registers were relatively undifferentiated, reflecting the fusion of various forms of hierarchy in state and society, and the moral/psychological use of the term barely existed. The earliest social definition of the verb *to depend (on)* in the *Oxford English Dictionary* (OED) is "to be connected with in a relation of subordination." A *dependent*, from at least 1588, was one "who depends on another for support, position, etc.; a retainer, attendant, subordinate, servant." A *dependency* was either a retinue or body of servants or a foreign territorial possession or colony. This family of terms applied widely in a hierarchical social context in which nearly everyone was subordinate to someone else but did not incur any individual stigma as a result.[13]

We can appreciate just how common dependency was in preindustrial society by examining its opposite. The term *independence* at first

13 Joan R. Gundersen, "Independence, Citizenship, and the American Revolution," *Signs: Journal of Women in Culture and Society* 13:1, 1987, 59–77.

applied primarily to aggregate entities, not to individuals; thus in the seventeenth century a nation or a church congregation could be independent. By the eighteenth century, however, an individual could be said to have an *independency*, meaning an ownership of property, a fortune that made it possible to live without laboring. (This sense of the term, which we would today call economic, survives in our expressions *to be independently wealthy* and *a person of independent means*.) To be dependent, in contrast, was to gain one's livelihood by working for someone else. This of course was the condition of most people, of wage laborers as well as serfs and slaves, of most men as well as most women.[14]

Dependency, therefore, was a normal as opposed to a deviant condition, a social relation as opposed to an individual trait. Thus, it did not carry any moral opprobrium. Neither English nor US dictionaries report any pejorative uses of the term before the early twentieth century. In fact, some leading preindustrial definitions were explicitly positive, implying trusting, relying on, counting on another—the predecessors of today's *dependable*.

Nevertheless, *dependency* did mean status inferiority and legal coverture, being a part of a unit headed by someone else who had legal standing. In a world of status hierarchies dominated by great landowners and their retainers, all members of a household other than its "head" were dependents, as were free or servile peasants on an estate. They were, as Peter Laslett put it, "caught up, so to speak, 'subsumed' . . . into the personalities of their fathers and masters."[15]

Dependency also had what we would today call political consequences. While the term did not mean precisely *unfree*, its context was a social order in which subjection, not citizenship, was the norm. *Independence* connoted unusual privilege and superiority, as in freedom from labor. Thus, throughout most of the European development of representative government, independence in the sense of property ownership was a prerequisite for political rights. When dependents began to claim rights and liberty, they perforce became revolutionaries.

*Dependency* was not then applied uniquely to characterize the relation of a wife to her husband. Women's dependency, like children's, meant being on a lower rung in a long social ladder; their husbands and fathers were above them but below others. For the agrarian majority,

---

14   In preindustrial society, moreover, the reverse dependence of the master upon his men was widely recognized. The historian Christopher Hill evoked that understanding when he characterized the "essence" of feudal society as "the bond of loyalty and dependence between lord and man." Here "dependence" means interdependence. Hill, *The World Turned Upside Down: Radical Ideas During the English Revolution,* New York: Viking, 1972, 32.

15   Peter Laslett, *The World We Have Lost: England Before the Industrial Age,* New York: Charles Scribner, 1971, 21.

moreover, there was no implication of women's unilateral economic dependency, because their labor, like that of children, was recognized as essential to the family economy; the women were economic dependents only in the sense that the men of their class were as well. In general, women's dependency in preindustrial society was less gender-specific than it later became; it was similar in kind to that of subordinate men, only multiplied. But so too were the lives of children, servants, and the elderly overlaid with multiple layers of dependency.

In practice, of course, these preindustrial arrangements did not always provide satisfactorily for the poor. In the fourteenth century, new, stronger states began to limit the freedom of movement of the destitute and to codify older, informal distinctions between those worthy and unworthy of assistance. When the English Poor Law of 1601 confirmed this latter distinction, it was already shameful to ask for public help. But the culture neither disapproved of dependency nor valorized individual independence. Rather, the aim of the statutes was to return the mobile, uprooted, and excessively "independent" poor to their local parishes or communities, and hence to enforce their traditional dependencies.

Nevertheless, dependency was not universally approved or uncontested. It was subject, rather, to principled challenges from at least the seventeenth century on, when liberal-individualist political arguments became common. The terms *dependence* and *independence* often figured centrally in political debates in this period, as they did, for example, in the Putney Debates of the English Civil War. Sometimes they even became key signifiers of social crisis, as in the seventeenth-century English controversy about "out-of-doors" servants, hired help who did not reside in the homes of their masters and who were not bound by indentures or similar legal understandings. In the discourse of the time, the anomalous "independence" of these men served as a general figure for social disorder, a lightening rod focusing diffuse cultural anxieties— much as the anomalous "dependence" of "welfare mothers" does today.

### 3. INDUSTRIAL "DEPENDENCY": THE WORKER AND HIS NEGATIVES

With the rise of industrial capitalism, the semantic geography of dependency shifted significantly. In the eighteenth and nineteenth centuries, *independence*, not *dependence*, figured centrally in political and economic discourse, and its meanings were radically democratized. But if we read the discourse about independence carefully, we see the shadow of a powerful anxiety about dependency.

What in preindustrial society had been a normal and unstigmatized condition became deviant and stigmatized. More precisely, certain dependencies became shameful while others were deemed natural and proper. In particular, as eighteenth- and nineteenth-century political culture intensified gender difference, new, explicitly gendered senses of *dependency* appeared—states considered proper for women, but degrading for men. Likewise, emergent racial constructions made some forms of dependency appropriate for the "dark races," but intolerable for "whites." Such differentiated valuations became possible as the term's preindustrial unity fractured. No longer designating only generalized subordination, *dependency* in the industrial era could be socio-legal or political or economic. With these distinctions came another major semantic shift: now *dependency* need not always refer to a social relation; it could also designate an individual character trait. Thus, the moral/psychological register was born.

These redefinitions were greatly influenced by Radical Protestantism, which elaborated a new positive image of individual independence and a critique of socio-legal and political dependency. In the Catholic and the early Protestant traditions, dependence on a master had been modeled on dependence on God. To the radicals of the English Civil War, or to Puritans, Quakers, and Congregationalists in the United States, in contrast, rejecting dependence on a master was akin to rejecting blasphemy and false gods.[16] From this perspective, status hierarchies no longer appeared natural or just. Political subjection and socio-legal subsumption were offenses against human dignity, defensible only under special conditions, if supportable at all. These beliefs informed a variety of radical movements throughout the industrial era, including abolition, feminism, and labor organizing, with substantial successes. In the nineteenth century, these movements abolished slavery and some of the legal disabilities of women. More thoroughgoing victories were won by white male workers who, in the eighteenth and nineteenth centuries, threw off their socio-legal and political dependency and won civil and electoral rights. In the age of democratic revolutions, the developing new concept of citizenship rested on independence; dependency was deemed antithetical to citizenship.

Changes in the civil and political landscape of dependence and independence were accompanied by even more dramatic changes in the economic register. When white workingmen demanded civil and electoral rights, they claimed to be independent. This entailed reinterpreting the meaning of wage labor so as to divest it of the association with dependency. That in turn required a shift in focus—from the experience or means of labor (e.g., ownership of tools or land, control of skills, and the organization of work) to its remuneration and how

---

16    Christopher Hill, *The Century of Revolution 1603–1714*, New York: W.W. Norton & Company, 1961.

that was spent. Radical workingmen, who had earlier rejected wage labor as "wage slavery," claimed a new form of manly independence within it. Their collective pride drew on another aspect of Protestantism: its work ethic, which valorized discipline and labor. Workers sought to reclaim these values within the victorious wage labor system; many of them—women as well as men—created and exercised a new kind of independence in their militancy and boldness toward employers. Through their struggles, economic independence came eventually to encompass the ideal of earning a family wage, a wage sufficient to maintain a household and to support a dependent wife and children. Thus, workingmen expanded the meaning of economic independence to include a form of wage labor in addition to property ownership and self-employment.[17]

This shift in the meaning of independence also transformed the meanings of dependency. As wage labor became increasingly normative—and increasingly definitive of independence—it was precisely those excluded from wage labor who appeared to personify dependency. In the new industrial semantics, there emerged three principal icons of dependency, all effectively negatives of the dominant image of "the worker," and each embodying a different aspect of non-independence.

The first icon of industrial dependency was "the pauper," who lived not on wages but on poor relief.[18] In the strenuous new culture of emergent capitalism, the figure of the pauper was like a bad double of the upstanding workingman, threatening the latter should he lag. The image of the pauper was elaborated largely in an emerging new register of dependency discourse—the moral/psychological register. Paupers were not simply poor but degraded, their character corrupted and their will sapped through reliance on charity. To be sure, the moral/psychological condition of pauperism was related to the economic condition of poverty, but the relationship was not simple, but complex. While

---

17   One might say that this redefinition foregrounded wage labor *as* a new form of property, namely, property in one's own labor power. This conception was premised on what C. B. Macpherson called "possessive individualism," the assumption of an individual's property in his (sic) own person. (See Macpherson, *The Political Theory of Possessive Individualism: Hobbes to Locke*, Oxford: Oxford University Press, 1962.) Leading to the construction of wages as an entitlement, this approach was overwhelmingly male. Allen Hunter (personal communication) describes it as a loss of systemic critique, a sense of independence gained by narrowing the focus to the individual worker and leaving behind aspirations for collective independence from capital.

18   In the sixteenth century the term "pauper" had meant simply a poor person and, in law, one who was allowed to sue or defend in a court without paying costs (OED). Two centuries later, it took on a more restricted definition, denoting a new class of persons who subsisted on poor relief instead of wages and who were held to be deviant and blameworthy.

nineteenth-century charity experts acknowledged that poverty could contribute to pauperization, they also held that character defects could cause poverty.[19] Toward the end of the century, as hereditarian (eugenic) thought caught on, the pauper's character defects were given a basis in biology. The pauper's dependency was figured as unlike the serf's in that it was unilateral, not reciprocal. To be a pauper was not to be subordinate within a system of productive labor; it was to be outside such a system altogether.

A second icon of industrial dependency was embodied alternately in the figures of "the colonial native" and "the slave." They, of course, were very much inside the economic system, their labor often fundamental to the development of capital and industry. Whereas the pauper represented the characterological distillation of economic dependency, natives and slaves personified political subjection.[20] Their images as "savage," "childlike," and "submissive" became salient as the old, territorial sense of dependency as a colony became intertwined with a new, racist discourse developed to justify colonialism and slavery.[21] There emerged a drift from an older sense of dependency as a relation of subjection imposed by an imperial power on an indigenous population to a newer sense of dependency as an inherent property or character trait of the people so subjected. In earlier usage, colonials were dependent because they had been conquered; in nineteenth-century imperialist culture, they were conquered because they were dependent. In this new conception, it was the intrinsic, essential dependency of natives and slaves that justified their colonization and enslavement.

The dependency of the native and the slave, like that of the pauper, was elaborated largely in the moral/psychological register. The character traits adduced to justify imperialism and slavery, however, arose

---

19    Linda Gordon, "Social Insurance and Public Assistance: The Influence of Gender in Welfare Thought in the United States, 1890–1935," *American Historical Review* 97:1, 1992, 19–54.

20    Actually, there are many variants within the family of images that personify political subjection in the industrial era. Among these are related but not identical stereotypes of the Russian serf, the Caribbean slave, the slave in the United States, and the American Indian. Moreover, there are distinct male and female stereotypes within each of those categories. We simplify here in order to highlight the features that are common to all these images, notably the idea of natural subjection rooted in race. We focus especially on stereotypes that portray African Americans as personifications of dependency because of their historic importance and contemporary resonance in the US language of social welfare.

21    The evolution of the term "native" neatly encapsulates this process. Its original meaning in English, dating from about 1450, was tied to dependency: "one born in bondage; a born thrall," but without racial meaning. Two centuries later it carried the additional meaning of colored or Black (OED).

less from individual temperament than from the supposed nature of human groups. Racialist thought was the linchpin for this reasoning. By licensing a view of "the Negro" as fundamentally *other*, this way of thinking provided the extraordinary justificatory power required to rationalize subjection at a time when liberty and equality were being proclaimed inalienable "rights of man" —for example, in that classic rejection of colonial status, the United States's "Declaration of Independence." Thus racism helped transform dependency as political subjection into dependency as psychology and forged enduring links between the discourse of dependency and racial oppression.

Like the pauper, the native and the slave were excluded from wage labor and thus were negatives of the image of the worker. They shared that characteristic, if little else, with the third major icon of dependency in the industrial era: the newly invented figure of "the housewife." As we saw, the independence of the white workingman presupposed the ideal of the family wage, a wage sufficient to maintain a household and to support a non-employed wife and children. Thus, for wage labor to create (white male) independence, (white) female economic dependence was required. Women were thus transformed "from partners to parasites."[22] But this transformation was by no means universal. In the United States, for example, the family wage ideal held greater sway among whites than among Blacks, and was at variance with actual practice for all of the poor and the working class. Moreover, both employed and non-employed wives continued to perform work once considered crucial to a family economy. Since few husbands actually were able to support a family single-handedly, most families continued to depend on the labor of women and children. Nevertheless, the family wage norm commanded great loyalty in the United States, partly because it was used by the organized working class as an argument for higher wages.[23]

Several different registers of dependency converged in the figure of the housewife. This figure melded woman's traditional socio-legal and political dependency with her more recent economic dependency in the industrial order. Continuing from preindustrial usage was the assumption that fathers headed households and that other household

---

22   Hilary Land, "The Family Wage," *Feminist Review* 6, 1980, 57. Jeanne Boydston, *Home and Work: Housework, Wages, and the Ideology of Labor in the Early Republic*, New York: Oxford University Press, 1991.

23   Gwendolyn S. Hughes, *Mothers in Industry*, New York: New Republic, 1925; Sophonisba P. Breckinridge, "The Home Responsibilities of Women Workers and the 'Equal Wage'," *Journal of Political Economy* 31, 1928, 521–43; *Women Workers Through the Depression: A Study of White Collar Employment Made by the American Woman's Association*, ed. Lorine Pruette, New York: Macmillan, 1934; and Linda Gordon, "Social Insurance and Public Assistance."

members were represented by them, as codified in the legal doctrine of coverture. The socio-legal and political dependency of wives enforced their new economic dependency, since under coverture even married women who were wage workers could not legally control their wages. But the connotations of female dependency were altered. Although erstwhile dependent white men gained political rights, most white women remained legally and politically dependent. The result was to feminize—and stigmatize—socio-legal and political dependency, making coverture appear increasingly obnoxious and stimulating agitation for the statutes and court decisions that eventually dismantled it.

Together, then, a series of new personifications of dependency combined to constitute the underside of the workingman's independence. Henceforth, those who aspired to full membership in society would have to distinguish themselves from the pauper, the native, the slave, and the housewife in order to construct their independence. In a social order in which wage labor was becoming hegemonic, it was possible to encapsulate all these distinctions simultaneously in the ideal of the family wage. On the one hand, and most overtly, the ideal of the family wage premised the white workingman's independence on his wife's subordination and economic dependence. But on the other hand, it simultaneously contrasted with counter-images of dependent men—first with degraded male paupers on poor relief and later with racist stereotypes of Negro men unable to dominate Negro women. The family wage, therefore, was a vehicle for elaborating meanings of dependence and independence that were deeply inflected by gender, race, and class.

In this new industrial semantics, white workingmen appeared to be economically independent, but their independence was largely illusory and ideological. Since few actually earned enough to support a family single-handedly, most depended in fact—if not in word—on their wives' and children's contributions. Equally important, the language of wage labor in capitalism denied workers' dependence on their employers, thereby veiling their status as subordinates in a unit headed by someone else. Thus, hierarchy that had been relatively explicit and visible in the peasant-landlord relation was mystified in the relationship of factory operative to factory owner. There was a sense, then, in which the economic dependency of the white workingman was spirited away through linguistic sleight of hand—somewhat like reducing the number of poor people by lowering the official poverty demarcating line.

By definition, then, economic inequality among white men no longer created dependency. But non-economic hierarchy among white men was considered unacceptable in the United States. Thus, *dependency* was redefined to refer exclusively to those non-economic relations of subordination deemed suitable only for people of color and for white women. The result was to differentiate dimensions of dependency that had been fused in preindustrial usage. Whereas all relations of subordination had previously counted as dependency relations, now capital-labor relations were exempted. Socio-legal and political hierarchy appeared to diverge from economic hierarchy, and only the former seemed incompatible with hegemonic views of society. It seemed to follow, moreover, that were socio-legal dependency and political dependency ever to be formally abolished, no social-structural dependency would remain. Any dependency that did persist could only be moral or psychological.

## 4. AMERICAN "WELFARE DEPENDENCY": 1890–1945

Informed by these general features of industrial-era semantics, a distinctive welfare-related use of *dependency* developed in the United States. Originating in the late-nineteenth-century discourse of pauperism, modified in the Progressive Era and stabilized in the period of the New Deal, this use of the term was fundamentally ambiguous, slipping easily, and repeatedly, from an economic meaning to a moral/psychological meaning.

The United States was especially hospitable to elaborating dependency as a defect of individual character. Because the country lacked a strong legacy of feudalism or aristocracy and thus a strong popular sense of reciprocal obligations between lord and man, the older, preindustrial meanings of dependency—as an ordinary, majority condition—were weak, and the pejorative meanings were stronger. In the colonial period, dependency was seen mainly as a voluntary condition, as in indentured servitude. But the American Revolution so valorized independence that it stripped dependency of its voluntarism, emphasized its powerlessness, and imbued it with stigma. One result was to change the meaning of women's social and legal dependency, making it distinctly inferior.[24]

The long American love affair with independence was politically double-edged. On the one hand, it helped nurture powerful labor and women's movements. On the other hand, the absence of a hierarchical social tradition in which subordination was understood to be structural, not characterological, facilitated hostility to public support for the poor. Also influential was the very nature of the American state, weak and decentralized in comparison to European states throughout the nineteenth century. All told, the United States proved fertile soil for the moral/psychological discourse of dependency.

---

24 Joan R. Gundersen, "Independence, Citizenship, and the American Revolution."

As discussed earlier, the most general definition of economic dependency in this era was simply non-wage-earning. By the end of the nineteenth century, however, that definition had divided into two: a "good" household dependency, predicated of children and wives, and an increasingly "bad" (or at least dubious) charity dependency, predicated of recipients of relief. Both senses had as their reference point the ideal of the family wage, and both were eventually incorporated into the discourse of the national state. The good, household sense was elaborated via the census[25] and by the Internal Revenue Service, which installed the category of dependent as the norm for wives. The already problematic charity sense became even more pejorative with the development of public assistance. The old distinction between the deserving and the undeserving poor intensified in the late nineteenth century's Gilded Age. Theoretically, the undeserving should not be receiving aid, but constant vigilance was required to ensure they did not slip in, disguising themselves as deserving. Dependence on assistance became increasingly stigmatized, and it was harder and harder to rely on relief without being branded a pauper.

Ironically, reformers in the 1890s introduced the word *dependent* into relief discourse as a substitute for *pauper* precisely in order to destigmatize the receipt of help. They first applied the word to children, the paradigmatic "innocent" victims of poverty.[26] Then, in the early twentieth century, Progressive-era reformers began to apply the term to adults, again to rid them of stigma. Only after World War II did *dependent* become the hegemonic word for a recipient of aid.[27] By then, however, the term's pejorative connotations were fixed.

The attempt to get rid of stigma by replacing *pauperism* with

25  Nancy Folbre, "The Unproductive Housewife: Her Evolution in Nineteenth-Century Economic Thought," *Signs: Journal of Women in Culture and Society* 16:3, 1991, 463–84.

26  For example, Amos Griswold Warner uses "dependent" only for children in *American Charities and Social Work*, New York: Thomas Y. Crowell, 1894 through 1930. The same is true of Edith Abbott and Sophonisba P. Breckinridge, *The Administration of the Aid-to-Mothers Law in Illinois*, Washington: U.S. Children's Bureau, Publication no. 82, 1921, 7; and the *Proceedings* of the National Conference of Charities and Correction (1890s through 1920s). This usage produced some curious effects because of its intersection with the dependency produced by the normative family. For example, charity experts debated the propriety of "keeping dependent children in their own homes." The children in question were considered dependent because their parent(s) could not support them; yet other children were deemed dependent precisely because their parents did support them.

27  Studies of welfare done in the 1940s still used the word "dependents" only in the sense of those supported by family heads; see, for example, Josephine Chapin Brown, *Public Relief 1929–1939*, New York: Henry Holt, 1940; Donald S. Howard, *The WPA and Federal Relief Policy*, New York: Russell Sage, 1943; and Frank J. Bruno, *Trends in Social Work*, New York: Columbia University Press, 1948.

*dependency* failed. Talk about economic dependency repeatedly slid into condemnation of moral/psychological dependency. Even during the Depression of the 1930s, experts worried that receipt of relief would create "habits of dependence" including, as one charity leader put it, "a belligerent dependency, an attitude of having a right and title to relief."[28] Because the hard times lasted so long and created so many newly poor people, there was a slight improvement in the status of recipients of aid. But attacks on "chiseling" and "corruption" continued to embarrass those receiving assistance, and many of the neediest welfare beneficiaries accepted public aid only after much hesitation and with great shame, so strong was the stigma of dependency.[29]

Most important, the New Deal intensified the dishonor of receiving help by consolidating a two-track welfare system. First-track programs like unemployment and old-age insurance offered aid as an entitlement, without stigma or supervision and hence without dependency. Such programs were constructed to create the misleading appearance that beneficiaries merely got back what they put in. They constructed an honorable status for recipients and are not called "welfare" even today. Intended to at least partially replace the white workingman's family wage, first-track programs excluded most minorities and white women. In contrast, second-track public assistance programs, among which Aid to Dependent Children (ADC), later Aid to Families with Dependent Children (AFDC), became the biggest and most well known, continued the private charity tradition of searching out the deserving few among the many chiselers. Funded from general tax revenues instead of from earmarked wage deductions, these programs created the appearance that claimants were getting something for nothing.[30] They established entirely different conditions for receiving aid: means-testing, morals-testing, moral supervision, home visits, extremely low stipends—in short, all the conditions associated with welfare dependency today.[31]

---

28 Lilian Brandt, *An Impressionistic View of the Winter of 1930–31 in New York City*, New York: Welfare Council of New York City, 1932, 23–4. See also Gertrude Vaile, untitled, in *College Women and the Social Sciences*, ed. Herbert Elmer Mills, New York: John Day, 1934, 26; and Mary L. Gibbons, "Family Life Today and Tomorrow," *Proceedings*, National Conference of Catholic Charities, 19, 1933, 133–68.

29 E. Wight Bakke, *Citizens Without Work: A Study of the Effects of Unemployment Upon Workers' Social Relations and Practices*, New Haven: Yale University Press, 1940, and *The Unemployed Worker: A Study of the Task of Making a Living Without a Job*, New Haven: Yale University Press, 1940.

30 Nancy Fraser and Linda Gordon, "Contract Versus Charity: Why Is There No Social Citizenship in the United States?"

31 Nancy Fraser, "Women, Welfare, and the Politics of Need Interpretation," in Fraser, *Unruly Practices*; Linda Gordon, "The New Feminist Scholarship on the Welfare

The racial and sexual exclusions of the first-track programs were not accidental. They were designed to win the support of Southern legislators who wanted to keep Blacks dependent in another sense, namely, on low wages or sharecropping.[32] Equally deliberate was the construction of the differential in legitimacy between the two tracks of the welfare system. The Social Security Board propagandized for Social Security Old Age Insurance (the program today called just "Social Security") precisely because, at first, it did not seem more earned or more dignified than public assistance. To make Social Security more acceptable, the Board worked to stigmatize public assistance, even pressuring states to keep stipends low.[33]

Most Americans today still distinguish between "welfare" and "non-welfare" forms of public provision and see only the former as creating dependency. The assumptions underlying these distinctions, however, had to be constructed politically. Old people became privileged (non-welfare) recipients only through decades of militant organization and lobbying. All programs of public provision, whether they are called "welfare" or not, shore up some dependencies and discourage others. Social Security subverted adults' sense of responsibility for their parents, for example. Public assistance programs, by contrast, aimed to buttress the dependence of minorities on low-wage labor, of wives on husbands, of children on their parents.

The conditions of second-track assistance made recipients view their dependence on public assistance as inferior to the supposed independence of wage labor.[34] Wage labor, meanwhile, had become so naturalized that its own inherent supervision could be overlooked;

State," in *Women, the State, and Welfare*, ed. Linda Gordon, Madison: University of Wisconsin Press, 1990, 9–35; and Barbara J. Nelson, "The Origins of the Two-Channel Welfare State: Workmen's Compensation and Mothers' Aid," in *Women, the State, and Welfare*, ed. Linda Gordon, 123–51. Starting in the 1960s, increasing numbers of Black women were able to claim AFDC, but prior to that they were largely excluded. At first, the language of the New Deal followed the precedent of earlier programs in applying the term "dependent" to children. De facto, however, the recipients of ADC were virtually exclusively solo mothers. Between the 1940s and 1960s the term's reference gradually shifted from the children to their mothers.

32   Jill Quadagno, "From Old-Age Assistance to Supplemental Social Security Income: The Political Economy of Relief in the South, 1935–1972," in *The Politics of Social Policy in the United States*, ed. Margaret Weir, Ann Shola Orloff, and Theda Skocpol, Princeton, NJ: Princeton University Press, 1988, 235–63.

33   Jerry R. Cates, *Insuring Inequality: Administrative Leadership in Social Security, 1935–54*, Ann Arbor: University of Michigan Press, 1983.

34   Jacqueline Pope, *Biting the Hand that Feeds Them: Organizing Women on Welfare at the Grass Roots Level*, New York: Praeger, 1989, 73, 144; Guida West, *The National Welfare Rights Movement: The Social Protest of Poor Women*, New York: Praeger, 1981; and Milwaukee County Welfare Rights Organization, *Welfare Mothers Speak Out*, New York: W.W. Norton & Company, 1972.

thus one ADC recipient complained, "Welfare life is a difficult experience . . . When you work, you don't have to report to anyone."[35] Yet the designers of ADC did not initially intend to drive white solo mothers into paid employment. Rather, they wanted to protect the norm of the family wage by making dependence on a male breadwinner continue to seem preferable to dependence on the state.[36] ADC occupied the strategic semantic space where the good, household sense of dependency and the bad, relief sense of dependency intersected. It enforced at once the positive connotations of the first and the negative connotations of the second.

Thus, the poor solo mother was enshrined as the quintessential *welfare dependent*.[37] That designation has thus become significant not only for what it includes, but also for what it excludes and occludes. Although it appears to mean relying on the government for economic support, not all recipients of public funds are equally considered dependent. Hardly anyone today calls recipients of Social Security retirement insurance *dependents*. Similarly, persons receiving unemployment insurance, agricultural loans, and home mortgage assistance are excluded from that categorization, as indeed are defense contractors and the beneficiaries of corporate bailouts and regressive taxation.

## 5. POSTINDUSTRIAL SOCIETY AND THE DISAPPEARANCE OF "GOOD" DEPENDENCY

With the transition to a postindustrial phase of capitalism, the semantic map of dependency is being redrawn yet again. Whereas industrial usage had cast some forms of dependency as natural and proper, postindustrial usage figures all forms as avoidable and blameworthy. No longer moderated by any positive countercurrents, the term's pejorative connotations are being strengthened. Industrial usage had recognized some forms of dependency to be rooted in relations of subordination; postindustrial usage, in contrast, focuses more intensely on the traits of individuals. The moral/psychological register is expanding, therefore, and its qualitative character is changing, with new psychological and therapeutic idioms displacing the explicitly racist and misogynous idioms of the industrial era. Yet dependency nonetheless remains feminized and racialized; the new psychological meanings have strong feminine associations, while currents once

---

35   Annie S. Barnes, *Single Parents in Black America: A Study in Culture and Legitimacy*, Bristol, Conn: Wyndham Hall Press, 1987, vi.

36   Linda Gordon, "Social Insurance and Public Assistance."

37   Men on "general relief" are sometimes also included in that designation; their treatment by the welfare system is usually as bad or worse.

associated with the native and the slave are increasingly inflecting the discourse about welfare.

One major influence here is the formal abolition of much of the legal and political dependency that was endemic to industrial society. Housewives, paupers, natives, and the descendants of slaves are no longer formally excluded from most civil and political rights; neither their subsumption nor their subjection is viewed as legitimate. Thus, major forms of dependency deemed proper in industrial usage are now considered objectionable, and postindustrial uses of the term carry a stronger negative charge.

A second major shift in the geography of postindustrial dependency is affecting the economic register. This is the decentering of the ideal of the family wage, which had been the gravitational center of industrial usage. The relative deindustrialization of the United States is restructuring the political economy, making the single-earner family far less viable. The loss of higher-paid "male" manufacturing jobs and the massive entry of women into low-wage service work is meanwhile altering the gender composition of employment.[38] At the same time, divorce is common and, thanks in large part to the feminist and gay and lesbian liberation movements, changing gender norms are helping to proliferate new family forms, making the male breadwinner/female homemaker model less attractive to many.[39] Thus, the family wage ideal is no longer hegemonic, but competes with alternative gender norms, family forms, and economic arrangements. It no longer goes without saying that a woman should rely on a man for economic support, nor that mothers should not also be "workers." Thus, another major form of dependency that was positively inflected in industrial semantics has become contested if not simply negative.

The combined result of these developments is to increase the stigma of dependency. With all legal and political dependency now illegitimate, and with wives' economic dependency now contested, there is no longer any self-evidently "good" adult dependency in postindustrial society. Rather, all dependency is suspect, and independence is enjoined upon everyone. Independence, however, remains identified with wage labor. That identification seems even to increase in a context where there is no longer any "good" adult personification of dependency who can be counterposed to "the worker." In this

38  Joan Smith, "The Paradox of Women's Poverty: Wage-Earning Women and Economic Transformation," *Signs: Journal of Women in Culture and Society* 10:2, 1984, 291–310.

39  Judith Stacey, "Sexism By a Subtler Name? Postindustrial Conditions and Postfeminist Consciousness in the Silicon Valley," *Socialist Review* 96, 1987, 7–28; and Kath Weston, *Families We Choose: Lesbians, Gays, Kinship*, New York: Columbia University Press, 1991.

context, the worker tends to become the universal social subject: everyone is expected to "work" and to be "self-supporting." Any adult not perceived as a worker shoulders a heavier burden of self-justification. Thus, a norm previously restricted to white workingmen applies increasingly to everyone. Yet this norm still carries a racial and gender subtext, as it supposes that the worker has access to a job paying a decent wage and is not also a primary parent.

If one result of these developments is an increase in dependency's negative connotations, another is its increased individualization. As we saw, talk of dependency as a character trait of individuals was already widespread in the industrial period, diminishing the preindustrial emphasis on relations of subordination. The importance of individualized dependency tends to be heightened, however, now that socio-legal dependency and political dependency are officially ended. Absent coverture and Jim Crow, it has become possible to claim that equality of opportunity exists and that individual merit determines outcomes. As we saw, the groundwork for that view was laid by industrial usage, which redefined dependency so as to exclude capitalist relations of subordination. With capitalist economic dependency already abolished by definition, and with legal and political dependency now abolished by law, postindustrial society appears to some conservatives and liberals to have eliminated every social-structural basis of dependency. Whatever dependency remains, therefore, can be interpreted as the fault of individuals. That interpretation does not go uncontested, to be sure, but the burden of argument has shifted. Now those who would deny that the fault lies in themselves must swim upstream against the prevailing semantic currents. Postindustrial dependency, thus, is increasingly individualized.

## 6. "WELFARE DEPENDENCY" AS POSTINDUSTRIAL PATHOLOGY

The worsening connotations of *welfare dependency* have been nourished by several streams from outside the field of welfare. New postindustrial medical and psychological discourses have associated dependency with pathology. In articles with titles such as "Pharmacist Involvement in a Chemical-Dependency Rehabilitation Program," social scientists began in the 1980s to write about *chemical, alcohol,* and *drug dependency,* all euphemisms for addiction.[40] Because welfare claimants are often—falsely—assumed to be addicts, the pathological

---

40 M. Haynes, "Pharmacist Involvement in a Chemical-Dependency Rehabilitation Program," *American Journal of Hospital Pharmacy* 45:10, 1988, 2099–2101.

connotations of *drug dependency* tend also to infect *welfare dependency*, increasing stigmatization.

A second important postindustrial current is the rise of new psychological meanings of dependency with very strong feminine associations. In the 1950s, social workers influenced by psychiatry began to diagnose dependence as a form of immaturity common among women, particularly among solo mothers (who were often, of course, welfare claimants). "Dependent, irresponsible, and unstable, they respond like small children to the immediate moment," declared the author of a 1954 discussion of out-of-wedlock pregnancy.[41] The problem was that women were supposed to be just dependent enough, and it was easy to tip over into excess in either direction. The norm, moreover, was racially marked, as white women were usually portrayed as erring on the side of excessive dependence, while Black women were typically charged with excessive independence.

Psychologized dependency became the target of some of the earliest second-wave feminism. Betty Friedan's 1963 classic *The Feminine Mystique* provided a phenomenological account of the housewife's psychological dependency and drew from it a political critique of her social subordination.[42] More recently, however, a burgeoning cultural-feminist, postfeminist, and anti-feminist self-help and pop-psychology literature has obfuscated the link between the psychological and the political. In Colette Dowling's 1981 book *The Cinderella Complex*, women's dependency was hypostatized as a depth-psychological gender structure: "women's hidden fear of independence" or the "wish to be saved."[43] The late 1980s saw a spate of books about "code-pendency," a supposedly prototypically female syndrome of supporting or "enabling" the dependency of someone else. In a metaphor that reflects the drug hysteria of the period, dependency here, too, is an addiction. Apparently, even if a woman manages to escape her gender's predilection to dependency, she is still liable to incur the blame for facilitating the dependency of her husband or children. This completes the vicious circle: the increased stigmatizing of dependency in the culture at large has also deepened contempt for those who care for dependents, reinforcing the traditionally low status of the female helping professions, such as nursing and social work.[44]

The 1980s saw a cultural panic about dependency. In 1980, the

---

41   Leontine Young, *Out of Wedlock*, New York: McGraw Hill, 1954, 87.

42   Betty Friedan, *The Feminine Mystique*, New York: W.W. Norton & Company, 1963.

43   Colette Dowling, *The Cinderella Complex: Women's Hidden Fear of Independence*, New York: Summit Books, 1981.

44   Virginia Sapiro, "The Gender Basis of American Social Policy," in *Women, the State, and Welfare*, ed. Linda Gordon, 36–54.

American Psychiatric Association codified "Dependent Personality Disorder" (DPD) as an official psychopathology. According to the 1987 edition of the Diagnostic and Statistical Manual of Mental Disorders (DSM-III-R),

> the essential feature of this disorder is a pervasive pattern of dependent and submissive behavior beginning by early childhood . . . People with this disorder are unable to make everyday decisions without an excessive amount of advice and reassurance from others, and will even allow others to make most of their important decisions . . . The disorder is apparently common and is diagnosed more frequently in females.[45]

The codification of DPD as an official psychopathology represents a new stage in the history of the moral/psychological register. Here the social relations of dependency disappear entirely into the personality of the dependent. Overt moralism also disappears in the apparently neutral, scientific, medicalized formulation. Thus, although the defining traits of the dependent personality match point for point the traits traditionally ascribed to housewives, paupers, natives, and slaves, all links to subordination have vanished. The only remaining trace of those themes is the flat, categorical, and uninterpreted observation that DPD is "diagnosed more frequently in females."[46]

If psychological discourse has further feminized and individualized dependency, other postindustrial developments have further racialized it. The increased stigmatization of welfare dependency followed a general increase in public provision in the United States, the removal of some discriminatory practices that had previously excluded minority women from participation in AFDC, especially in the South, and the transfer of many white women to first-track programs as social-insurance coverage expanded. By the 1970s the figure of the Black solo mother had come to epitomize welfare dependency. As a result, the new discourse about welfare draws on older symbolic currents that linked dependency with racist ideologies.

The ground was laid by a long, somewhat contradictory stream of discourse about "the Black family," in which African-American gender and kinship relations were measured against white middle-class norms and deemed pathological. One supposedly pathological element was "the excessive independence" of Black women, an ideologically distorted allusion to long traditions of wage work, educational

---

45  American Psychiatric Association, *Diagnostic and Statistical Manual of Mental Disorders*, 3rd edition revised, Washington, DC: American Psychiatric Association, 1987, 353–4.
46  Ibid.

achievement, and community activism. The 1960s and 1970s discourse about poverty recapitulated traditions of misogyny toward African-American women; in Daniel Moynihan's diagnosis, for example, "matriarchal" families had "emasculated" Black men and created a "culture of poverty" based on a "tangle of [family] pathology."[47] This discourse placed Black AFDC claimants in a double-bind: they were pathologically independent with respect to men and pathologically dependent with respect to government.

By the 1980s, however, the racial imagery of dependency had shifted. The Black welfare mother who haunted the white imagination ceased to be the powerful matriarch. Now the preeminent stereotype is the unmarried teenage mother caught in the "welfare trap" and rendered drone-like and passive. This new icon of welfare dependency is younger and weaker than the matriarch. She is often evoked in the phrase *children having children*, which can express feminist sympathy or anti-feminist contempt, Black appeals for parental control or white-racist eugenic anxieties.

Many of these postindustrial discourses coalesced in early 1990s. Then-Vice President Dan Quayle brought together the pathologized, feminized, and racialized currents in his comment on the May 1992 Los Angeles riot: "Our inner cities are filled with children having children . . . with people who are dependent on drugs and on the narcotic of welfare."[48]

Thus postindustrial culture has called up a new personification of dependency: the Black, unmarried, teenaged, welfare-dependent mother. This image has usurped the symbolic space previously occupied by the housewife, the pauper, the native, and the slave, while absorbing and condensing their connotations. Black, female, a pauper, not a worker, a housewife and mother, yet practically a child herself—the new stereotype partakes of virtually every quality that has been coded historically as antithetical to independence. Condensing multiple, often contradictory meanings of dependency, it is a powerful ideological trope that simultaneously organizes diffuse cultural anxieties and dissimulates their social bases.

## 7. POSTINDUSTRIAL POLICY AND THE POLITICS OF DEPENDENCY

Despite the worsening economic outlook for many Americans in the last few decades, there has been no cultural revaluation of welfare. Families

47   Lee Rainwater and William L. Yancey, *The Moynihan Report and the Politics of Controversy*, Cambridge, MA: MIT Press, 1967.

48   Dan Quayle, "Excerpts From Vice President's Speech on Cities and Poverty," *New York Times*, May 20, 1992, A11.

working harder for less often resent those who appear to them not to be working at all. Apparently lost, at least for now, are the struggles of the 1960s that aimed to recast AFDC as an entitlement in order to promote recipients' independence. Instead, the honorific term *independent* remains firmly centered on wage labor, no matter how impoverished the worker. *Welfare dependency*, in contrast, has been inflated into a behavioral syndrome and made to seem more contemptible.

Contemporary policy discourse about welfare dependency is thoroughly inflected by these assumptions. It divides into two major streams. The first continues the rhetoric of pauperism and the culture of poverty. It is used in both conservative and liberal, victim-blaming or non-victim-blaming ways, depending on the causal structure of the argument. The contention is that poor, dependent people have something more than lack of money wrong with them. The flaws can be located in biology, psychology, upbringing, neighborhood influence; they can be cast as cause or as effect of poverty, or even as both simultaneously. Conservatives, such as George Gilder and Lawrence Mead, argue that welfare causes moral/psychological dependency.[49] Liberals, such as William Julius Wilson and Christopher Jencks, blame social and economic influences, but agree that claimants' culture and behavior are problematic.[50]

A second stream of thought begins from neoclassical economic premises. It assumes a "rational man" facing choices in which welfare and work are both options. For these policy analysts, the moral/psychological meanings of dependency are present but uninterrogated, assumed to be undesirable. Liberals of this school, such as many of the social scientists associated with the Institute for Research on Poverty at the University of Wisconsin, grant that welfare inevitably has some bad, dependency-creating effects, but claim that these are outweighed by other, good effects like improved conditions for children, increased societal stability, and relief of suffering. Conservatives of this school, such as Charles Murray, disagree.[51] The two camps argue above all about the question of incentives. Do AFDC stipends encourage women to have more out-of-wedlock children? Do they discourage them from accepting jobs? Can reducing or withholding stipends serve as a stick to

49   George Gilder, *Wealth and Poverty*, New York: Basic Books, 1981; and Lawrence Mead, *Beyond Entitlement: The Social Obligations of Citizenship*, New York: Free Press, 1986.

50   William Julius Wilson, *The Truly Disadvantaged: The Inner City, the Underclass, and Public Policy*, Chicago: University of Chicago Press, 1987; and Christopher Jencks, *Rethinking Social Policy: Race, Poverty, and the Underclass*, Cambridge, Mass.: Harvard University Press, 1992.

51   Charles Murray, *Losing Ground: American Social Policy, 1950–1980*, New York: Basic Books, 1984.

encourage recipients to stay in school, keep their children in school, get married?

Certainly, there are real and significant differences here, but there are also important similarities. Liberals and conservatives of both schools rarely situate the notion of dependency in its historical or economic context; nor do they interrogate its presuppositions. Neither group questions the assumption that independence is an unmitigated good or its identification with wage labor. Many poverty and welfare analysts equivocate between an official position that *dependency* is a value-neutral term for receipt of (or need for) welfare and a usage that makes it a synonym for *pauperism*.

These assumptions permeate the public sphere. In the current round of alarms about welfare dependency, it is increasingly claimed that "welfare mothers ought to work," a usage that tacitly defines work as wage-earning and childrearing as non-work. Here we run up against contradictions in the discourse of dependency: when the subject under consideration is teenage pregnancy, these mothers are cast as children; when the subject is welfare, they become adults who should be self-supporting. It is only in the last decade that welfare experts have reached a consensus on the view that AFDC recipients should be employed. The older view, which underlay the original passage of ADC, was that children need a mother at home—although in practice there was always a class double standard, since full-time maternal domesticity was a privilege that had to be purchased, not an entitlement poor women could claim. However, as waged work among mothers of young children has become more widespread and normative, the last defenders of a welfare program that permitted recipients to concentrate full-time on childraising were silenced.

None of the negative imagery about welfare dependency has gone uncontested, of course. From the 1950s through the 1970s, many of these presuppositions were challenged, most directly in the mid-1960s by an organization of women welfare claimants, the National Welfare Rights Organization. NWRO women cast their relation with the welfare system as active rather than passive, a matter of claiming rights rather than receiving charity. They also insisted that their domestic labor was socially necessary and praiseworthy. Their perspective helped reconstruct the arguments for welfare, spurring poverty lawyers and radical intellectuals to develop a legal and political-theoretical basis for welfare as an entitlement and right. Edward Sparer, a legal strategist for the welfare rights movement, challenged the usual understanding of dependency:

> The charge of antiwelfare politicians is that welfare makes the recipient "dependent." What this means is that the recipient depends on the

welfare check for his [sic] material subsistence rather than upon some other source . . . whether that is good or bad depends on whether a better source of income is available . . . The real problem . . . is something entirely different. The recipient and the applicant traditionally have been dependent on the whim of the caseworker.[52]

The cure for welfare dependency, then, was welfare rights. Had the NWRO not been greatly weakened by the late 1970s, the revived discourse of pauperism in the 1980s could not have become hegemonic.

Even in the absence of a powerful National Welfare Rights Organization, many AFDC recipients maintained their own oppositional interpretation of welfare dependency. They complained not only of stingy allowances but also of infantilization due to supervision, loss of privacy, and a maze of bureaucratic rules that constrained their decisions about housing, jobs, and even (until the 1960s) sexual relations. In the claimants' view, welfare dependency is a social condition, not a psychological state, a condition they analyze in terms of power relations. It is what a left-wing English dictionary of social welfare calls *enforced dependency*, "the creation of a dependent class" as a result of "enforced reliance . . . for necessary psychological or material resources."[53]

This idea of enforced dependency was central to another, related challenge to the dominant discourse. During the period in which NWRO activism was at its height, New Left revisionist historians developed an interpretation of the welfare state as an apparatus of social control. They argued that what apologists portrayed as helping practices were actually modes of domination that created enforced dependency. The New Left critique bore some resemblance to the NWRO critique, but the overlap was only partial. The historians of social control told their story mainly from the perspective of the "helpers" and cast recipients as almost entirely passive. They thereby occluded the agency of actual or potential welfare claimants in articulating needs, demanding rights, and making claims.[54]

Still another contemporary challenge to mainstream uses of *dependency* arose from a New Left school of international political economy.

52    Edward V. Sparer, "The Right to Welfare," in *The Rights of Americans: What They Are—What They Should Be*, ed. Norman Dorsen, New York: Pantheon, 1971, 71.

53    Noel and Rita Timms, *Dictionary of Social Welfare*, London: Routledge & Kegan Paul, 1982, 55–6.

54    For a fuller discussion of the social control critique, see Linda Gordon, "The New Feminist Scholarship on the Welfare State." On needs claims see Chapter 2 of this volume, "Struggle over Needs," and Barbara J. Nelson, "The Origins of the Two-Channel Welfare State."

The context was the realization, after the first heady days of postwar decolonization, that politically independent former colonies remained economically dependent. In *dependency theory*, radical theorists of "underdevelopment" used the concept of dependency to analyze the global neocolonial economic order from an anti-racist and anti-imperialist perspective. In so doing, they resurrected the old preindustrial meaning of dependency as a subjected territory, seeking thereby to divest the term of its newer moral/psychological accretions and to retrieve the occluded dimensions of subjection and subordination. This usage remains strong in Latin America as well as in US social-scientific literature, where we find articles such as "Institutionalizing Dependency: The Impact of Two Decades of Planned Agricultural Modernization."[55]

What all these oppositional discourses share is a rejection of the dominant emphasis on dependency as an individual trait. They seek to shift the focus back to the social relations of subordination. But they do not have much impact on mainstream talk about welfare in the United States today. On the contrary, with economic dependency now a synonym for poverty, and with moral/psychological dependency now a personality disorder, talk of dependency as a social relation of subordination has become increasingly rare. Power and domination tend to disappear.[56]

## 8. CONCLUSION

*Dependency*, once a general-purpose term for all social relations of subordination, is now differentiated into several analytically distinct registers. In the economic register, its meaning has shifted from gaining one's livelihood by working for someone else to relying for support on charity or welfare; wage labor now confers independence. In the socio-legal register, the meaning of dependency as subsumption is unchanged, but its scope of reference and connotations have altered: once a socially approved majority condition, it first became a group-based status deemed proper for some classes of persons but not others and then shifted again to designate (except in the case of children) an anomalous, highly stigmatized status of deviant and incompetent individuals. Likewise, in the political register, dependency's meaning as subjection to an

---

55   M. Gates, "Institutionalizing Dependency: The Impact of Two Decades of Planned Agricultural Modernization," *Journal of Developing Areas* 22:3, 1988, 293–320.

56   For an account of the further individualization of dependency in subsequent neoliberal discourse, see Nancy Fraser, "Clintonism, Welfare and the Antisocial Wage: The Emergence of a Neoliberal Political Imaginary," *Rethinking Marxism* 6:1, 1993, 1–15.

external governing power has remained relatively constant, but its evaluative connotations worsened as individual political rights and national sovereignty became normative. Meanwhile, with the emergence of a newer moral/psychological register, properties once ascribed to social relations came to be posited instead as inherent character traits of individuals or groups, and the connotations here, too, have worsened. This last register now claims an increasingly large proportion of the discourse, as if the social relations of dependency were being absorbed into personality. Symptomatically, erstwhile relational understandings have been hypostatized in a veritable portrait gallery of dependent personalities: initially housewives, paupers, natives, and slaves; then poor, solo, Black teenage mothers.

These shifts in the semantics of dependency reflect some major socio-historical developments. One is the progressive differentiation of the official economy—that which is counted in the domestic national product—as a seemingly autonomous system that dominates social life. Before the rise of capitalism, all forms of work were woven into a net of dependencies, which constituted a single, continuous fabric of social hierarchies. The whole set of relations was constrained by moral understandings, as in the preindustrial idea of a moral economy. In the patriarchal families and communities that characterized the preindustrial period, women were subordinated and their labor often controlled by others, but their labor was visible, understood, and valued. With the emergence of religious and secular individualism, on the one hand, and of industrial capitalism, on the other, a sharp, new dichotomy was constructed in which economic dependency and economic independence were unalterably opposed to one another. A crucial corollary of this dependence/independence dichotomy, and of the hegemony of wage labor in general, was the occlusion and devaluation of women's unwaged domestic and parenting labor.

The genealogy of dependency also expresses the modern emphasis on individual personality. This is the deepest meaning of the spectacular rise of the moral/psychological register, which constructs yet another version of the independence/dependence dichotomy. In the moral/psychological version, social relations are hypostatized as properties of individuals or groups. Fear of dependency, both explicit and implicit, posits an ideal, independent personality in contrast to which those considered dependent are deviant. This contrast bears traces of a sexual division of labor that assigns men primary responsibility as providers or breadwinners and women primary responsibility as caretakers and nurturers and then treats the derivative personality patterns as fundamental. It is as if male breadwinners absorbed into their personalities the independence associated with their ideologically interpreted economic role, whereas the persons of female nurturers became saturated with the dependency of those for whom they care. In this way, the opposition between the independent personality and the dependent personality maps onto a whole series of hierarchical oppositions and dichotomies that are central in modern capitalist culture: masculine/feminine, public/private, work/care, success/love, individual/community, economy/family, and competitive/self-sacrificing.

A genealogy cannot tell us how to respond politically to today's discourse about welfare dependency. It does suggest, however, the limits of any response that presupposes rather than challenges the definition of the problem that is implicit in that expression. An adequate response would need to question our received valuations and definitions of dependence and independence in order to allow new, emancipatory social visions to emerge. Some contemporary welfare-rights activists adopt this strategy, continuing the NWRO tradition. Pat Gowens, for example, elaborates a feminist reinterpretation of dependency:

> The vast majority of mothers of *all classes and all educational levels* "depends" on another income. It may come from child support . . . or from a husband who earns $20,000 while she averages $7,000. But "dependence" more accurately defines dads who count on women's unwaged labor to raise children and care for the home. Surely, "dependence" doesn't define the single mom who does it all: child-rearing, homemaking, and bringing in the money (one way or another). When caregiving is valued and paid, when dependence is not a dirty word, and interdependence is the norm—only then will we make a dent in poverty.[57]

57  Pat Gowens, "Welfare, Learnfare—Unfair! A Letter to My Governor," *Ms. Magazine*, September–October 1991, 90–91.

4

# After the Family Wage:
# A Postindustrial Thought Experiment*

The crisis of the welfare state has many roots—global economic trends, massive movements of refugees and immigrants, popular hostility to taxes, the weakening of trade unions and labor parties, the rise of national and "racial"-ethnic antagonisms, the decline of solidaristic ideologies, and the collapse of state socialism. One absolutely crucial factor, however, is the crumbling of the old gender order. Existing welfare states are premised on assumptions about gender that are increasingly out of phase with many people's lives and self-understandings. As a result, they do not provide adequate social protections, especially for women and children.

The gender order that is now disappearing descends from the industrial era of capitalism and reflects the social world of its origin. It was centered on the ideal of *the family wage*. In this world people were supposed to be organized into heterosexual, male-headed nuclear families, which lived principally from the man's labor market earnings. The male head of the household would be paid a family wage, sufficient to support children and a wife-and-mother, who performed domestic labor without pay. Of course, countless lives never fit this pattern. Still, it provided the normative picture of a proper family.

The family-wage ideal was inscribed in the structure of most industrial-era welfare states.[1] That structure had three tiers, with social-insurance

* Research for this essay was supported by the Center for Urban Affairs and Policy Research, Northwestern University. For helpful comments, I am indebted to Rebecca Blank, Joshua Cohen, Fay Cook, Barbara Hobson, Axel Honneth, Jenny Mansbridge, Linda Nicholson, Ann Shola Orloff, John Roemer, Ian Shapiro, Tracy Strong, Peter Taylor-Gooby, Judy Wittner, Eli Zaretsky, and the members of the Feminist Public Policy Work Group of the Center for Urban Affairs and Policy Research, Northwestern University.

1    Mimi Abramowitz, *Regulating the Lives of Women: Social Welfare Policy from Colonial Times to the Present*, Boston: South End Press, 1988; Nancy Fraser, "Women, Welfare, and the Politics of Need Interpretation," in Fraser, *Unruly Practices: Power,*

programs occupying the first rank. Designed to protect people from the vagaries of the labor market (and to protect the economy from shortages of demand), these programs replaced the breadwinner's wage in case of sickness, disability, unemployment, or old age. Many countries also featured a second tier of programs, providing direct support for full-time female homemaking and mothering. A third tier served the "residuum." Largely a holdover from traditional poor relief, public assistance programs provided paltry, stigmatized, means-tested aid to needy people who had no claim to honorable support because they did not fit the family-wage scenario.[2]

Today, however, the family-wage assumption is no longer tenable—either empirically or normatively. We are currently experiencing the death throes of the old, industrial gender order with the transition to a new, *postindustrial* phase of capitalism. The crisis of the welfare state is bound up with these epochal changes. It is rooted in part in the collapse of the world of the family wage, and of its central assumptions about labor markets and families.

In the labor markets of postindustrial capitalism, few jobs pay wages sufficient to support a family single-handedly; many, in fact, are temporary or part-time and do not carry standard benefits.[3] Women's

---

*Discourse, and Gender in Contemporary Social Theory*, Minneapolis: University of Minnesota Press, 1989; Linda Gordon, "What Does Welfare Regulate?" *Social Research* 55:4, Winter 1988, 609–30; Hilary Land, "Who Cares for the Family?" *Journal of Social Policy* 7:3, July 1978, 257–84. An exception to the built-in family-wage assumption is France, which from early on accepted high levels of female waged work. See Jane Jenson, "Representations of Gender: Policies to 'Protect' Women Workers and Infants in France and the United States before 1914," in *Women, the State, and Welfare*, ed. Linda Gordon, Madison: University of Wisconsin Press, 1990.

2   This account of the tripartite structure of the welfare state represents a modification of the account I proposed in "Women, Welfare, and the Politics of Need Interpretation." There I followed Barbara Nelson in positing a two-tier structure of ideal-typically "masculine" social insurance programs and ideal-typically "feminine" family support programs. (See her "Women's Poverty and Women's Citizenship: Some Political Consequences of Economic Marginality," *Signs: Journal of Women in Culture and Society* 10:2, Winter 1984, 209–31, and "The Origins of the Two-Channel Welfare State: Workmen's Compensation and Mothers' Aid," in *Women, the State, and Welfare*, ed. Linda Gordon.) Although that view was a relatively accurate picture of the US social-welfare system, I now consider it analytically misleading. The United States is unusual in that the second and third tiers are conflated. What was for many decades the main program of means-tested poor relief—Aid to Families with Dependent Children (AFDC)—was also the main program supporting women's childraising. Analytically, however, these are best understood as two distinct tiers of social welfare. When social insurance is added, we get a three-tier welfare state.

3   David Harvey, *The Condition of Postmodernity: An Inquiry into the Origins of Cultural Change*, Oxford: Blackwell, 1989; Scott Lash and John Urry, *The End of*

employment is increasingly common, moreover—although far less well-paid than men's.[4] Postindustrial families, meanwhile, are less conventional and more diverse.[5] Heterosexuals are marrying less and later, and divorcing more and sooner, while gays and lesbians are pioneering new kinds of domestic arrangements.[6] Gender norms and family forms are highly contested. Thanks in part to the feminist and gay-and-lesbian liberation movements, many people no longer prefer the male breadwinner/female homemaker model. One result of these trends is a steep increase in solo-mother families: growing numbers of women, both divorced and never married, are struggling to support themselves and their families without access to a male breadwinner's wage. Their families have high rates of poverty.

In short, a new world of economic production and social reproduction is emerging—a world of less stable employment and more diverse families. Though no one can be certain about its ultimate shape, this much seems clear: the emerging world, no less than the world of the family wage, will require a welfare state that effectively insures people against uncertainties. It is clear, too, that the old forms of welfare state, built on assumptions of male-headed families and relatively stable jobs, are no longer suited to providing this protection. We need something new, a postindustrial welfare state suited to radically new conditions of employment and reproduction.

What, then, should a postindustrial welfare state look like? Conservatives have lately had a lot to say about "restructuring the welfare state," but their vision is counterhistorical and contradictory; they seek to reinstate the male breadwinner/female homemaker family for the middle class, while demanding that poor single mothers "work." Neoliberal proposals have recently emerged in the United States but they, too, are inadequate in the current context. Punitive, androcentric, and obsessed with employment despite the absence of good jobs, they are unable to provide security in a postindustrial world.[7] Both these approaches ignore one crucial thing: A postindustrial welfare

*Organized Capitalism*, Cambridge: Polity Press, 1987; Robert Reich, *The Work of Nations: Preparing Ourselves for 21st Century Capitalism*, New York: Knopf, 1991.

4 Joan Smith, "The Paradox of Women's Poverty: Wage-earning Women and Economic Transformation," *Signs: Journal of Women in Culture and Society* 9:2, Winter 1984, 291–310.

5 Judith Stacey, "Sexism By a Subtler Name? Postindustrial Conditions and Postfeminist Consciousness in the Silicon Valley," *Socialist Review* no. 96, 1987, 7–28.

6 Kath Weston, *Families We Choose: Lesbians, Gays, Kinship*, New York: Columbia University Press, 1991.

7 Nancy Fraser, "Clintonism, Welfare, and the Antisocial Wage: The Emergence of a Neoliberal Political Imaginary," *Rethinking Marxism* 6:1, Spring 1993, 9–23.

state, like its industrial predecessor, must support a gender order. But the only kind of gender order that can be acceptable today is one premised on *gender justice*.

Feminists, therefore, are in a good position to generate an emancipatory vision for the coming period. They, more than anyone, appreciate the importance of gender relations to the current crisis of the industrial welfare state and the centrality of gender justice to any satisfactory resolution. Feminists also appreciate the importance of carework for human well-being and the effects of its social organization on women's standing. They are attuned, finally, to potential conflicts of interest within families and to the inadequacy of androcentric definitions of work.

To date, however, feminists have tended to shy away from systematic reconstructive thinking about the welfare state. Nor have we yet developed a satisfactory account of gender justice that can inform an emancipatory vision. We need now to undertake such thinking. We should ask: What new, postindustrial gender order should replace the family wage? And what sort of welfare state can best support such a new gender order? What account of gender justice best captures our highest aspirations? And what vision of social welfare comes closest to embodying it?

Two different sorts of answers are presently conceivable, I think, both of which qualify as feminist. The first I call the *Universal Breadwinner* model. Implicit in the current political practice of most US feminists and liberals, this vision aims to foster gender justice by promoting women's employment; its centerpiece is state provision of employment-enabling services such as day care. The second possible answer I call the *Caregiver Parity* model. Implicit in the current political practice of most Western European feminists and social democrats, this approach aims to promote gender justice chiefly by supporting informal carework; its centerpiece is state provision of caregiver allowances.

Which of these two approaches should command our loyalties in the coming period? Which expresses the most attractive vision of a postindustrial gender order? Which best embodies the ideal of gender justice? In this chapter, I outline a framework for thinking systematically about these questions. I analyze highly idealized versions of Universal Breadwinner and Caregiver Parity in the manner of a thought experiment. I postulate, contrary to fact, a world in which both these models are feasible, in that their economic and political preconditions are in place. Assuming very favorable conditions, then, I assess the respective strengths and weaknesses of each.

The result is not a standard policy analysis, for neither Universal Breadwinner nor Caregiver Parity will in fact be realized in the near future, and my discussion is not directed primarily at policy-making elites. My intent, rather, is theoretical and political in a broader sense. I aim, first, to clarify some dilemmas surrounding "equality" and "difference" by reconsidering what is meant by gender justice. In so doing, I also aim to spur increased reflection on feminist strategies and goals by spelling out some assumptions that are implicit in current practice and subjecting them to critical scrutiny.

My discussion proceeds in four parts. In a first section, I propose an analysis of gender justice that generates a set of evaluative standards. Then, in the second and third sections, I apply those standards to Universal Breadwinner and Caregiver Parity, respectively. I conclude, in the fourth section, that neither of those approaches, even in an idealized form, can deliver full gender justice. To have a shot at *that*, I contend, we must develop a new vision of a postindustrial welfare state, which effectively dismantles the gender division of labor.

## 1. GENDER JUSTICE: A COMPLEX CONCEPTION

In order to evaluate alternative visions of a postindustrial welfare state, we need some normative criteria. Gender justice, I have said, is one indispensable standard. But in what precisely does it consist?

Feminists have so far associated gender justice with either equality or difference, where "equality" means treating women exactly like men, and where "difference" means treating women differently inso-far as they differ from men. Theorists have debated the relative merits of these two approaches as if they represented two antithetical poles of an absolute dichotomy. These arguments have generally ended in stalemate. Proponents of "difference" have successfully shown that equality strategies typically presuppose "the male as norm," thereby disadvantaging women and imposing a distorted standard on every-one. Egalitarians have argued just as cogently, however, that difference approaches typically rely on essentialist notions of femininity, thereby reinforcing existing stereotypes and confining women within existing gender divisions.[8] Neither equality nor difference, then, is a workable conception of gender justice.

Feminists have responded to this stalemate in several different ways. Some have tried to resolve the dilemma by reconceiving one or another of its horns; they have reinterpreted difference or equality in what they consider a more defensible form. Others have concluded "a plague on both your houses" and sought some third, wholly other, normative principle. Still others have tried to embrace the dilemma as

---

8  Some of the most sophisticated discussions are found in *Feminist Legal Theory: Readings in Law and Gender*, eds. Katharine T. Bartlett and Rosanne Kennedy, Boulder, CO: Westview Press, 1991.

an enabling paradox, a resource to be treasured, not an impasse to be gotten round. Many feminists, finally, have retreated altogether from normative theorizing—into cultural positivism, piecemeal reformism, or postmodern antinomianism.

None of these responses is satisfactory. Normative theorizing remains an indispensable intellectual enterprise for feminism, indeed for all emancipatory social movements. We need a vision or picture of where we are trying to go and a set of standards for evaluating various proposals as to how we might get there. The equality/difference impasse is real, moreover, and cannot be simply sidestepped or embraced. Nor is there any "wholly other" third term that can magically catapult us beyond it. What, then, should feminist theorists do?

I propose we reconceptualize gender justice as a complex idea, not a simple one. This means breaking with the assumption that gender justice can be identified with any single value or norm, whether it be equality, difference, or something else. Instead, we should treat it as a complex notion comprising a plurality of distinct normative principles. The plurality will include some notions associated with the equality side of the debate, as well as some associated with the difference side. It will also encompass still other normative ideas that neither side has accorded due weight. Wherever they come from, however, the important point is this: each of several distinct norms must be respected simultaneously in order that gender justice be achieved. Failure to satisfy any one of them means failure to realize the full meaning of gender justice.

In what follows, I assume that gender justice is complex in this way. And I propose an account of it that is designed for the specific purpose of evaluating alternative pictures of a postindustrial welfare state. For issues other than welfare, a somewhat different package of norms might be called for. Nevertheless, I believe that the general idea of treating gender justice as a complex conception is widely applicable. The analysis here may serve as a paradigm case demonstrating the usefulness of this approach.

For this particular thought experiment, in any case, I unpack the idea of gender justice as a compound of seven distinct normative principles. Let me enumerate them one by one:

1. *The Anti-Poverty Principle*: The first and most obvious objective of social-welfare provision is to prevent poverty. Preventing poverty is crucial to achieving gender justice now, after the family wage, given the high rates of poverty in solo-mother families and the vastly increased likelihood that US women and children will live in such families.[9] If it accomplishes nothing else, a welfare state should at least

---

9 David T. Ellwood, *Poor Support: Poverty in the American Family*, New York: Basic Books, 1988.

relieve suffering by meeting otherwise unmet basic needs. Arrangements, such as those in the United States, that leave women, children,
and men in poverty, are unacceptable according to this criterion. Any
postindustrial welfare state that prevented such poverty would constitute a major advance. So far, however, this does not say enough. The
anti-poverty principle might be satisfied in a variety of different ways,
not all of which are acceptable. Some ways, such as the provision of
targeted, isolating, and stigmatized poor relief for solo-mother families, fail to respect several of the following normative principles, which
are also essential to gender justice in social welfare.

2. *The Anti-Exploitation Principle*: Anti-poverty measures are important not only in themselves but also as a means to another basic
objective: preventing exploitation of vulnerable people.[10] This principle, too, is central to achieving gender justice after the family wage.
Needy women with no other way to feed themselves and their children, for example, are liable to exploitation—by abusive husbands, by
sweatshop foremen, and by pimps. In guaranteeing relief of poverty,
then, welfare provision should also aim to mitigate exploitable
dependency.[11] The availability of an alternative source of income
enhances the bargaining position of subordinates in unequal relationships. The non-employed wife who knows she can support herself
and her children outside of her marriage has more leverage within it;
her "voice" is enhanced as her possibilities of "exit" increase.[12] The
same holds for the low-paid nursing-home attendant in relation to
her boss.[13] For welfare measures to have this effect, however, support
must be provided as a matter of right. When receipt of aid is highly
stigmatized or discretionary, the anti-exploitation principle is not

---

10   Robert Goodin, *Reasons for Welfare: The Political Theory of the Welfare State*,
Princeton, NJ: Princeton University Press, 1988.

11   Not all dependencies are exploitable. In *Reasons for Welfare*, 175–6, Robert
Goodin specifies the following four conditions that must be met if a dependency is
to be exploitable: 1) the relationship must be asymmetrical; 2) the subordinate party
must need the resource that the superordinate supplies; 3) the subordinate must
depend on some particular superordinate for the supply of needed resources; 4) the
superordinate must enjoy discretionary control over the resources that the
subordinate needs from him/her.

12   Albert O. Hirschman, *Exit, Voice, and Loyalty: Responses to Decline in Firms,
Organizations, and States*, Cambridge, MA: Harvard University Press, 1970; Susan
Moller Okin, *Justice, Gender, and the Family*, New York: Basic Books, 1989; Barbara
Hobson, "No Exit, No Voice: Women's Economic Dependency and the Welfare
State," *Acta Sociologica* 33:3, Fall 1990, 235–50.

13   Frances Fox Piven and Richard A. Cloward, *Regulating the Poor*, New
York: Random House, 1971; Gosta Esping-Andersen, *The Three Worlds of Welfare
Capitalism*, Princeton, NJ: Princeton University Press, 1990.

satisfied.[14] At best the claimant would trade exploitable dependence on a husband or a boss for exploitable dependence on a caseworker's whim.[15] The goal should be to prevent at least three kinds of exploitable dependencies: exploitable dependence on an individual family member, such as a husband or an adult child; exploitable dependence on employers and supervisors; and exploitable dependence on the personal whims of state officials. Rather than shuttle people back and forth among these exploitable dependencies, an adequate approach must prevent all three simultaneously.[16] This principle rules out arrangements that channel a homemaker's benefits through her husband. It is likewise incompatible with arrangements that provide essential goods, such as health insurance, only in forms linked conditionally to scarce employment. Any postindustrial welfare state that satisfied the anti-exploitation principle would represent a major improvement over current US arrangements. But even it might not be satisfactory. Some ways of satisfying this principle would fail to respect several of the following normative principles, which are also essential to gender justice in social welfare.

*The Three Equality Principles*: A postindustrial welfare state could prevent women's poverty and exploitation and yet still tolerate severe gender inequality. Such a welfare state is not satisfactory. A further dimension of gender justice in social provision is redistribution, reducing inequality between women and men. Some feminists, as we saw, have criticized equality; they have argued that it entails treating women exactly like men according to male-defined standards, and that this necessarily disadvantages women. That argument expresses a legitimate worry, which I shall address under another rubric below. But it does not undermine the ideal of equality *per se*. The worry pertains only to certain inadequate ways of conceiving equality, which I do not presuppose here. At least three distinct conceptions of equality escape the objection. These are essential to gender justice in social welfare.

---

14  Robert Goodin, *Reasons for Welfare*.

15  Edward V. Sparer, "The Right to Welfare," in *The Rights of Americans: What They are—What They Should Be*, ed. Norman Dorsen, New York: Pantheon, 1970.

16  Ann Shola Orloff, "Gender and the Social Rights of Citizenship: The Comparative Analysis of Gender Relations and Welfare States," *The American Sociological Review* 58:3, June 1993, 303–28. The anti-exploitation objective should not be confused with current US attacks on "welfare dependency," which are highly ideological. These attacks define "dependency" exclusively as receipt of public assistance. They ignore the ways in which such receipt can promote claimants' independence by preventing exploitable dependence on husbands and employers. For a critique of such views, see Chapter 3 of this volume, Fraser and Gordon, "A Genealogy of 'Dependency.'"

*3. Income Equality*: One form of equality that is crucial to gender justice concerns the distribution of real per capita income. This sort of equality is highly pressing now, after the family wage, when US women's earnings are approximately 70 percent of men's, when much of women's labor is not compensated at all, and when many women suffer from "hidden poverty" due to unequal distribution within families.[17] As I interpret it, the principle of income equality does not require absolute leveling. But it does rule out arrangements that reduce women's incomes after divorce by nearly half, while men's incomes nearly double.[18] It likewise rules out unequal pay for equal work and the wholesale undervaluation of women's labor and skills. The income-equality principle requires a substantial reduction in the vast discrepancy between men's and women's incomes. In so doing, it tends, as well, to help equalize the life-chances of children, as a majority of US children are currently likely to live at some point in solo-mother families.[19]

*4. Leisure-Time Equality*: Another kind of equality that is crucial to gender justice concerns the distribution of leisure time. This sort of equality is highly pressing now, after the family wage, when many women, but relatively few men, do both paid work and unpaid primary carework and when women suffer disproportionately from "time poverty."[20] One recent British study found that 52 percent of women surveyed, compared to 21 percent of men, said they "felt tired most of the time."[21] The leisure-time-equality principle rules out welfare arrangements that would equalize incomes while requiring a double shift of work from women, but only a single shift from men. It likewise rules out arrangements that would require women, but not men, to do either the "work of claiming" or the time-consuming "patchwork" of piecing together income from several sources and of coordinating services from different agencies and associations.[22]

---

17    Ruth Lister, "Women, Economic Dependency, and Citizenship," *Journal of Social Policy* 19:4, 1990, 445–67; Amartya Sen, "More Than 100 Million Women Are Missing," *New York Review of Books* 37:20, December 20, 1990, 61–6.

18    Lenore Weitzman, *The Divorce Revolution: The Unexpected Social Consequences for Women and Children in America*, New York: Free Press, 1985.

19    David T. Ellwood, *Poor Support*, 45.

20    Lois Bryson, "Citizenship, Caring and Commodification," unpublished paper presented at conference on Crossing Borders: International Dialogues on Gender, Social Politics and Citizenship, Stockholm, May 27–29, 1994; Arlie Hochschild, *The Second Shift: Working Parents and the Revolution at Home*, New York: Viking Press, 1989; Juliet Schor, *The Overworked American: The Unexpected Decline of Leisure*, New York: Basic Books, 1991.

21    Ruth Lister, "Women, Economic Dependency, and Citizenship."

22    Laura Balbo, "Crazy Quilts," in *Women and the State*, ed. Ann Showstack Sassoon, London: Hutchinson, 1987.

5. *Equality of Respect*: Equality of respect is also crucial to gender justice. This kind of equality is especially pressing now, after the family wage, when postindustrial culture routinely represents women as sexual objects for the pleasure of male subjects. The principle of equal respect rules out social arrangements that objectify and deprecate women—even if those arrangements prevent poverty and exploitation, and even if in addition they equalize income and leisure time. It is incompatible with welfare programs that trivialize women's activities and ignore women's contributions—hence with "welfare reforms" in the United States that assume AFDC claimants do not "work." Equality of respect requires recognition of women's personhood and of women's work.

A postindustrial welfare state should promote equality in all three of these dimensions. Such a state would constitute an enormous advance over present arrangements, but even it might not go far enough. Some ways of satisfying the equality principles would fail to respect the following principle, which is also essential to gender justice in social welfare.

6. *The Anti-Marginalization Principle*: A welfare state could satisfy all the preceding principles and still function to marginalize women. By limiting support to generous mothers' pensions, for example, it could render women independent, well provided for, well rested, and respected, but enclaved in a separate domestic sphere, removed from the life of the larger society. Such a welfare state would be unacceptable. Social policy should promote women's full participation on a par with men in all areas of social life—in employment, in politics, in the associational life of civil society. The anti-marginalization principle requires provision of the necessary conditions for women's participation, including day care, elder care, and provision for breast-feeding in public. It also requires the dismantling of masculinist work cultures and woman-hostile political environments. Any postindustrial welfare state that provided these things would represent a great improvement over current arrangements. Yet even it might leave something to be desired. Some ways of satisfying the anti-marginalization principle would fail to respect the last principle, which is also essential to gender justice in social welfare.

7. *The Anti-Androcentrism Principle*: A welfare state that satisfied many of the foregoing principles could still entrench some obnoxious gender norms. It could assume the androcentric view that men's current life-patterns represent the human norm and that women ought to assimilate to them. (This is the real issue behind the previously noted worry about equality.) Such a welfare state is unacceptable. Social policy should not require women to become like men, nor to fit into institutions designed for men, in order to enjoy comparable levels of well-being. Policy

should aim instead to restructure androcentric institutions so as to welcome human beings who can give birth and who often care for relatives and friends, treating them not as exceptions, but as ideal-typical participants. The anti-androcentrism principle requires decentering masculinist norms—in part by revaluing practices and traits that are currently undervalued because they are associated with women. It entails changing men as well as changing women.

Here, then, is an account of gender justice in social welfare. On this account, gender justice is a complex idea comprising seven distinct normative principles, each of which is necessary and essential. No postindustrial welfare state can realize gender justice unless it satisfies them all.

How, then, do the principles interrelate? Here everything depends on context. Some institutional arrangements permit simultaneous satisfaction of several principles with a minimum of mutual interference; other arrangements, in contrast, set up zero-sum situations, in which attempts to satisfy one principle interfere with attempts to satisfy another. Promoting gender justice after the family wage, therefore, means attending to multiple aims that are potentially in conflict. The goal should be to find approaches that avoid trade-offs and maximize prospects for satisfying all—or at least most—of the seven principles.

In the following sections, I use this approach to assess two alternative models of a postindustrial welfare state. First, however, I want to flag four sets of relevant issues. One concerns the social organization of carework. Precisely how this work is organized is crucial to human well-being in general and to the social standing of women in particular. In the era of the family wage, carework was treated as the private responsibility of individual women. Today, however, it can no longer be treated in that way. Some other way of organizing it is required, but a number of different scenarios are conceivable. In evaluating postindustrial welfare state models, then, we must ask: How is responsibility for carework allocated between such institutions as the family, the market, civil society, and the state? And how is responsibility for this work assigned within such institutions—by gender? by class? by "race"-ethnicity? by age?

A second set of issues concerns the bases of entitlement to provision. Every welfare state assigns its benefits according to a specific mix of distributive principles, which defines its basic moral quality. That mix, in each case, needs to be scrutinized. Usually it contains varying proportions of three basic principles of entitlement: need, desert, and citizenship. Need-based provision is the most redistributive, but it risks isolating and stigmatizing the needy; it has been the basis of traditional poor relief and of modern public assistance, the least honorable forms of provision. The most honorable, in contrast, is entitlement based on desert, but it tends to be anti-egalitarian and exclusionary. Here one receives benefits according to one's "contributions," usually tax payments, work, and service—where "tax payments" means wage deductions paid into a special fund, "work" means primary labor-force employment, and "service" means the military, all interpretations of those terms that disadvantage women. Desert has usually been seen as the primary basis of earnings-linked social insurance in the industrial welfare state.[23] The third principle, citizenship, allocates provision on the basis of membership in society. It is honorable, egalitarian, and universalist, but exclusionary vis-à-vis non-citizen immigrants and those without papers. It is also expensive, and hence hard to sustain at high levels of quality and generosity; some theorists worry, too, that it encourages free-riding, which they define, however, androcentrically.[24] Citizenship-based entitlements are most often found in social-democratic countries, where they may include single-payer universal health insurance systems and universal family or child allowances; they are virtually unknown in the United States—except for public education. In examining models of postindustrial welfare states, then, one must look closely at the construction of entitlement. It makes considerable difference to women's and children's well-being, for example, whether day care places are distributed as citizenship entitlements or as desert-based entitlements, i.e., whether or not they are conditional on prior employment. It likewise matters, to take another example, whether carework is supported on the basis of need, in the form of a means-tested benefit for the poor, or whether it is supported on the basis of desert, as return for "work" or "service," now interpreted non-androcentrically, or whether, finally, it is supported on the basis of citizenship under a universal Basic Income scheme.

A third set of issues concerns differences among women. Gender is the principal focus of this chapter, to be sure, but it cannot be treated *en bloc*. The lives of women and men are cross-cut by several other salient social divisions, including class, "race"-ethnicity, sexuality, and

---

23   Actually, there is a heavy ideological component in the usual view that public assistance is need-based, while social insurance is desert-based. Benefit levels in social insurance do not strictly reflect "contributions." Moreover, all government programs are financed by "contributions" in the form of taxation. Public assistance programs are financed from general revenues, both federal and state. Welfare recipients, like others, "contribute" to these funds, for example, through payment of sales taxes. See Nancy Fraser and Linda Gordon, "Contract versus Charity: Why Is There No Social Citizenship in the United States?" *Socialist Review* 22:3, July–September 1992, 45–68.

24   The free-rider worry is usually posed androcentrically as a worry about shirking paid employment. Little attention is paid, in contrast, to a far more widespread problem, namely, men's free-riding on women's unpaid domestic labor. A welcome exception is Peter Taylor-Gooby, "Scrounging, Moral Hazard, and Unwaged Work: Citizenship and Human Need," unpublished typescript, 1993.

age. Models of postindustrial welfare states, then, will not affect all women—nor all men—in the same way; they will generate different outcomes for differently situated people. For example, some policies will affect women who have children differently from those who do not; some, likewise, will affect women who have access to a second income differently from those who do not; and some, finally, will affect women employed full time differently from those employed part time, and differently yet again from those who are not employed. For each model, then, we must ask: which groups of women would be advantaged and which groups disadvantaged?

A fourth set of issues concerns desiderata for postindustrial welfare states other than gender justice. Gender justice, after all, is not the only goal of social welfare. Also important are non-justice goals, such as efficiency, community, and individual liberty. In addition there remain other justice goals, such as "racial"-ethnic justice, generational justice, class justice, and justice among nations. All of these issues are necessarily backgrounded here. Some of them, however, such as "racial"-ethnic justice, could be handled via parallel thought experiments: one might define "racial"-ethnic justice as a complex idea, analogous to the way gender justice is treated here, and then use it, too, to assess competing visions of a postindustrial welfare state.

With these considerations in mind, let us now examine two strikingly different feminist visions of a postindustrial welfare state. And let us ask: Which comes closest to achieving gender justice in the sense I have elaborated here?

## 2. THE UNIVERSAL BREADWINNER MODEL

In one vision of postindustrial society, the age of the family wage would give way to the age of the *Universal Breadwinner*. This is the vision implicit in the current political practice of most US feminists and liberals. (It was also assumed in the former Communist countries!) It aims to achieve gender justice principally by promoting women's employment. The point is to enable women to support themselves and their families through their own wage-earning. The breadwinner role is to be universalized, in sum, so that women, too, can be citizen-workers.

Universal Breadwinner is a very ambitious postindustrial scenario, requiring major new programs and policies. One crucial element is a set of employment-enabling services, such as day care and elder care, aimed at freeing women from unpaid responsibilities so they could take full-time employment on terms comparable to men.[25] Another

---

25  Employment-enabling services could be distributed according to need, desert,

essential element is a set of workplace reforms aimed at removing
equal-opportunity obstacles, such as sex discrimination and sexual
harassment. Reforming the workplace requires reforming the culture,
however—eliminating sexist stereotypes and breaking the cultural
association of breadwinning with masculinity. Also required are policies to help change socialization, so as, first, to reorient women's
aspirations away from domesticity and toward employment, and
second, to reorient men's expectations toward acceptance of women's
new role. None of this would work, however, without one additional
ingredient: macroeconomic policies to create full-time, high paying,
permanent jobs for women.[26] These would have to be true breadwinner jobs in the primary labor force, carrying full, first-class
social-insurance entitlements. Social insurance, finally, is central to
Universal Breadwinner. The aim here is to bring women up to parity
with men in an institution that has traditionally disadvantaged them.

How would this model organize carework? The bulk of such work
would be shifted from the family to the market and the state, where it
would be performed by employees for pay.[27] Who, then, are these
employees likely to be? In many countries today, including the United
States, paid institutional carework is poorly remunerated, feminized,
and largely racialized and/or performed by immigrants.[28] But such
arrangements are precluded in this model. If the model is to succeed

---

or citizenship, but citizenship accords best with the spirit of the model. Means-tested
day care targeted for the poor cannot help but signify a failure to achieve genuine
breadwinner status; and desert-based day care sets up a catch-22: one must already be
employed in order to get what is needed for employment. Citizenship-based entitlement
is best, then, but it must make services available to all, including to immigrants. This
rules out Swedish-type arrangements, which fail to guarantee sufficient day care places
and are plagued by long queues. For the Swedish problem, see Barbara Hobson,
"Economic Dependency and Women's Social Citizenship: Some Thoughts on Esping-
Andersen's Welfare State Regimes," unpublished typescript, 1993.

26    That incidentally would be to break decisively with US policy, which has
assumed since the New Deal that job creation is principally for men. Bill Clinton's
1992 campaign proposals for "industrial" and "infrastructural investment" policies
were no exception in this regard. See Nancy Fraser, "Clintonism, Welfare, and the
Antisocial Wage."

27    Government could itself provide carework services in the form of public
goods or it could fund marketized provision through a system of vouchers.
Alternatively, employers could be mandated to provide employment-enabling
services for their employees, either through vouchers or in-house arrangements.
The state option means higher taxes, of course, but it may be preferable nevertheless.
Mandating employer responsibility creates a disincentive to hire workers with
dependents, to the likely disadvantage of women.

28    Evelyn Nakano Glenn, "From Servitude to Service Work: Historical
Continuities in the Racial Division of Paid Reproductive Labor," *Signs: Journal of
Women in Culture and Society* 18:1, Autumn 1992, 1–43.

in enabling *all* women to be breadwinners, it must upgrade the status and pay attached to carework employment, making it, too, into primary labor-force work. Universal Breadwinner, then, is necessarily committed to a policy of "comparable worth"; it must redress the widespread undervaluation of skills and jobs currently coded as feminine and/or "non-white," and it must remunerate such jobs with breadwinner-level pay.

Universal Breadwinner would link many benefits to employment and distribute them through social insurance, with levels varying according to earnings. In this respect, the model resembles the industrial-era welfare state.[29] The difference is that many more women would be covered on the basis of their own employment records. And many more women's employment records would look considerably more like men's.

Not all adults can be employed, however. Some will be unable to work for medical reasons, including some not previously employed. Others will be unable to get jobs. Some, finally, will have carework responsibilities that they are unable or unwilling to shift elsewhere. Most of these last will be women. To provide for these people, Universal Breadwinner must include a residual tier of social welfare that provides need-based, means-tested wage replacements.[30]

Universal Breadwinner is far removed from present realities. It requires massive creation of primary labor-force jobs—jobs sufficient to support a family single-handedly. That, of course, is wildly askew of current postindustrial trends, which generate jobs not for breadwinners but for "disposable workers."[31] Let us assume for the sake of the thought experiment, however, that its conditions of possibility could be met. And let us consider whether the resulting postindustrial welfare state could claim title to gender justice.

*Anti-Poverty*: We can acknowledge straight off that Universal Breadwinner would do a good job of preventing poverty. A policy that

---

29 It, too, conditions entitlement on desert and defines "contribution" in traditional androcentric terms as employment and wage deductions.

30 Exactly what else must be provided inside the residual system will depend on the balance of entitlements outside it. If health insurance is provided universally as a citizen benefit, for example, then there need be no means-tested health system for the non-employed. If, however, mainstream health insurance is linked to employment, then a residual health care system will be necessary. The same holds for unemployment, retirement, and disability insurance. In general, the more that is provided on the basis of citizenship, instead of on the basis of desert, the less has to be provided on the basis of need. One could even say that desert-based entitlements create the necessity of need-based provision; thus, employment-linked social insurance creates the need for means-tested public assistance.

31 Peter Kilborn, "New Jobs Lack the Old Security in Time of 'Disposable Workers,'" *New York Times*, March 15 1993, A1, A6.

created secure breadwinner-quality jobs for all employable women and men—while providing the services that would enable women to take such jobs—would keep most families out of poverty. And generous levels of residual support would keep the rest out of poverty through transfers.[32]

*Anti-Exploitation*: The model should also succeed in preventing exploitable dependency for most women. Women with secure breadwinner jobs are able to exit unsatisfactory relations with men. And those who do not have such jobs but know they can get them will also be less vulnerable to exploitation. Failing that, the residual system of income support provides back-up protection against exploitable dependency—assuming that it is generous, nondiscretionary, and honorable.[33]

*Income Equality*: Universal Breadwinner is only fair, however, at achieving income equality. Granted, secure breadwinner jobs for women—plus the services that would enable women to take them—would narrow the gender wage gap.[34] Reduced inequality in earnings, moreover, translates into reduced inequality in social-insurance benefits. And the availability of exit options from marriage should encourage a more equitable distribution of resources within it. But the model is not otherwise egalitarian. It contains a basic social fault line dividing breadwinners from others, to the considerable disadvantage of the others—most of whom would be women. Apart from comparable worth, moreover, it does not reduce pay inequality among breadwinner jobs. To be sure, the model reduces the weight of gender in assigning individuals to unequally compensated breadwinner jobs; but it thereby increases the weight of other variables, presumably class, education, "race"-ethnicity, and age. Women—and men—who are disadvantaged in relation to those axes of social differentiation will earn less than those who are not.

*Leisure-Time Equality*: The model is quite poor, moreover, with respect to equality of leisure time, as we know from the Communist experience. It assumes that all of women's current domestic and carework responsibilities can be shifted to the market and/or the state. But that assumption is patently unrealistic. Some things, such as

---

32   Failing that, however, several groups are especially vulnerable to poverty in this model: those who cannot work, those who cannot get secure, permanent, full-time, good-paying jobs—disproportionately women and/or people of color; and those with heavy, hard-to-shift, unpaid carework responsibilities—disproportionately women.

33   Failing that, however, the groups mentioned in the previous note remain especially vulnerable to exploitation—by abusive men, by unfair or predatory employers, by capricious state officials.

34   Exactly how much remains depends on the government's success in eliminating discrimination and in implementing comparable worth.

childbearing, attending to family emergencies, and much parenting work cannot be shifted—short of universal surrogacy and other presumably undesirable arrangements. Other things, such as cooking and (some) housekeeping, could be shifted—provided we were prepared to accept collective living arrangements or high levels of commodification. Even those tasks that are shifted, finally, do not disappear without a trace, but give rise to burdensome new tasks of coordination. Women's chances for equal leisure, then, depend on whether men can be induced to do their fair share of this work. On this, the model does not inspire confidence. Not only does it offer no disincentives to free-riding, but in valorizing paid work, it implicitly denigrates unpaid work, thereby fueling the motivation to shirk.[35] Women without partners would in any case be on their own. And those in lower-income households would be less able to purchase replacement services. Employed women would have a second shift on this model, then, albeit a less burdensome one than some have now; and there would be many more women employed full time. Universal Breadwinner, in sum, is not likely to deliver equal leisure. Anyone who does not free-ride in this possible postindustrial world is likely to be harried and tired.

*Equality of Respect*: The model is only fair, moreover, at delivering equality of respect. Because it holds men and women to the single standard of the citizen-worker, its only chance of eliminating the gender respect gap is to admit women to that status on the same terms as men. This, however, is unlikely to occur. A more likely outcome is that women would retain more connection to reproduction and domesticity than men, thus appearing as breadwinners manqué. In addition, the model is likely to generate another kind of respect gap. By putting a high premium on breadwinner status, it invites disrespect for others. Participants in the means-tested residual system will be liable to stigmatization; and most of these will be women. Any employment-centered model, even a feminist one, has a hard time constructing an honorable status for those it defines as "non-workers."

*Anti-Marginalization*: This model is also only fair at combating women's marginalization. Granted, it promotes women's participation in employment, but its definition of participation is narrow. Expecting full-time employment of all who are able, the model may actually impede participation in politics and civil society. Certainly, it does nothing to promote women's participation in those arenas. It

---

35 Universal Breadwinner presumably relies on persuasion to induce men to do their fair share of unpaid work. The chances of that working would be improved if the model succeeded in promoting cultural change and in enhancing women's voice within marriage. But it is doubtful that this alone would suffice, as the Communist experience suggests.

fights women's marginalization, then, in a one-sided, "workerist" way.

*Anti-Androcentrism*: Lastly, the model performs poorly in overcoming androcentrism. It valorizes men's traditional sphere—employment— and simply tries to help women fit in. Traditionally female carework, in contrast, is treated instrumentally; it is what must be sloughed off in order to become a breadwinner. It is not itself accorded social value. The ideal-typical citizen here is the breadwinner, now nominally gender-neutral. But the content of the status is implicitly masculine; it is the male half of the old breadwinner/homemaker couple, now universalized and required of everyone. The female half of the couple has simply disappeared. None of her distinctive virtues and capacities has been preserved for women, let alone universalized to men. The model is androcentric.

Not surprisingly, Universal Breadwinner delivers the best outcomes to women whose lives most closely resemble the male half of the old family-wage ideal couple. It is especially good to childless women and to women without other major domestic responsibilities that cannot easily be shifted to social services. But for those women, as well as for others, it falls short of full gender justice.

## 3. THE CAREGIVER PARITY MODEL

In a second vision of postindustrial society, the era of the family wage would give way to the era of Caregiver Parity. This is the picture implicit in the political practice of most Western European feminists and social democrats. It aims to promote gender justice principally by supporting informal carework. The point is to enable women with significant domestic responsibilities to support themselves and their families either through carework alone or through carework plus part-time employment. (Women without significant domestic responsibilities would presumably support themselves through employment.) The aim is not to make women's lives the same as men's, but rather to "make difference costless."[36] Thus, childbearing, childrearing, and informal domestic labor are to be elevated to parity with formal paid labor. The caregiver role is to be put on a par with the breadwinner role—so that women and men can enjoy equivalent levels of dignity and well-being.

Caregiver Parity is also extremely ambitious. On this model, many (though not all) women will follow the current US female practice of alternating spells of full-time employment, spells of full-time

---

36  Christine A. Littleton, "Reconstructing Sexual Equality," in *Feminist Legal Theory*, eds. Katharine T. Bartlett and Rosanne Kennedy.

carework, and spells that combine part-time carework with part-time employment. The aim is to make such a life-pattern costless. To this end, several major new programs are necessary. One is a program of caregiver allowances to compensate childbearing, childraising, housework, and other forms of socially necessary domestic labor; the allowances must be sufficiently generous at the full-time rate to support a family—hence equivalent to a breadwinner wage.[37] Also required is a program of workplace reforms. These must facilitate the possibility of combining supported carework with part-time employment and of making transitions between different life-states. The key here is flexibility. One obvious necessity is a generous program of mandated pregnancy and family leave so that caregivers can exit and enter employment without losing security or seniority. Another is a program of retraining and job search for those not returning to old jobs. Also essential is mandated flex-time so that caregivers can shift their hours to accommodate their carework responsibilities, including shifts between full- and part-time employment. Finally, in the wake of all this flexibility, there must be programs to ensure continuity of all the basic social-welfare benefits, including health, unemployment, disability, and retirement insurance.

This model organizes carework very differently from Universal Breadwinner. Whereas that approach shifted carework to the market and the state, this one keeps the bulk of such work in the household and supports it with public funds. Caregiver Parity's social-insurance system also differs sharply. To assure continuous coverage for people alternating between carework and employment, benefits attached to both must be integrated in a single system. In this system, part-time jobs and supported carework must be covered on the same basis as full-time jobs. Thus, a woman finishing a spell of supported carework would be eligible, in the event she could not find a suitable job, for unemployment insurance benefits on the same basis as a recently laid-off employee. And a supported careworker who became disabled

---

37   Caregiver allowances could be distributed on the basis of need, as a means-tested benefit for the poor—as they have always been in the United States. But that would contravene the spirit of Caregiver Parity. One cannot consistently claim that the caregiver life is equivalent in dignity to the breadwinner life, while supporting it only as a last-resort stop-gap against poverty. (This contradiction has always bedeviled mothers' pensions—and later Aid to Dependent Children—in the United States. Although these programs were intended by some advocates to exalt motherhood, they sent a contradictory message by virtue of being means-tested and morals-tested.) Means-tested allowances, moreover, would impede easy transitions between employment and carework. Since the aim is to make caregiving as deserving as breadwinning, caregiver allowances must be based on desert. Treated as compensation for socially necessary "service" or "work," they alter the standard androcentric meanings of those terms.

would receive disability payments on the same basis as a disabled employee. Years of supported carework would count on a par with years of employment toward eligibility for retirement pensions. Benefit levels would be fixed in ways that treat carework and employment equivalently. [38]

Caregiver Parity also requires another, residual tier of social welfare. Some adults will be unable to do either carework or waged work, including some without prior work records of either type. Most of these people will probably be men. To provide for them, the model must offer means-tested wage-and-allowance replacements.[39] Caregiver Parity's residual tier should be smaller than Universal Breadwinner's, however; nearly all adults should be covered in the integrated breadwinner-caregiver system of social insurance.

Caregiver Parity, too, is far removed from current US arrangements. It requires large outlays of public funds to pay caregiver allowances, hence major structural tax reform and a sea-change in political culture. Let us assume for the sake of the thought experiment, however, that its conditions of possibility could be met. And let us consider whether the resulting postindustrial welfare state could claim title to gender justice.

*Anti-Poverty*: Caregiver Parity would do a good job of preventing poverty—including for those women and children who are currently most vulnerable. Sufficiently generous allowances would keep solo-mother families out of poverty during spells of full-time carework. And a combination of allowances and wages would do the same during spells of part-time supported carework and part-time

---

38   In *Justice, Gender, and the Family*, Susan Okin has proposed an alternative way to fund carework. In her scheme the funds would come from what are now considered to be the earnings of the caregiver's partner. A man with a non-employed wife, for example, would receive a paycheck for one-half of "his" salary; his employer would cut a second check in the same amount payable directly to the wife. Intriguing as this idea is, one may wonder whether it is really the best way to promote a wife's independence from her husband, as it ties her income so directly to his. In addition, Okin's proposal does not provide any carework support for women without employed partners. Caregiver Parity, in contrast, provides public support for all who perform informal carework. Who, then, are its beneficiaries likely to be? With the exception of pregnancy leave, all the model's benefits are open to everyone; so men as well as women can opt for a "feminine" life. Women, however, are considerably more likely to do so. Although the model aims to make such a life costless, it includes no positive incentives for men to change. Some men, of course, may simply prefer such a life and will choose it when offered the chance; most will not, however, given current socialization and culture. We shall see, moreover, that Caregiver Parity contains some hidden disincentives to male caregiving.

39   In this respect, it resembles the Universal Breadwinner model: whatever additional essential goods are normally offered on the basis of desert must be offered here too on the basis of need.

employment.[40] Since each of these options would carry the basic social-insurance package, moreover, women with "feminine" work-patterns would have considerable security.[41]

*Anti-Exploitation*: Caregiver Parity should also succeed in preventing exploitation for most women, including for those who are most vulnerable today. By providing income directly to non-employed wives, it reduces their economic dependence on husbands. It also provides economic security to single women with children, reducing their liability to exploitation by employers. Insofar as caregiver allowances are honorable and nondiscretionary, finally, recipients are not subject to caseworkers' whims.[42]

*Income Equality*: Caregiver Parity performs quite poorly, however, with respect to income equality, as we know from the Nordic experience. Although the system of allowances-plus-wages provides the equivalent of a basic minimum breadwinner wage, it also institutes a "mommy track" in employment—a market in flexible, noncontinuous full- and/or part-time jobs. Most of these jobs will pay considerably less even at the full-time rate than comparable breadwinner-track jobs. Two-partner families will have an economic incentive to keep one partner on the breadwinner track rather than to share spells of carework between them; and given current labor markets, making the breadwinner the man will be most advantageous for heterosexual couples. Given current culture and socialization, moreover, men are generally unlikely to choose the mommy track in the same proportions as women. So the two employment tracks will carry traditional gender associations. Those associations are likely in turn to produce discrimination against women in the breadwinner track. Caregiver Parity may make difference cost less, then, but it will not make difference costless.

*Leisure-Time Equality*: Caregiver Parity does somewhat better, however, with respect to equality of leisure time. It makes it possible for all women to avoid the double shift if they choose, by opting for full- or part-time supported carework at various stages in their lives. (Currently, this choice is available only to a small percentage of privileged US women.) We just saw, however, that this choice is not truly costless. Some women with families will not want to forego the

---

40  Wages from full-time employment must also be sufficient to support a family with dignity.

41  Adults with neither carework nor employment records would be most vulnerable to poverty in this model; most of these would be men. Children, in contrast, would be well protected.

42  Once again, it is adults with neither carework nor employment records who are most vulnerable to exploitation in this model; and the majority of them would be men.

benefits of breadwinner-track employment and will try to combine it with carework. Those not partnered with someone on the caregiver track will be significantly disadvantaged with respect to leisure time, and probably in their employment as well. Men, in contrast, will largely be insulated from this dilemma. On leisure time, then, the model is only fair.

*Equality of Respect*: Caregiver Parity is also only fair at promoting equality of respect. Unlike Universal Breadwinner, it offers two different routes to that end. Theoretically, citizen-workers and citizen-caregivers are statuses of equivalent dignity. But are they really on a par with one another? Caregiving is certainly treated more respectfully in this model than in current US society, but it remains associated with femininity. Breadwinning likewise remains associated with masculinity. Given those traditional gender associations, plus the economic differential between the two lifestyles, caregiving is unlikely to attain true parity with breadwinning. In general, it is hard to imagine how "separate but equal" gender roles could provide genuine equality of respect today.

*Anti-Marginalization*: Caregiver Parity performs poorly, moreover, in preventing women's marginalization. By supporting women's informal carework, it reinforces the view of such work as women's work and consolidates the gender division of domestic labor. By consolidating dual labor markets for breadwinners and caregivers, moreover, the model marginalizes women within the employment sector. By reinforcing the association of caregiving with femininity, finally, it may also impede women's participation in other spheres of life, such as politics and civil society.

*Anti-Androcentrism*: Yet Caregiver Parity is better than Universal Breadwinner at combating androcentrism. It treats caregiving as intrinsically valuable, not as a mere obstacle to employment, thus challenging the view that only men's traditional activities are fully human. It also accommodates "feminine" life-patterns, thereby rejecting the demand that women assimilate to "masculine" patterns. But the model still leaves something to be desired. Caregiver Parity stops short of affirming the universal value of activities and life-patterns associated with women. It does not value caregiving enough to demand that men do it, too; it does not ask men to change. Thus, Caregiver Parity represents only one-half of a full-scale challenge to androcentrism. Here, too, its performance is only fair.

In general, Caregiver Parity improves the lot of women with significant carework responsibilities. But for those women, as well as for others, it fails to deliver full gender justice.

## 4. TOWARD A UNIVERSAL CAREGIVER MODEL

Both Universal Breadwinner and Caregiver Parity are highly utopian visions of a postindustrial welfare state. Either one of them would represent a major improvement over current US arrangements. Yet neither is likely to be realized soon. Both models assume background preconditions that are strikingly absent today. Both presuppose major political-economic restructuring, including significant public control over corporations, the capacity to direct investment to create high-quality permanent jobs, and the ability to tax profits *and wealth* at rates sufficient to fund expanded high-quality social programs. Both models also assume broad popular support for a postindustrial welfare state that is committed to gender justice.

If both models are utopian in this sense, neither is utopian enough. Neither Universal Breadwinner nor Caregiver Parity can actually make good on its promise of gender justice—even under very favorable conditions. Although both are good at preventing women's poverty and exploitation, both are only fair at redressing inequality of respect: Universal Breadwinner holds women to the same standard as men, while constructing arrangements that prevent them from meeting it fully; Caregiver Parity, in contrast, sets up a double standard to accommodate gender difference, while institutionalizing policies that fail to assure equivalent respect for "feminine" activities and life-patterns. When we turn to the remaining principles, moreover, the two models' strengths and weaknesses diverge. Universal Breadwinner fails especially to promote equality of leisure time and to combat androcentrism, while Caregiver Parity fails especially to promote income equality and to prevent women's marginalization. Neither model, in addition, promotes women's full participation on a par with men in politics and civil society. And neither values female-associated practices enough to ask men to do them too; neither asks men to change. Neither model, in sum, provides everything feminists want. Even in a highly idealized form, neither delivers full gender justice.

If these were the only possibilities, we would face a very difficult set of tradeoffs. Suppose, however, we reject this Hobson's choice and try to develop a third alternative. The trick is to envision a postindustrial welfare state that combines the best of Universal Breadwinner with the best of Caregiver Parity, while jettisoning the worst features of each. What third alternative is possible?

So far we have examined—and found wanting—two initially plausible approaches: one aiming to make women more like men are now; the other leaving men and women pretty much unchanged, while aiming to make women's difference costless. A third possibility is to *induce men to become more like most women are now*—viz., people who do primary carework.

Consider the effects of this one change on the models we have just examined. If men were to do their fair share of carework, Universal Breadwinner would come much closer to equalizing leisure time and eliminating androcentrism, while Caregiver Parity would do a much better job of equalizing income and reducing women's marginalization. Both models, in addition, would tend to promote equality of respect. If men were to become more like women are now, in sum, both models would begin to approach gender justice.

The key to achieving gender justice in a postindustrial welfare state, then, is to make women's current life-patterns the norm for everyone. Women today often combine breadwinning and caregiving, albeit with great difficulty and strain. A postindustrial welfare state must ensure that men do the same, while redesigning institutions so as to eliminate the difficulty and strain.

We might call this vision *Universal Caregiver*.

What, then, might such a welfare state look like? Unlike Caregiver Parity, its employment sector would not be divided into two different tracks; all jobs would be designed for workers who are caregivers, too; all would have a shorter work week than full-time jobs have now; and all would have the support of employment-enabling services. Unlike Universal Breadwinner, however, employees would not be assumed to shift all carework to social services. Some informal carework would be publicly supported and integrated on a par with paid work in a single social-insurance system. Some would be performed in households by relatives and friends, but such households would not necessarily be heterosexual nuclear families. Other supported carework would be located outside households altogether—in civil society. In state-funded but locally organized institutions, childless adults, older people, and others without kin-based responsibilities would join parents and others in democratic, self-managed carework activities.

A Universal Caregiver welfare state would promote gender justice by effectively dismantling the gendered opposition between breadwinning and caregiving. It would integrate activities that are currently separated from one another, eliminate their gender-coding, and encourage men to perform them too. This, however, is tantamount to a wholesale restructuring of the institution of gender. The construction of breadwinning and caregiving as separate roles, coded masculine and feminine respectively, is a principal undergirding of the current gender order. To dismantle those roles and their cultural coding is in effect to overturn that order. It means subverting the existing gender division of labor and reducing the salience of gender as a structural principle of social organization.[43] At the limit, it suggests deconstructing gender.[44] By deconstructing the opposition between breadwinning and caregiving, moreover, Universal Caregiver would simultaneously deconstruct the associated opposition between bureaucratized public institutional settings and intimate private domestic settings. Treating civil society as an additional site for carework, it would overcome both the "workerism" of Universal Breadwinner and the domestic privatism of Caregiver Parity. Thus, Universal Caregiver promises expansive new possibilities for enriching the substance of social life and for promoting equal participation.

Only by embracing the Universal Caregiver vision, moreover, can we mitigate potential conflicts among our seven component principles of gender justice and minimize the need for trade-offs. Rejecting this approach, in contrast, makes such conflicts, and hence trade-offs, more likely. *Achieving gender justice in a postindustrial welfare state, then, requires deconstructing gender.*

Much more work needs to be done to develop this third—Universal Caregiver—vision of a postindustrial welfare state. A key is to develop policies that discourage free-riding. *Contra* conservatives, the real free-riders in the current system are not poor solo mothers who shirk employment. Instead they are men of all classes who shirk carework and domestic labor, as well as corporations who free-ride on the labor of working people, both underpaid and unpaid.

A good statement of the Universal Caregiver vision comes from the Swedish Ministry of Labor: "To make it possible for both men and women to combine parenthood and gainful employment, a new view of the male role and a radical change in the organization of working life are required."[45] The trick is to imagine a social world in which citizens' lives integrate wage-earning, caregiving, community activism, political participation, and involvement in the associational life of civil society—while also leaving time for some fun. This world is not likely to come into being in the immediate future. But it is the only imaginable postindustrial world that promises true gender justice. And unless we are guided by this vision now, we will never get any closer to achieving it.

---

43  Susan Okin, *Justice, Gender, and the Family.*

44  Joan Williams, "Deconstructing Gender," in *Feminist Legal Theory*, eds. Katharine T. Bartlett and Rosanne Kennedy.

45  Quoted in Ruth Lister, "Women, Economic Dependency, and Citizenship," 463.

# PART II

Feminism Tamed:
From Redistribution to Recognition
in the Age of Identity

5

# Against Symbolicism:
# The Uses and Abuses of Lacanianism
# for Feminist Politics*

This chapter grew out of an experience of severe puzzlement. For several years I watched with growing incomprehension as a large and influential body of feminist scholars created an interpretation of Jacques Lacan's theory of the symbolic order, which they sought to use for feminist purposes. I myself had felt a disaffinity with Lacanian thought, as much intellectual as political. So, while many of my fellow feminists were adapting quasi-Lacanian ideas to theorize the discursive construction of subjectivity in film and literature, I was relying on alternative models to develop an account of language that could inform a feminist social theory.[1] For a long while, I avoided any explicit, meta-theoretical discussion of these matters. I explained neither to myself nor to my colleagues why I looked to the discourse models of writers like Foucault, Bourdieu, Bakhtin, Habermas, and Gramsci instead of to those of Lacan, Kristeva, Saussure, and Derrida.[2] In this essay, I want to provide such an explanation. I will try to explain why I think feminists should eschew the versions of discourse theory that they attribute to Lacan and the related theories attributed to Julia Kristeva. I will also try to identify some places where I think we can find more satisfactory alternatives.

* I am grateful for helpful comments and suggestions from Jonathan Arac, David Levin, Paul Mattick, Jr., John McCumber, Diana T. Meyers, and Eli Zaretsky

1 See Chapter 2 of this volume, "Struggle over Needs."
2 I group these writers together not because all are Lacanians—clearly only Kristeva and Lacan himself are—but rather because, disclaimers notwithstanding, all continue the structuralist reduction of discourse to symbolic system. I shall develop this point later in this chapter..

## 1. WHAT DO FEMINISTS WANT IN A DISCOURSE THEORY?

Let me begin by posing two questions: What might a theory of discourse contribute to feminism? And what, therefore, should feminists look for in a theory of discourse? I suggest that a conception of discourse can help us understand at least four things, all of which are interrelated. First, it can help us understand how people's social identities are fashioned and altered over time. Second, it can help us understand how, under conditions of inequality, social groups in the sense of collective agents are formed and unformed. Third, a conception of discourse can illuminate how the cultural hegemony of dominant groups in society is secured and contested. Fourth and finally, it can shed light on the prospects for emancipatory social change and political practice. Let me elaborate.

First, consider the uses of a conception of discourse for understanding social identities. The basic idea here is that people's social identities are complexes of meanings, networks of interpretation. To have a social identity, to be a woman or a man, for example, just *is* to live and to act under a set of descriptions. These descriptions, of course, are not simply secreted by people's bodies; nor are they simply exuded by people's psyches. Rather, they are drawn from the fund of interpretive possibilities available to agents in specific societies. It follows that, in order to understand the gender dimension of social identity, it does not suffice to study biology or psychology. Instead, one must study the historically specific social practices through which cultural descriptions of gender are produced and circulated.[3]

Moreover, social identities are exceedingly complex. They are knitted together from a plurality of different descriptions arising from a plurality of different signifying practices. Thus, no one is simply a woman; one is rather, for example, a white, Jewish, middle-class woman, a philosopher, a lesbian, a socialist, and a mother.[4] Because everyone acts in a plurality of social contexts, moreover, the different descriptions comprising any individual's social identity fade in and out of focus. Thus, one is not always a woman in the same degree; in

---

3   To appreciate the importance of history, consider how little the fund of interpretive possibilities available to me, a late twentieth-century North American, overlaps with that available to the thirteenth-century Chinese woman I may want to imagine as my sister. And yet in both cases, hers and mine, the interpretive possibilities are established in the medium of social discourse. It is in the medium of discourse that each of us encounters an interpretation of what it is to be a person, as well as a menu of possible descriptions specifying the particular sort of person each is to be.

4   See Elizabeth V. Spelman, *Inessential Woman*, Boston: Beacon Press, 1988.

some contexts, one's womanhood figures centrally in the set of descriptions under which one acts; in others, it is peripheral or latent.[5] Finally, it is not the case that people's social identities are constructed once and for all and definitively fixed. Rather, they alter over time, shifting with shifts in agents' practices and affiliations. Even the way in which one is a woman will shift—as it does, to take a dramatic example, when one becomes a feminist. In short, social identities are discursively constructed in historically specific social contexts; they are complex and plural; and they shift over time. One use of a conception of discourse for feminist theorizing, then, is in understanding social identities in their full socio-cultural complexity, thus in demystifying static, single variable, essentialist views of gender identity.

A second use of a conception of discourse for feminist theorizing is in understanding the formation of social groups. How does it happen, under conditions of domination, that people come together, arrange themselves under the banner of *collective* identities, and constitute themselves as collective social agents? How do class formation and, by analogy, gender formation occur?

Clearly, group formation involves shifts in people's social identities and therefore also in their relation to social discourse. One thing that happens here is that pre-existing strands of identities acquire a new sort of salience and centrality. These strands, previously submerged among many others, are reinscribed as the nub of new self-definitions and affiliations.[6] For example, in the current wave of feminist ferment, many of us who had previously been "women" in some taken-for-granted way have now become "women" in the very different sense of a discursively self-constituted political collectivity. In the process, we have remade entire regions of social discourse. We have invented new terms for describing social reality—for example, "sexism," "sexual harassment," "marital, date, and acquaintance rape," "labor force sex-segregation," "the double shift," and "wife-battery." We have also invented new language games such as consciousness-raising and new, institutionalized public spheres such as the Society for Women in Philosophy.[7] The point is that the formation of social

5   See Denise Riley, *"Am I That Name?" Feminism and the Category of "Women" in History*, Minneapolis: University of Minnesota Press, 1988.

6   See Jane Jenson, "Paradigms and Political Discourse: Labor and Social Policy in the USA and France before 1914," Working Paper Series, Center for European Studies, Harvard University, Winter 1989.

7   See Chapter 3 of this volume, "Struggle over Needs," and Riley, *"Am I That Name?"* On the struggle to create such new public spheres, see Nancy Fraser, "Rethinking the Public Sphere: A Contribution to the Critique of Actually Existing Democracy," in *Habermas and the Public Sphere*, ed. Craig Calhoun, Cambridge, MA:

groups proceeds by struggles over social discourse. Thus, a conception of discourse is useful here, both for understanding group formation and for coming to grips with the closely related issue of socio-cultural hegemony.

"Hegemony" is the Italian Marxist Antonio Gramsci's term for the discursive face of power. It is the power to establish the "common sense" or "doxa" of a society, the fund of self-evident descriptions of social reality that normally go without saying.[8] This includes the power to establish authoritative definitions of social situations and social needs, the power to define the universe of legitimate disagreement, and the power to shape the political agenda. Hegemony, then, expresses the advantaged position of dominant social groups with respect to discourse. It is a concept that allows us to recast the issues of social identity and social groups in the light of societal inequality. How do pervasive axes of dominance and subordination affect the production and circulation of social meanings? How does stratification along lines of gender, "race," and class affect the discursive construction of social identities and the formation of social groups?

The notion of hegemony points to the intersection of power, inequality, and discourse. However, it does not entail that the ensemble of descriptions that circulate in society comprise a monolithic and seamless web, nor that dominant groups exercise an absolute, top-down control of meaning. On the contrary, "hegemony" designates a process wherein cultural authority is negotiated and contested. It presupposes that societies contain a plurality of discourses and discursive sites, a plurality of positions and perspectives from which to speak. Of course, not all of these have equal authority. Yet conflict and contestation are part of the story. Thus, one use of a conception of discourse for feminist theorizing is to shed light on the processes by which the socio-cultural hegemony of dominant groups is achieved and contested. What are the processes by which definitions and interpretations inimical to women's interests acquire cultural authority? What are the prospects for mobilizing counter-hegemonic feminist definitions and interpretations to create broad oppositional groups and alliances?

The link between these questions and emancipatory political practice is, I believe, fairly obvious. A conception of discourse that lets us examine identities, groups, and hegemony in the ways I have been

MIT Press, 1991, 109–142, and "Tales from the Trenches: On Women Philosophers, Feminist Philosophy, and SPEP," *Journal of Speculative Philosophy* 26:2, 2012, 175–84.

8   Antonio Gramsci, *Selections from the Prison Notebooks of Antonio Gramsci*, eds. and trans. Quinton Hoare and Geoffrey Nowell Smith, New York: International Publishers, 1972.

describing would be of considerable use to feminist practice. It would valorize the empowering dimensions of discursive struggles without leading to "culturalist" retreats from political engagement.[9] In addition, the right kind of conception would counter the disabling assumption that women are just passive victims of male dominance. That assumption over-totalizes male dominance, treating men as the only social agents and rendering inconceivable our own existence as feminist theorists and activists. In contrast, the sort of conception I have been proposing would help us understand how, even under conditions of subordination, women participate in the making of culture.

## 2. LACANIANISM AND THE LIMITS OF STRUCTURALISM

In light of the foregoing, what sort of conception of discourse will be useful for feminist theorizing? What sort of conception best illuminates social identities, group formation, hegemony, and emancipatory practice?

In the postwar period, two approaches to theorizing language became influential among political theorists. The first is the *structuralist model*, which studies language as a symbolic system or code. Derived from Saussure, this model is presupposed in the version of Lacanian theory I shall be concerned with here; in addition, it is abstractly negated but not entirely superseded in deconstruction and in related forms of French "women's writing." The second influential approach to theorizing language may be called the *pragmatics model*, which studies language at the level of discourses, as historically specific social practices of communication. Espoused by such thinkers as Mikhail Bakhtin, Michel Foucault, and Pierre Bourdieu, this model is operative in some but not all dimensions of the work of Julia Kristeva and Luce Irigaray. In the present section of this chapter, I shall argue that the first, structuralist model is of only limited usefulness for feminist theorizing.

Let me begin by noting that there are good *prima facie* reasons for feminists to be suspicious of the structuralist model. This model constructs its object of study by abstracting from exactly what we need to focus on, namely, the social practice and social context of communication. Indeed, the abstraction from practice and context are among the founding gestures of Saussurean linguistics. Saussure

---

9  For a critique of "cultural feminism" as a retreat from political struggle, see Alice Echols, "The New Feminism of Yin and Yang," in *Powers of Desire: The Politics of Sexuality*, eds. Ann Snitow, Christine Stansell, and Sharon Thompson, New York: Monthly Review Press, 1983.

began by splitting signification into *langue*, the symbolic system or code, and *parole*, speakers' uses of language in communicative practice or speech. He then made the first of these, *langue*, the proper object of the new science of linguistics, and relegated the second, *parole*, to the status of a devalued remainder.[10] At the same time, Saussure insisted that the study of *langue* be synchronic rather than diachronic; he thereby posited his object of study as static and atemporal, abstracting it from historical change. Finally, the founder of structuralist linguistics posited that *langue* was indeed a single system; he made its unity and systematicity consist in the putative fact that every signifier, every material, signifying element of the code, derives its meaning positionally through its difference from all of the others.

Together, these founding operations render the structuralist approach of limited utility for feminist purposes.[11] Because it abstracts from *parole*, the structuralist model brackets questions of practice, agency, and the speaking subject. Thus, it cannot shed light on the discursive practices through which social identities and social groups are formed. Because this approach brackets the diachronic, moreover, it will not tell us anything about shifts in identities and affiliations over time. Similarly, because it abstracts from the social context of communication, the model brackets issues of power and inequality. Thus, it cannot illuminate the processes by which cultural hegemony is secured and contested. Finally, because the model theorizes the fund of available linguistic meanings as a single symbolic system, it lends itself to a monolithic view of signification that denies tensions and contradictions among social meanings. In short, by reducing discourse to a "symbolic system," the structuralist model evacuates social agency, social conflict, and social practice.[12]

Let me now try to illustrate these problems by means of a brief discussion of Lacanianism. By "Lacanianism," I do not mean the actual thought of Jacques Lacan, which is far too complex to tackle here. I

---

10   Fernand de Saussure, *Course in General Linguistics*, trans. Wade Baskin, New York: Columbia University Press, 2011. For a persuasive critique of this move, see Pierre Bourdieu, *Outline of a Theory of Practice*, Cambridge: Cambridge University Press, 1977. Similar objections to Bourdieu's are found in Julia Kristeva's "The System and the Speaking Subject," in *The Kristeva Reader*, ed. Toril Moi, New York: Columbia University Press, 1986, to be discussed below, and in the Soviet Marxist critique of Russian formalism from which Kristeva's views derive.

11   I leave it to linguists to decide whether it is useful for other purposes.

12   These criticisms pertain to what may be called "global" structuralisms, that is, approaches that treat the whole of language as a single symbolic system. They are not intended to rule out the potential utility of approaches that analyze structural relations in limited, socially situated, culturally and historically specific sublanguages or discourses. On the contrary, it is possible that approaches of this latter sort can be usefully articulated with the pragmatic model discussed below.

mean, rather, an ideal-typical neo-structuralist reading of Lacan that is widely credited among English-speaking feminists.[13] In discussing "Lacanianism," I shall bracket the question of the fidelity of this reading, which could be faulted for overemphasizing the influence of Saussure at the expense of other, countervailing influences, such as Hegel.[14] For my purposes, however, this ideal-typical, Saussurean reading of Lacan is useful precisely because it evinces with unusual clarity the difficulties that beset many conceptions of discourse that are widely considered "poststructuralist" but that remain wedded in important respects to structuralism. Because their attempts to break free of structuralism remain abstract, such conceptions tend finally to recycle it. Lacanianism, as discussed here, is a paradigm case of "neo-structuralism."[15]

At first sight, neo-structuralist Lacanianism seems to promise some advantages for feminist theorizing. By conjoining the Freudian problematic of the construction of gendered subjectivity to the Saussurean model of structural linguistics, it seems to provide each with its needed corrective. The introduction of the Freudian problematic promises to supply the speaking subject that is missing in Saussure and thereby to reopen the excluded questions about identity, speech, and social practice. Conversely, the use of the Saussurean model promises to remedy some of Freud's deficiencies. By insisting that gender identity is *discursively* constructed, Lacanianism appears to eliminate lingering vestiges of biologism in Freud, to treat gender as sociocultural all the way down, and to render it in principle more open to change.

Upon closer inspection, however, the promised advantages fail to materialize. Instead, Lacanianism begins to look viciously circular. On the one hand, it purports to describe the process by which individuals acquire gendered subjectivity through their painful conscription as young children into a pre-existing phallocentric symbolic order. Here the structure of the symbolic order is presumed to determine

---

13   In earlier versions of this chapter, I was not as careful as I should have been in distinguishing "Lacanianism" from Lacan. In taking greater pains to make this distinction here, however, I do not mean to imply that I believe Lacan to be free of difficulties. On the contrary, I suspect that many of the basic critical points made here against "Lacanianism" tell against Lacan as well. But a much longer, more complex textual argument would be required to demonstrate this.

14   For the tensions between the Hegelian and Saussurean dimensions in Lacan's thought, see Peter Dews, *Logics of Disintegration: Poststructuralist Thought and the Claims of Critical Theory*, London: Verso Books, 1987.

15   For the notion of "neo-structuralism," see Manfred Frank, *What Is Neo-Structuralism?* trans. Sabine Wilke and Richard Gray, Minneapolis: University of Minnesota Press, 1989.

the character of individual subjectivity. But, on the other hand, the
theory also purports to show that the symbolic order must necessarily
be phallocentric since the attainment of subjectivity requires submis-
sion to "the Father's Law." Here, conversely, the nature of individual
subjectivity, as dictated by an autonomous psychology, is presumed to
determine the character of the symbolic order.

One result of this circularity is an apparently ironclad determinism.
As Dorothy Leland has noted, the theory casts the developments it
describes as necessary, invariant, and unalterable.[16] Phallocentrism,
woman's disadvantaged place in the symbolic order, the encoding of
cultural authority as masculine, the impossibility of describing a
nonphallic sexuality—in short, any number of historically contingent
trappings of male dominance—now appear as invariable features of
the human condition. Women's subordination, then, is inscribed as
the inevitable destiny of civilization.

I can spot several spurious steps in this reasoning, some of which
have their roots in the presupposition of the structuralist model. First,
to the degree Lacanianism has succeeded in eliminating biologism—
and that is dubious for reasons I shall not go into here[17]—it has replaced
it with psychologism, the untenable view that autonomous psychological imperatives given independently of culture and history can
dictate the way they are interpreted and acted on within culture and
history. Lacanianism falls prey to psychologism to the extent that it
claims that the phallocentricity of the symbolic order is required by
the demands of an enculturation process that is itself independent of
culture.[18]

If one half of Lacanianism's circular argument is vitiated by psychologism, then the other half is vitiated by what I shall call *symbolicism*.
By symbolicism I mean, first, the homogenizing reification of diverse
signifying practices into a monolithic and all-pervasive "symbolic
order," and second, the endowing of that order with an exclusive and

---

16   Dorothy Leland, "Lacanian Psychoanalysis and French Feminism," in
*Revaluing French Feminism: Critical Essays on Difference, Agency, and Culture*, eds.
Nancy Fraser and Sandra Bartky, Bloomington: Indiana University Press, 1991.

17   Here I believe one can properly speak of Lacan. Lacan's claim to have
overcome biologism rests on his insistence that the phallus is not the penis. However,
many feminist critics have shown that he fails to prevent the collapse of the symbolic
signifier into the organ. The clearest indication of this failure is his claim, in "The
Meaning of the Phallus," that the phallus becomes the master signifier because of its
"turgidity" which suggests "the transmission of vital flow" in copulation. See
Jacques Lacan, "The Meaning of the Phallus," in *Feminine Sexuality: Jacques Lacan
and the école freudienne*, eds. Juliet Mitchell and Jacqueline Rose, New York: W.W.
Norton & Company, 1982.

18   A version of this argument is made by Dorothy Leland in "Lacanian
Psychoanalysis and French Feminism."

unlimited causal power to fix people's subjectivities once and for all. Symbolism, then, is an operation whereby the structuralist abstraction *langue* is troped into a quasi-divinity, a normative "symbolic order" whose power to shape identities dwarfs to the point of extinction that of mere historical institutions and practices.

Actually, as Deborah Cameron has noted, Lacan himself equivocates on the expression "the symbolic order."[19] Sometimes he uses this expression relatively narrowly to refer to Saussurean *langue*, the structure of language as a system of signs. In this narrow usage, Lacanianism would be committed to the implausible view that the sign system itself determines individuals' subjectivities independently of the social context and social practice of its uses. At other times, Lacan uses the expression "the symbolic order" far more broadly to refer to an amalgam that includes not only linguistic structures, but also cultural traditions and kinship structures, the latter mistakenly equated with social structure in general.[20] In this broad usage, Lacanianism would conflate the ahistorical structural abstraction *langue* with variable historical phenomena like family forms and childrearing practices; cultural representations of love and authority in art, literature, and philosophy; the gender division of labor; forms of political organization and of other institutional sources of power and status. The result would be a conception of "the symbolic order" that essentializes and homogenizes contingent historical practices and traditions, erasing tensions, contradictions, and possibilities for change. This would be a conception, moreover, that is so broad that the claim that *it* determines the structure of subjectivity risks collapsing into an empty tautology.[21]

The combination of psychologism and symbolism in Lacanianism results in a conception of discourse that is of limited usefulness for feminist theorizing. To be sure, this conception offers an account of the discursive construction of social identity. However, it is not an account that can make sense of the complexity and multiplicity of

---

19  Deborah Cameron, *Feminism and Linguistic Theory*, New York: St. Martin's Press, 1985.

20  For the declining significance of kinship as a social structural component of modern capitalist societies, see Chapter 7 of this volume, "Heterosexism, Misrecognition, and Capitalism." Also Linda J. Nicholson, *Gender and History: The Limits of Social Theory in the Age of the Family*, New York: Columbia University Press, 1986.

21  In fact, the main function of this broad usage seems to be ideological. For it is only by collapsing into a single category what is supposedly ahistorical and necessary and what is historical and contingent that Lacanianism could endow its claim about the inevitability of phallocentrism with a deceptive appearance of plausibility.

social identities, the ways they are woven from a plurality of discursive strands. Granted, Lacanianism stresses that the apparent unity and simplicity of ego identity is imaginary, that the subject is irreparably split both by language and drives. But this insistence on fracture does not lead to an appreciation of the diversity of the socio-cultural discursive practices from which identities are woven. It leads, rather, to a unitary view of the human condition as inherently tragic.

In fact, Lacanianism differentiates identities only in binary terms, along the single axis of having or lacking the phallus. As Luce Irigaray has shown, this phallic conception of sexual difference is not an adequate basis for understanding femininity[22]—nor, I would add, masculinity. Still less, then, is it able to shed light on other dimensions of social identities, including ethnicity, color, and social class. Nor could the theory be emended to incorporate these manifestly historical phenomena, given its postulation of an ahistorical, tension-free "symbolic order" equated with kinship.[23]

Moreover, Lacanianism's account of identity construction cannot account for identity shifts over time. It is committed to the general psychoanalytic proposition that gender identity (the only kind of identity it considers) is basically fixed once and for all with the resolution of the Oedipus complex. Lacanianism equates this resolution with the child's entry into a fixed, monolithic, and all-powerful symbolic order. Thus, it actually increases the degree of identity fixity found in classical Freudian theory. It is true, as Jacqueline Rose points out, that the theory stresses that gender identity is always precarious, that its apparent unity and stability are always threatened by repressed libidinal drives.[24] But this emphasis on precariousness is not an opening onto genuine historical thinking about shifts in people's social identities. On the contrary, it is an insistence on a permanent, ahistorical condition, since for Lacanianism the only alternative to fixed gender identity is psychosis.

If Lacanianism cannot provide an account of social identity that is useful for feminist theorizing, then it is unlikely to help us understand the formation of social groups. For Lacanianism, affiliation falls under the rubric of the imaginary. To affiliate with others, to

---

22   See "The Blind Spot in an Old Dream of Symmetry," in Luce Irigaray, *Speculum of the Other Woman*, trans. Gillian C. Gill, Ithaca: Cornell University Press, 1985. Here Irigaray shows how the use of a phallic standard to conceptualize sexual difference casts woman negatively as "lack."

23   For an illuminating discussion of this issue as it emerges in relation to the very different—feminist object-relations—version of psychoanalysis developed in the US by Nancy Chodorow, see Elizabeth V. Spelman, *Inessential Woman*.

24   Jacqueline Rose, "Introduction—II," in *Feminine Sexuality: Jacques Lacan and the école freudienne*.

align oneself with others in a social movement, would be to fall prey to the illusions of the imaginary ego. It would be to deny loss and lack, to seek an impossible unification and fulfillment. Thus, from the perspective of Lacanianism, collective movements would by definition be vehicles of delusion; they could not even in principle be emancipatory.[25]

Moreover, insofar as group formation depends on linguistic innovation, it is untheorizable from the perspective of Lacanianism. Because Lacanianism posits a fixed, monolithic symbolic system and a speaker who is wholly subjected to it, it is inconceivable that there could ever be any linguistic innovation. Speaking subjects could only ever reproduce the existing symbolic order; they could not possibly alter it.

From this perspective, the question of cultural hegemony is blocked from view. There can be no question as to how the cultural authority of dominant groups in society is established and contested, no question of unequal negotiations between different social groups occupying different discursive positions. For Lacanianism, on the contrary, there is simply "*the* symbolic order," a single universe of discourse that is so systematic, so all-pervasive, so monolithic that one cannot even conceive of such things as alternative perspectives, multiple discursive sites, struggles over social meanings, contests between hegemonic and counterhegemonic definitions of social situations, conflicts of interpretation of social needs. One cannot even conceive, really, of a plurality of different speakers.

With the way blocked to a political understanding of identities, groups, and cultural hegemony, the way is also blocked to an understanding of political practice. For one thing, there is no conceivable agent of such practice. Lacanianism posits a view of the person as a non-sutured congeries of three moments, none of which can qualify as a political agent. The speaking subject is simply the grammatical "I," a shifter wholly subjected to the symbolic order; it can only and forever reproduce that order. The ego is an imaginary projection, deluded about its own stability and self-possession, hooked on an impossible narcissistic desire for unity and self-completion; it therefore can only and forever tilt at windmills. Finally, there is the ambiguous unconscious, sometimes an ensemble of repressed libidinal drives, sometimes the face of language as Other, but never anything that could count as a social agent.

---

25 Even Lacanian feminists have been known on occasion to engage in this sort of movement-baiting. It seems to me that, in her introductory chapter to *The Daughter's Seduction*, Jane Gallop comes perilously close to dismissing the politics of a feminist movement informed by ethical commitments as "imaginary." See Jane Gallop, *The Daughter's Seduction: Feminism and Psychoanalysis*, Ithaca: Cornell University Press, 1982.

This discussion shows, I think, that Lacanianism suffers from many conceptual shortcomings.[26] I have stressed those deficiencies that have their roots in the presupposition of the structuralist conception of language. Lacanianism seemed to promise a way to get beyond structuralism by introducing the concept of the speaking subject. This in turn seemed to hold out the promise of a way of theorizing discursive practice. However, as I hope I have shown, these promises remain unfulfilled. The speaking subject introduced by Lacanianism is not the agent of discursive practice. It is simply an effect of the symbolic order conjoined to some repressed libidinal drives. Thus, the introduction of the speaking subject has not succeeded in dereifying linguistic structure. On the contrary, a reified conception of language as system has colonized the speaking subject.

## 3. JULIA KRISTEVA BETWEEN STRUCTURALISM AND PRAGMATICS

So far, I have been arguing that the structuralist model of language is of limited usefulness for feminist theorizing. Now I want to suggest that the pragmatics model is more promising. Indeed, there are good *prima facie* reasons for feminists to prefer a pragmatics approach to the study of language. Unlike the structuralist approach, the pragmatics view studies language as social practice in social context. This model takes discourses, not structures, as its object. Discourses are historically specific, socially situated, signifying practices. They are the communicative frames in which speakers interact by exchanging speech acts. Yet discourses are themselves set within social institutions and action contexts. Thus, the concept of a discourse links the study of language to the study of society.

The pragmatics model offers several potential advantages for feminist theorizing. First, it treats discourses as contingent, positing that they arise, alter, and disappear over time. Thus, the model lends itself to historical contextualization, and it allows us to thematize change. Second, the pragmatics approach understands signification as action

---

26    I have focused here on conceptual as opposed to empirical issues, and I have not directly addressed the question, is Lacanianism true? Yet recent research on the development of subjectivity in infants seems not to support its views. It now appears that even at the earliest stages children are not passive, blank slates on which symbolic structures are inscribed, but rather active participants in the interactions that construct their experience. See, for example, Beatrice Beebe and Frank Lachman, "Mother-Infant Mutual Influence and Precursors of Psychic Structure," in ed. Arnold Goldberg, *Frontiers in Self Psychology: Progress in Self Psychology*, Vol. 3, Hillsdale, NJ: Analytic Press, 1988, 3–25. I am grateful to Paul Mattick, Jr. for alerting me to this work.

rather than as representation. It is concerned with how people "do things with words." Thus, the model allows us to see speaking subjects not simply as effects of structures and systems, but rather as socially situated agents. Third, the pragmatics model treats discourses in the plural. It starts from the assumption that there exist a plurality of different discourses in society, hence a plurality of communicative sites from which to speak. Because it posits that individuals assume different discursive positions as they move from one discursive frame to another, this model lends itself to a theorization of social identities as non-monolithic. Then, too, the pragmatics approach rejects the assumption that the totality of social meanings in circulation constitutes a single, coherent, self-reproducing "symbolic system." Instead, it allows for conflicts among social schemas of interpretation and among the agents who deploy them. Finally, because it links the study of discourses to the study of society, the pragmatics approach allows us to focus on power and inequality. In short, the pragmatics approach has many of the features we need in order to understand the complexity of social identities, the formation of social groups, the securing and contesting of cultural hegemony, and the possibility and actuality of political practice.

Let me illustrate the uses of the pragmatics model for feminist theorizing by considering the ambiguous case of Julia Kristeva. Kristeva's case is instructive in that she began her career as a critic of structuralism and a proponent of a pragmatics alternative. Having fallen under the sway of Lacanianism, however, she has not maintained a consistent orientation to pragmatics. Instead, she has ended up producing a strange, hybrid theory, one that oscillates between structuralism and pragmatics. In what follows, I shall argue that the political-theoretically fruitful aspects of Kristeva's thought are linked to its pragmatic dimensions, while the impasses she arrives at derive from structuralist lapses.

Kristeva's intention to break with structuralism is most clearly and succinctly announced in a brilliant 1973 essay called "The System and the Speaking Subject."[27] Here she argues that, because it conceives language as a symbolic system, structuralist semiotics is necessarily incapable of understanding oppositional practice and change. To remedy these lacunae, she proposes a new approach oriented to "signifying practices." These she defines as norm-governed, but not necessarily all-powerfully constraining, and as situated in "historically determined relations of production." As a complement to this concept of signifying practices, Kristeva also proposes a new concept of the "speaking subject." This subject is socially and historically situated, to

---

27    Kristeva, "The System and the Speaking Subject."

be sure, but it is not wholly subjected to the reigning social and discursive conventions. It is a subject, rather, who is capable of innovative practice.

In a few bold strokes, then, Kristeva rejects the exclusion of context, practice, agency, and innovation, and she proposes a new model of discursive pragmatics. Her general idea is that speakers act in socially situated, norm-governed signifying practices. In so doing, they sometimes transgress the established norms in force. Transgressive practice gives rise to discursive innovations and these in turn may lead to actual change. Innovative practice may subsequently be normalized in the form of new or modified discursive norms, thereby "renovating" signifying practices.[28]

The uses of this sort of approach for feminist theorizing should by now be apparent. Yet there are also some warning signs of possible problems. First, there is Kristeva's antinomian bent—her tendency, at least in this early quasi-Maoist phase of her career, to valorize transgression and innovation *per se* irrespective of its content and direction.[29] The flip side of this attitude is a penchant for inflecting norm-conforming practice as simply negative, irrespective of the content of the norms. Obviously, this attitude is not particularly helpful for feminist theorizing, which requires ethical distinctions between oppressive and emancipatory social norms.

A second potential problem here is Kristeva's aestheticizing bent, her association of valorized transgression with "poetic practice." Kristeva tends to treat avant-garde aesthetic production as the privileged site of innovation. By contrast, communicative practice in everyday life appears as conformism *simpliciter.* This tendency to enclave or regionalize innovative practice is not useful for feminist theorizing. We need to recognize and assess the emancipatory potential of oppositional practice *wherever* it appears—in bedrooms, on shopfloors, in the caucuses of the American Philosophical Association.

The third and most serious problem is Kristeva's additive approach to theorizing. By this I mean her penchant for remedying theoretical problems by simply *adding* to deficient theories instead of by scrapping or overhauling them. This, I submit, is how she ends up handling

---

28   "Renovation" and "renewal" are standard English translations of Kristeva's term, "renouvellement." Yet they lack some of the force of the French. Perhaps this explains why Anglophone readers have not always noticed the change-making aspect of her account of transgression, why they have instead tended to treat it as pure negation with no positive consequences. For an example of this interpretation, see Judith Butler, "The Body Politics of Julia Kristeva," in *Revaluing French Feminism.*

29   This tendency fades in Kristeva's later writings, where it is replaced by an equally one-sided, undiscriminating, conservative emphasis on the "totalitarian" dangers lurking in every attempt at uncontrolled innovation.

certain features of structuralism; rather than eliminating certain structuralist notions altogether, she simply adds other, anti-structuralist notions alongside them.

Kristeva's additive, dualistic style of theorizing is apparent in the way she analyzes and classifies signifying practices. She takes such practices to consist in varying proportions of two basic ingredients. One of these is "the symbolic," a linguistic register keyed to the transmission of propositional content via the observance of grammatical and syntactical rules. The other is "the semiotic," a register keyed to the expression of libidinal drives via intonation and rhythm and not bound by linguistic rules. The symbolic, then, is the axis of discursive practice that helps reproduce the social order by imposing linguistic conventions on anarchic desires. The semiotic, in contrast, expresses a material, bodily source of revolutionary negativity, the power to break through convention and initiate change. According to Kristeva, all signifying practices contain some measure of each of these two registers of language, but with the signal exception of poetic practice, the symbolic register is always the dominant one.

In her later work, Kristeva provides a psychoanalytically grounded gender subtext to her distinction between the symbolic and the semiotic. Following Lacanianism, she associates the symbolic with the paternal, and she describes it as a monolithically phallocentric, rule-bound order to which subjects submit as the price of sociality when they resolve the Oedipus complex by accepting the Father's Law. But then Kristeva breaks with Lacanianism in insisting on the underlying persistence of a feminine, maternal element in all signifying practice. She associates the semiotic with the pre-oedipal and the maternal, and she valorizes it as a point of resistance to paternally-coded cultural authority, a sort of oppositional feminine beach-head within discursive practice.

This way of analyzing and classifying signifying practices may seem at first sight to have some potential utility for feminist theorizing. It seems to contest the presumption of Lacanianism that language is monolithically phallocentric and to identify a locus of feminist opposition to the dominance of masculine power. However, on closer inspection, this appearance of feminist potential turns out to be largely illusory. In fact, Kristeva's analysis of signifying practices betrays her best pragmatics intentions. The decomposition of such practices into symbolic and semiotic constituents does not lead beyond structuralism. The "symbolic," after all, is a repetition of the reified, phallocentric symbolic order of Lacanianism. And while the "semiotic" is a force that momentarily disrupts that symbolic order, it does not constitute an alternative to it. On the contrary, as Judith Butler has shown, the contest between the two modes of signification is stacked in favor of the symbolic: the semiotic is by definition transitory and subordinate, always doomed in advance to reabsorption by the symbolic order.[30] Moreover, and more fundamentally problematic, I think, is the fact that the semiotic is defined parasitically over against the symbolic as the latter's mirror image and abstract negation. Simply adding the two together, then, cannot and does not lead to pragmatics. Rather, it yields an amalgam of structure and anti-structure. Moreover, this amalgam is, in Hegel's phrase, a "bad infinity," since it leaves us oscillating ceaselessly between a structuralist moment and an anti-structuralist moment without ever getting to anything else.

Thus, by resorting to an additive mode of theorizing, Kristeva surrenders her promising pragmatic conception of signifying practice to a quasi-Lacanian neo-structuralism. In the process, she ends up reproducing some of Lacanianism's most unfortunate conceptual shortcomings. She, too, lapses into symbolicism, treating the symbolic order as an all-powerful causal mechanism and conflating linguistic structure, kinship structure, and social structure in general.[31] On the other hand, Kristeva sometimes does better than Lacanianism in appreciating the historical specificity and complexity of particular cultural traditions, especially in those portions of her work that analyze cultural representations of gender in such traditions. Even there, however, she often lapses into psychologism; for example, she mars her potentially very interesting studies of cultural representations of femininity and maternity in Christian theology and in Italian Renaissance painting by falling back on reductive schemes of interpretation that treat the historical material as reflexes of autonomous, ahistorical, psychological imperatives like "castration anxiety" and "feminine paranoia."[32]

All told, then, Kristeva's conception of discourse surrenders many of the potential advantages of pragmatics for feminist theorizing. In the end, she loses the pragmatic stress on the contingency and historicity of discursive practices, their openness to possible change. Instead, she lapses into a quasi-structuralist emphasis on the recuperating power of a reified symbolic order and thereby surrenders the possibility of explaining change. Likewise, her theory loses the pragmatic stress on the plurality of discursive practices. Instead, it lapses into a quasi-structuralist homogenizing and binarizing orientation, one that distinguishes practices along the sole axis of proportion of semiotic to symbolic,

---

30    Butler, "The Body Politics of Julia Kristeva."

31    For an example, see Julia Kristeva, *Powers of Horror: An Essay on Abjection*, trans. Leon S. Roudiez, New York: Columbia University Press, 1982.

32    See Julia Kristeva, "Stabat Mater," in *The Kristeva Reader*, ed. Toril Moi, and "Motherhood According to Giovanni Bellini" in Julia Kristeva, *Desire in Language: A Semiotic Approach to Art and Literature*, ed. Leon S. Roudiez, New York: Columbia University Press, 1980.

feminine to masculine, and thereby surrenders the potential for under-standing complex identities. In addition, Kristeva loses the pragmatic stress on social context. Instead, she lapses into a quasi-structuralist conflation of "symbolic order" with social context and thereby surren-ders the capacity to link discursive dominance to societal inequality. Finally, her theory loses the pragmatic stress on interaction and social conflict. Instead, as Andrea Nye has shown, it focuses almost exclu-sively on *intra*subjective tensions and thereby surrenders its ability to understand *inter*subjective phenomena, including affiliation, on the one hand, and social struggle, on the other.[33]

This last point can be brought home by considering Kristeva's account of the speaking subject. Far from being useful for feminist theorizing, her view replicates many of the disabling features of Laca-nianism. Her subject, like the latter's, is split into two halves, neither of which is a potential political agent. The subject of the symbolic is an oversocialized conformist, thoroughly subjected to symbolic conven-tions and norms. To be sure, its conformism is put "on trial" by the rebellious, desiring ensemble of bodily-based drives associated with the semiotic. But, as before, the mere addition of an anti-structuralist force does not actually lead beyond structuralism. Meanwhile, the semiotic "subject" cannot itself be an agent of feminist practice for several reasons. First, it is located beneath, rather than within, culture and society; so it is unclear how its practice could be *political* practice.[34] Second, it is defined exclusively in terms of the transgression of social norms; thus, it cannot engage in the reconstructive moment of femi-nist politics, a moment essential to social transformation. Finally, it is defined in terms of the shattering of social identity, and so it cannot figure in the reconstruction of the new, politically constituted, *collective* identities and solidarities that are essential to feminist politics.

By definition, then, neither half of Kristeva's split subject can be a feminist political agent. Nor, I submit, can the two halves be joined together. They tend rather simply to cancel one another out, the one forever shattering the identitarian pretensions of the other, the second forever recuperating the first and reconstituting itself as before. The upshot is a paralyzing oscillation between identity and non-identity without any determinate practical issue. Here, then, is another "bad infinity," an amalgam of structuralism and its abstract negation.

If there are no individual agents of emancipatory practice in Kris-teva's universe, then there are no such collective agents either. This

33  For a brilliant critical discussion of Kristeva's philosophy of language, one to which the present account is much indebted, see Andrea Nye, "Woman Clothed with the Sun," *Signs: Journal of Women in Culture and Society* 12:4, 1987, 664–86.

34  Butler makes this point in "The Body Politics of Julia Kristeva."

can be seen by examining one last instance of her additive pattern of thinking, namely, her treatment of the feminist movement itself. This topic is most directly addressed in an essay called "Women's Time," for which Kristeva is best known in feminist circles.[35] Here, she identifies three "generations" of feminist movements: first, an egalitarian, reform-oriented, humanist feminism, aiming to secure women's full participation in the public sphere, a feminism best personified perhaps by Simone de Beauvoir; second, a culturally-oriented gynocentric feminism, aiming to foster the expression of a non-male-defined feminine sexual and symbolic specificity, a feminism represented by the proponents of *écriture féminine* and *parler femme*; and finally, Kristeva's own, self-proclaimed brand of feminism—in my view, actually postfeminism—a radically nominalist, anti-essentialist approach that stresses that "women" do not exist and that collective identities are dangerous fictions.[36]

Despite the explicitly tripartite character of this categorization, the deep logic of Kristeva's thinking about feminism conforms to her additive, dualistic pattern. For one thing, the first, egalitarian humanist moment of feminism drops out of the picture, as Kristeva erroneously assumes that its program has already been achieved. In the end, accordingly, she concerns herself with two "generations" of feminism only. In addition, despite her explicit criticisms of gynocentrism, there is a strand of her thought that implicitly partakes of it—I mean Kristeva's quasi-biologistic, essentializing identification of women's femininity with maternity. Maternity, for her, is the way that women, as opposed to men, touch base with the pre-oedipal, semiotic residue. (Men do it by writing avant-garde poetry; women do it by having babies.) Here, Kristeva dehistoricizes and psychologizes motherhood, conflating conception, pregnancy, birthing, nursing, and childrearing, abstracting all of them from socio-political context, and erecting her own essentialist stereotype of femininity. But then she reverses herself and recoils from her construct, insisting that "women" don't exist, that feminine identity is fictitious, and that feminist movements therefore tend toward the religious and the proto-totalitarian. The overall pattern of Kristeva's thinking about feminism, then, is additive and dualistic: she ends up alternating

---

35  Reprinted in *The Kristeva Reader*, ed. Toril Moi.

36  I take the terms "humanist feminism" and "gynocentric feminism" from Iris Young, "Humanism, Gynocentrism and Feminist Politics," in Young, *Throwing Like a Girl and Other Essays in Feminist Philosophy and Social Theory*, Bloomington: Indiana University Press, 1990. I take the term "nominalist feminism" from Linda Alcoff, "Cultural Feminism versus Poststructuralism: The Identity Crisis in Feminist Theory," *Signs: Journal of Women in Culture and Society* 13:3, Spring 1988, 405–36.

essentialist gynocentric moments with anti-essentialist nominalistic moments, moments that consolidate an ahistorical, undifferentiated, maternal feminine gender identity with moments that repudiate women's identities altogether.

With respect to feminism, then, Kristeva leaves us oscillating between a regressive version of gynocentric-maternalist essentialism, on the one hand, and a postfeminist anti-essentialism, on the other. Neither of these is useful for feminist theorizing. In Denise Riley's terms, the first *overfeminizes* women by defining us maternally. The second *underfeminizes* us by insisting that "women" do not exist and by dismissing the feminist movement as a proto-totalitarian fiction.[37] Simply putting the two together, moreover, does not overcome the limits of either. On the contrary, it constitutes another "bad infinity"—another proof of the limited usefulness for feminist theorizing of an approach that merely conjoins an abstract negation of structuralism to a structuralist model left otherwise intact.

## 4. CONCLUSION

I hope the foregoing has provided a reasonably vivid and persuasive illustration of my most general point, namely, the superior utility for feminist theorizing of pragmatics over structuralist approaches to the study of language. Instead of reiterating the advantages of pragmatics models, I shall close with one specific example of their uses for feminist theorizing.

As I argued, pragmatics models insist on the social context and social practice of communication, and they study a plurality of historically changing discursive sites and practices. As a result, these approaches offer us the possibility of thinking of social identities as complex, changing, and discursively constructed. This in turn seems to me our best hope for avoiding some of Kristeva's difficulties. Complex, shifting, discursively constructed social identities provide an alternative to reified, essentialist conceptions of gender identity, on the one hand, and to simple negations and dispersals of identity, on the other. They thus permit us to navigate safely between the twin shoals of essentialism and nominalism, between reifying women's social identities under stereotypes of femininity, on the one hand, and dissolving them into sheer nullity and oblivion, on the other.[38] I am

37  For the terms "underfeminization" and "overfeminization," see Riley, *"Am I That Name?"* For a useful critique of Kristeva's equation of collective liberation movements with "totalitarianism," see Ann Rosalind Jones, "Julia Kristeva on Femininity: The Limits of a Semiotic Politics," *Feminist Review* 18, 1984, 56–73.

38  On this point, see Nancy Fraser and Linda J. Nicholson, "Social Criticism without Philosophy: An Encounter between Feminism and Postmodernism," in *Feminism/Postmodernism*, ed. Nicholson, New York: Routledge, 1993.

claiming, therefore, that with the help of a pragmatics conception of discourse we can accept the critique of essentialism without becoming postfeminists. This seems to me to be an invaluable help, for it will not be time to speak of postfeminism until we can legitimately speak of postpatriarchy.[39]

39  I borrow this line from Toril Moi, who uttered it in another context in her talk at a conference on "Convergence in Crisis: Narratives of the History of Theory," Duke University, September 24–27, 1987.

# 6

# Feminist Politics in the Age of Recognition: A Two-Dimensional Approach to Gender Justice

Feminist theory tends to follow the zeitgeist. In the 1970s, when second-wave feminism emerged out of the New Left, its most influential theories of gender reflected the still-potent influence of Marxism. Whether sympathetic or antagonistic to class analysis, these theories located gender relations on the terrain of political economy, even as they sought to expand that terrain to encompass housework, reproduction, and sexuality. Soon thereafter, chafing under the limits of labor-centered paradigms, additional currents of feminist theorizing emerged in dialogue with psychoanalysis. In the Anglophone world, object-relations theorists began to conceptualize gender as an "identity." On the European continent, meanwhile, Lacanians rejected the term "gender relations" as too sociological and replaced it with "sexual difference," which they conceptualized in relation to subjectivity and the symbolic order. In neither case was the initial intention to supplant Marxism *per se*; rather, both currents saw themselves as enriching and deepening materialist paradigms that too often lapsed into vulgar economism. By the 1990s, however, the New Left was only a memory, and Marxism seemed to many a dead letter. In that context, lines of thought that had begun by presuming Marxism's relevance took on another valence. Joining the larger exodus of intellectuals from Marxism, most feminist theorists took "the cultural turn." With the exception of a few holdouts, even those who rejected psychoanalysis came to understand gender as an identity or a "cultural construction." Today, accordingly, gender theory is largely a branch of cultural studies. As such, it has further attenuated, if not wholly lost, its historic links to Marxism—and to social theory and political economy more generally.

As always, the vicissitudes of theory follow those of politics. The shift, over the last thirty years, from quasi-Marxist, labor-centered understandings of gender to culture- and identity-based conceptions coincides with a parallel shift in feminist politics. Whereas the '68 generation hoped, among other things, to restructure the political economy so as to abolish the gender division of labor, subsequent feminists formulated other, less material aims. Some, for example, sought recognition of sexual difference, while others preferred to deconstruct the categorial opposition between masculine and feminine. The result was a shift in the center of gravity of feminist politics. Once centered on labor and violence, gender struggles have focused increasingly on identity and representation in recent years. The effect has been to subordinate social struggles to cultural struggles, the politics of redistribution to the politics of recognition. That was not, once again, the original intention. It was assumed, rather, by cultural feminists and deconstructionists alike that feminist cultural politics would synergize with struggles for social equality. But that assumption, too, has fallen prey to the zeitgeist. In "the network society," the feminist turn to recognition has dovetailed all too neatly with a hegemonic neoliberalism that wants nothing more than to repress socialist memory.[1]

Of course, feminism is hardly alone in this trajectory. On the contrary, the recent history of gender theory reflects a wider shift in the grammar of political claims-making. On the one hand, struggles for recognition have exploded everywhere—witness battles over multiculturalism, human rights, and national autonomy. On the other hand, struggles for egalitarian redistribution are in relative decline—witness the weakening of trade unions and the co-optation of labor and socialist parties in "the third way." The result is a tragic historical irony. The shift from redistribution to recognition has occurred just as an aggressively globalizing US-led capitalism is exacerbating economic inequality.[2]

For feminism, accordingly, this shift has been double-edged. On the one hand, the turn to recognition represents a broadening of gender struggle and a new understanding of gender justice. No longer restricted to questions of distribution, gender justice now encompasses issues of representation, identity, and difference. The result is a major advance over reductive economistic paradigms that had

---

1   For elaboration of this claim, see Chapters 9 ("Feminism, Capitalism, and the Cunning of History") and 10 ("Between Marketization and Social Protection") in this volume.

2   For a fuller discussion, see Nancy Fraser, "From Redistribution to Recognition? Dilemmas of Justice in a 'Postsocialist' Age," *New Left Review* 212, 1995, 68–93; reprinted in Fraser, *Justice Interruptus: Critical Reflections on the "Postsocialist" Condition*, New York: Routledge, 1997. See also Fraser, "Social Justice in the Age of Identity Politics: Redistribution, Recognition, and Participation," in Nancy Fraser and Axel Honneth, *Redistribution or Recognition? A Political-Philosophical Exchange*, London: Verso Books, 2003.

difficulty conceptualizing harms rooted not in the division of labor, but in androcentric patterns of cultural value. On the other hand, it is no longer clear that feminist struggles for recognition are serving to deepen and enrich struggles for egalitarian redistribution. Rather, in the context of an ascendant neoliberalism, they may be serving to displace the latter. In that case, the recent gains would be entwined with a tragic loss. Instead of arriving at a broader, richer paradigm that could encompass both redistribution and recognition, we would have traded one truncated paradigm for another—a truncated economism for a truncated culturalism. The result would be a classic case of combined and uneven development: the remarkable recent feminist gains on the axis of recognition would coincide with stalled progress—if not outright losses—on the axis of distribution.

That, at least, is my reading of present trends. In what follows, I shall outline an approach to gender theory and feminist politics that responds to this diagnosis and aims to forestall its full realization. What I have to say divides into four parts. First, I shall propose an analysis of gender that is broad enough to house the full range of feminist concerns, those central to the old socialist-feminism as well as those rooted in the cultural turn. To complement this analysis, I shall propose, second, a correspondingly broad conception of justice, capable of encompassing both distribution and recognition, and third, a non-identitarian account of recognition, capable of synergizing with redistribution. Finally, I shall examine some practical problems that arise when we try to envision institutional reforms that could redress maldistribution and misrecognition simultaneously. In all four sections, I break with those feminist approaches that focus exclusively on gender. Rather, I situate gender struggles as one strand among others in a broader political project aimed at institutionalizing democratic justice across multiple axes of social differentiation.

## 1. GENDER: A TWO-DIMENSIONAL CONCEPT

To avoid truncating the feminist problematic, and unwittingly colluding with neoliberalism, feminists today need to revisit the concept of gender. What is needed is a broad and capacious conception, which can accommodate at least two sets of concerns. On the one hand, such a conception must incorporate the labor-centered problematic associated with socialist-feminism; on the other hand, it must also make room for the culture-centered problematic associated with putatively "post-Marxian" strands of feminist theorizing. Rejecting sectarian formulations that cast those two problematics as mutually antithetical, feminists need to develop an account of gender that encompasses the concerns of both. As we shall see, this requires theorizing both the gendered character of the political economy and the androcentrism of the cultural order, without reducing either one of them to the other. At the same time, it also requires theorizing two analytically distinct dimensions of sexism, one centered on distribution, the other centered on recognition. The result will be a *two-dimensional conception of gender*. Only such a conception can support a viable feminist politics in the present era.

Let me explain. The approach I propose requires viewing gender bifocally—simultaneously through two different lenses. Viewed through one lens, gender has affinities with class; viewed through the other, it is more akin to status. Each lens brings into focus an important aspect of women's subordination, but neither is sufficient on its own. A full understanding becomes available only when the two lenses are superimposed. At that point, gender appears as a categorial axis that spans two dimensions of social ordering, the dimension of *distribution* and the dimension of *recognition*.

From the distributive perspective, gender appears as a class-like differentiation, rooted in the economic structure of society. A basic organizing principle of the division of labor, it underlies the fundamental division between paid "productive" labor and unpaid "reproductive" and domestic labor, assigning women primary responsibility for the latter. Gender also structures the division within paid labor between higher-paid, male-dominated manufacturing and professional occupations and lower-paid, female-dominated "pink collar" and domestic service occupations. The result is an economic structure that generates gender-specific forms of distributive injustice.

From the recognition perspective, in contrast, gender appears as a status differentiation, rooted in the status order of society. Gender codes pervasive cultural patterns of interpretation and evaluation, which are central to the status order as a whole. Thus, a major feature of gender injustice is androcentrism: an institutionalized pattern of cultural value that privileges traits associated with masculinity, while devaluing everything coded as "feminine," paradigmatically—but not only—women. Pervasively institutionalized, androcentric value patterns structure broad swaths of social interaction. Expressly codified in many areas of law (including family law and criminal law), they inform legal constructions of privacy, autonomy, self-defense, and equality. They are also entrenched in many areas of government policy (including reproductive, immigration, and asylum policy) and in standard professional practices (including medicine and psychotherapy). Androcentric value patterns also pervade popular culture and everyday interaction. As a result, women suffer gender-specific forms of *status subordination*, including sexual harassment, sexual assault, and domestic violence; trivializing, objectifying, and demeaning stereotypical depictions in the media; disparagement in everyday life; exclusion or marginalization in public spheres and deliberative bodies; and denial of the full rights and equal protections of citizenship. These harms are injustices of misrecognition. They are relatively independent of political economy and are not merely "superstructural." Thus, they cannot be overcome by redistribution alone but require additional, independent remedies of recognition.

When the two perspectives are combined, gender emerges as a two-dimensional category. It contains both a political-economic face that brings it within the ambit of redistribution, and also a cultural-discursive face that brings it simultaneously within the ambit of recognition. Moreover, neither dimension is merely an indirect effect of the other. To be sure, the distributive and recognition dimensions interact with each other. But gender maldistribution is not simply a by-product of status hierarchy; nor is gender misrecognition wholly a by-product of economic structure. Rather, each dimension has some relative independence from the other. Neither can be redressed entirely indirectly, therefore, through remedies addressed exclusively to the other. It is an open question whether the two dimensions are of equal weight. But redressing gender injustice, in any case, requires changing both the economic structure and the status order of contemporary society. Neither alone will suffice.

The two-dimensional character of gender wreaks havoc on the idea of an either/or choice between the politics of redistribution and the politics of recognition. That construction assumes that women are either a class or a status group, but not both; that the injustice they suffer is either maldistribution or misrecognition, but not both; that the remedy is either redistribution or recognition, but not both. Gender, we can now see, explodes this whole series of false antitheses. Here we have a category that is a compound of both status and class. Not only is gender "difference" constructed simultaneously from both economic differentials and institutionalized patterns of cultural value, but both maldistribution and misrecognition are fundamental to sexism. The implication for feminist politics is clear. To combat the subordination of women requires an approach that combines a politics of redistribution with a politics of recognition.[3]

---

3  Gender, moreover, is not unusual in this regard. "Race," too, is a two-dimensional category, a compound of status and class. Class, also, may well best be understood two-dimensionally, contra orthodox economistic theories. And even sexuality, which looks at first sight like the paradigm case of pure recognition, has an undeniable economic dimension. Thus, it may well turn out that virtually all real-world axes of injustice are two-dimensional. Virtually all perpetrate both maldistribution and misrecognition in forms where neither of those injustices can be redressed entirely indirectly but where each requires some practical attention. As

## 2. GENDER JUSTICE AS PARTICIPATORY PARITY

Developing such an approach requires a conception of justice as broad and capacious as the preceding view of gender. Such a conception, too, must accommodate at least two sets of concerns. On the one hand, it must encompass the traditional concerns of distributive justice, especially poverty, exploitation, inequality, and class differentials. At the same time, it must also encompass concerns of recognition, especially disrespect, cultural imperialism, and status hierarchy. Rejecting sectarian formulations that cast distribution and recognition as mutually incompatible understandings of justice, such a conception must accommodate both. As we shall see, this means theorizing maldistribution and misrecognition by reference to a common normative standard, without reducing either one to the other. The result, once again, will be a *two-dimensional conception of justice*. Only such a conception can comprehend the full magnitude of sexist injustice.

The conception of justice I propose centers on the principle of *parity of participation*. According to this principle, justice requires social arrangements that permit all (adult) members of society to interact with one another *as peers*. For participatory parity to be possible, at least two conditions must be satisfied. First, the distribution of material resources must be such as to ensure participants' independence and "voice." This "objective" condition precludes forms and levels of economic dependence and inequality that impede parity of participation. Precluded, therefore, are social arrangements that institutionalize deprivation, exploitation, and gross disparities in wealth, income, and leisure time, thereby denying some people the means and opportunities to interact with others as peers. In contrast, the second condition for participatory parity is "intersubjective." It requires that institutionalized patterns of cultural value express equal respect for all participants and ensure equal opportunity for achieving social esteem. This condition precludes institutionalized value patterns that systematically depreciate some categories of people and the qualities associated with them. Precluded, therefore, are institutionalized value patterns that deny some people the status of full partners in interaction—whether by burdening them with excessive ascribed "difference" or by failing to acknowledge their distinctiveness.

Both conditions are necessary for participatory parity. Neither alone is sufficient. The first brings into focus concerns traditionally associated with the theory of distributive justice, especially concerns

---

a practical matter, therefore, overcoming injustice in virtually every case requires both redistribution and recognition. For a fuller discussion, see Fraser, "Social Justice in the Age of Identity Politics."

pertaining to the economic structure of society and to economically defined class differentials. The second brings into focus concerns recently highlighted in the philosophy of recognition, especially concerns pertaining to the status order of society and to culturally defined hierarchies of status. Yet neither condition is merely an epiphenomenal effect of the other. Rather, each has some relative independence. Thus, neither can be achieved wholly indirectly, via reforms addressed exclusively to the other. The result is a two-dimensional conception of justice that encompasses *both* redistribution and recognition, without reducing either one to the other.[4]

This approach suits the conception of gender proposed earlier. By construing redistribution and recognition as two mutually irreducible dimensions of justice, it broadens the usual understanding of justice to encompass both the class and status aspects of gender subordination. By submitting both dimensions to the overarching norm of participatory parity, moreover, it supplies a single normative standard for assessing the justice of the gender order. Insofar as the economic structure of society denies women the resources they need for full participation in social life, it institutionalizes sexist maldistribution. Insofar, likewise, as the status order of society constitutes women as less than full partners in interaction, it institutionalizes sexist misrecognition. In either case, the result is a morally indefensible gender order.

Thus, the norm of participatory parity serves to identify—and condemn—gender injustice along two dimensions. But the standard also applies to other axes of social differentiation, including class, "race," sexuality, ethnicity, nationality, and religion. Insofar as social arrangements impede parity of participation along any of these axes, whether via maldistribution or misrecognition, they violate the requirements of justice. The result, as we shall see shortly, is a normative standard that is capable of adjudicating some of the hardest political dilemmas feminists face today. These dilemmas arise at the intersection of multiple axes of subordination, when for example efforts to remedy the unjust treatment of a religious minority seem to conflict head-on with efforts to remedy sexism. In the following section of the present essay, I shall show how the principle of participatory parity serves to resolve such dilemmas.

First, however, let me clarify my use of the term "parity," as it differs from recent French uses of that term. Four points of divergence are especially worth noting. First, in France *parité* designates a law mandating that women occupy half of all slots on electoral lists in campaigns for seats in legislative assemblies. There, accordingly, it

---

4 For a fuller argument, see Fraser, "Social Justice in the Age of Identity Politics."

means strict numerical equality in gender representation in electoral contests. For me, parity is not a matter of numbers. Rather, it is a qualitative condition, the condition of being a *peer*, of being on a *par* with others, of interacting with them on an equal footing. That condition is not guaranteed by mere numbers, as we know from former Communist countries, some of which came close to achieving parity in the French sense while remaining very far from achieving it in mine. To be sure, the severe under-representation of women in legislative assemblies and other formal political institutions usually signifies qualitative disparities of participation in social life. But numerical quotas are not necessarily or always the best solution. Thus, my conception deliberately leaves open (for democratic deliberation) the question of exactly what degree of representation or level of equality is necessary to ensure participatory parity.

The reason has to do with the second difference between my view of parity and the French one, a difference concerning scope. In France, the requirement of *parité* concerns one dimension of justice only, namely, the dimension of recognition. There, accordingly, it is apparently assumed that the chief obstacle to women's full participation in political life is an androcentric value hierarchy in the party structure and that the principal remedy is the constitutional requirement that women occupy half the slots on electoral lists. For me, in contrast, the requirement of participatory parity applies to both dimensions of social justice, hence to distribution as well as recognition. And I assume that the obstacle to parity can be (and often is) maldistribution as well as misrecognition. In the case of gender disparity in political representation, then, I assume that what is required is not only the deinstitutionalization of androcentric value hierarchies but also the restructuring of the division of labor to eliminate women's "double shift," which constitutes a formidable distributive obstacle to their full participation in political life.

The third key difference is also a matter of scope, but in a different sense. In France, *parité* applies to one arena of interaction only: electoral campaigns for seats in legislative assemblies. For me, in contrast, parity applies throughout the whole of social life. Thus, justice requires parity of participation in a multiplicity of interaction arenas, including labor markets, sexual relations, family life, public spheres, and voluntary associations in civil society. In each arena, however, participation means something different. For example, participation in the labor market means something qualitatively different from participation in sexual relations or in civil society. In each arena, therefore, the meaning of parity must be tailored to the kind of participation at issue. No single formula, quantitative or otherwise, can suffice for every case. What precisely is required to achieve participatory parity depends in part on the nature of the social interaction in question.

The fourth key difference concerns scope in yet another sense. In France, *parité* applies to one axis of social differentiation only, namely, the axis of gender. Thus, the law does not mandate proportional representation of other categories of subordinated people, such as racial/ethnic or religious minorities. Nor apparently are its supporters concerned about its impact on such representation. For me, in contrast, justice requires participatory parity across all major axes of social differentiation—not only gender, but also "race," ethnicity, sexuality, religion, and nationality.[5] And as I shall explain in the following section, this entails that proposed reforms be evaluated from multiple perspectives—hence that proponents must consider whether measures aimed at redressing one sort of disparity are likely to end up exacerbating another.[6]

In general, then, my notion of justice as participatory parity is far broader than the French *parité*. Unlike the latter, it provides a normative standard for assessing the justice of *all* social arrangements along *two* dimensions and across *multiple* axes of social differentiation. As such, it represents a fitting counterpart to a conception of gender that encompasses not only the status-oriented dimension of recognition, but also the class-like dimension of distribution.

## 3. RETHINKING RECOGNITION: BEYOND IDENTITY POLITICS

Now let us consider the implications of these conceptions for feminist politics, beginning with the politics of recognition. Usually, this is viewed as identity politics. From the standard perspective, what requires recognition is feminine gender identity. Misrecognition consists in the depreciation of such identity by a patriarchal culture and the consequent damage to women's sense of self. Redressing this harm requires engaging in a feminist politics of recognition. Such a

---

5 Thus, I reject the essentialist accounts of sexual difference, invoked by some French feminist philosophers to justify *parité*.

6 There is also a fifth difference, which concerns modality. The French law mandates *parité* of actual participation. For me, in contrast, the moral requirement is that members of society be ensured the *possibility* of parity, if and when they choose to participate in a given activity or interaction. There is no requirement that everyone actually participate in any such activity. To take an example from the United States: separatist groups such as the Amish are perfectly entitled to withdraw from participation in the larger society. What they cannot do, however, is deprive their children of the chance to acquire the social competences they would need to participate as peers in case they should later choose to exit the Amish community and join the social mainstream.

politics aims to repair internal self-dislocation by contesting demeaning androcentric pictures of femininity. Women must reject such pictures in favor of new self-representations of their own making. Having refashioned their collective identity, moreover, they must display it publicly in order to gain the respect and esteem of the society-at-large. The result, when successful, is "recognition," a positive relation to oneself. On the identity model, then, a feminist politics of recognition means identity politics.

Without doubt, this identity model contains some genuine insights concerning the psychological effects of sexism. Yet, as I have argued elsewhere, it is deficient on at least two major counts. First, it tends to reify femininity and to obscure crosscutting axes of subordination. As a result, it often recycles dominant gender stereotypes, while promoting separatism and political correctness. Second, the identity model treats sexist misrecognition as a freestanding cultural harm. As a result, it obscures the latter's links to sexist maldistribution, thereby impeding efforts to combat both aspects of sexism simultaneously.[7] For these reasons, feminists need an alternative approach.

The concepts of gender and justice proposed here imply an alternative feminist politics of recognition. From this perspective, recognition is a question of *social status*. What requires recognition is not feminine identity but the status of women as full partners in social interaction. Misrecognition, accordingly, does not mean the depreciation and deformation of femininity. Rather, it means social subordination in the sense of being prevented from participating as a peer in social life. To redress the injustice requires a feminist politics of recognition, to be sure, but this does not mean identity politics. On the status model, rather, it means a politics aimed at overcoming subordination by establishing women as full members of society, capable of participating on a par with men.

Let me explain. The status approach requires examining institutionalized patterns of cultural value for their effects on the relative *standing* of women. If and when such patterns constitute women as *peers*, capable of participating on a par with men in social life, then we can speak of *reciprocal recognition* and *status equality*. When, in contrast, institutionalized patterns of cultural value constitute women as inferior, excluded, wholly other, or simply invisible, hence as less than full partners in social interaction, then we must speak of *sexist misrecognition* and *status subordination*. On the status model, therefore, sexist misrecognition is a social relation of subordination relayed through

7  For a fuller critique of the identity model, see Nancy Fraser, "Rethinking Recognition: Overcoming Displacement and Reification in Cultural Politics," *New Left Review* 3, May/June 2000, 107–20.

*institutionalized patterns of cultural value.* It occurs when social institutions regulate interaction according to androcentric parity-impeding norms. Examples include criminal laws that ignore marital rape, social-welfare programs that stigmatize single mothers as sexually irresponsible scroungers, and asylum policies that regard genital mutilation as a "cultural practice" like any other. In each of these cases, interaction is regulated by an androcentric pattern of cultural value. In each case, the result is to deny women the status of full partners in interaction, capable of participating on a par with men.

Viewed in terms of status, therefore, misrecognition constitutes a serious violation of justice. Wherever and however it occurs, a claim for recognition is in order. But note precisely what this means: aimed not at valorizing femininity, but rather at overcoming subordination, claims for recognition seek to establish women as full partners in social life, able to interact with men as peers. They aim, that is, *to deinstitutionalize androcentric patterns of value that impede gender parity and to replace them with patterns that foster it.*[8]

In general, then, the status model makes possible a *non-identitarian* politics of recognition. Such a politics applies to gender, to be sure. But it also applies to other axes of subordination, including "race," sexuality, ethnicity, nationality, and religion. As a result, it enables feminists to adjudicate cases in which claims for recognition posed along one axis of subordination run up against claims posed along another.

Of special interest to feminists are cases in which claims for the recognition of minority cultural practices seem to conflict with gender justice. In such cases, the principle of participatory parity must be applied twice. It must be applied, once, at the *intergroup* level, to assess the effects of institutionalized patterns of cultural value on the relative standing of minorities vis-à-vis majorities. Then, it must be applied again, at the *intragroup* level, to assess the internal effects of the minority practices for which recognition is being claimed. Taken together, these two levels constitute a double requirement. Claimants must show, first, that the institutionalization of majority cultural norms denies them participatory parity and, second, that the practices whose recognition they seek do not themselves deny participatory parity to others, as well as to some of their own members.

Consider the French controversy over the *foulard.* Here the issue is whether policies forbidding Muslim girls to wear headscarves in state schools constitute unjust treatment of a religious minority. In this case, those claiming recognition of the *foulard* must establish two

---

8  For a fuller account of the status model, see Fraser, "Social Justice in the Age of Identity Politics."

points: they must show, first, that the ban on the scarf constitutes an unjust majority communitarianism, which denies educational parity to Muslim girls; and second, that an alternative policy permitting the *foulard* would not exacerbate female subordination—in Muslim communities or in society-at-large. The first point, concerning French majority communitarianism, can be established without difficulty, it seems, as no analogous prohibition bars the wearing of Christian crosses in state schools; thus, the current policy denies equal standing to Muslim citizens. The second point, concerning the non-exacerbation of female subordination, has proved controversial, in contrast, as some republicans have argued that the *foulard* is a marker of women's subordination and must therefore be denied state recognition. Disputing this interpretation, however, some multiculturalists have rejoined that the scarf's meaning is highly contested in French Muslim communities today, as are gender relations more generally; thus, instead of construing it as univocally patriarchal, which effectively accords male supremacists sole authority to interpret Islam, the state should treat the *foulard* as a symbol of Muslim identity in transition, one whose meaning is contested, as is French identity itself, as a result of transcultural interactions in a multicultural society. From this perspective, permitting the *foulard* in state schools could be a step toward, not away from, gender parity.

In my view, the multiculturalists have the stronger argument here. (This is *not* the case, incidentally, for those seeking recognition for what they call "female circumcision"—actually, genital mutilation, which clearly denies parity in sexual pleasure and in health to women and girls.) But that is not the point I wish to stress here. The point, rather, is that the argument is rightly cast in terms of parity of participation. This is precisely where the controversy should be joined. Participatory parity is the proper standard for warranting claims for recognition (and redistribution). It enables a non-identitarian feminist politics that can adjudicate conflicts between claims centered on gender and those focused on other, cross-cutting axes of subordination.[9]

---

9  This standard cannot be applied monologically, however, in the manner of a decision procedure. It must be applied dialogically, through democratic processes of public debate. In such debates, participants argue about whether existing institutionalized patterns of cultural value impede parity of participation and about whether proposed alternatives would foster it. Thus, participatory parity serves as an idiom of public contestation and deliberation about questions of justice. More strongly, it represents *the principal idiom of public reason*, the preferred language for conducting democratic political argumentation on issues of both distribution and recognition. I discuss this issue in "Social Justice in the Age of Identity Politics."

## 4. INTEGRATING REDISTRIBUTION AND RECOGNITION IN FEMINIST POLITICS

Now let us turn to the broader implications for feminist politics. As we saw, a feminist politics for today must be two-dimensional, combining a politics of recognition with a politics of redistribution. Only such a politics can avoid truncating the feminist agenda and colluding with neoliberalism.

Yet devising such a feminist politics is no easy matter. It is not sufficient to proceed additively, as if one could simply add a politics of redistribution to a politics of recognition. That would be to treat the two dimensions as if they occupied two separate spheres. In fact, however, distribution and recognition are thoroughly imbricated with one another. And neither claims for redistribution nor claims for recognition can be insulated from each other. On the contrary, they impinge on one another in ways that can give rise to unintended—and unwanted—effects.

Consider, first, that feminist claims for redistribution impinge on recognition. Redistributive policies aimed at mitigating women's poverty, for instance, have status implications that can harm the intended beneficiaries. For example, public assistance programs aimed specifically at "female-headed families" often insinuate the lesser value of "childrearing" vis-à-vis "wage-earning" and of "welfare mothers" vis-à-vis "tax payers."[10] At their worst, they mark single mothers as sexually irresponsible scroungers, thereby adding the insult of misrecognition to the injury of deprivation. In general, redistributive policies affect women's status and identities, as well as their economic position. These effects must be thematized and scrutinized, lest one end up fueling sexist misrecognition in the course of trying to remedy sexist maldistribution. Redistributive policies have sexist misrecognition effects when a culturally pervasive androcentric devaluation of caregiving inflects support for single-mother families as "getting something for nothing."[11] In this context, feminist struggles for redistribution cannot succeed unless they are joined with struggles for cultural change aimed at revaluing caregiving and the feminine associations that code it. In short: *no redistribution without recognition.*

---

10  See Nancy Fraser, "Clintonism, Welfare, and the Antisocial Wage: The Emergence of a Neoliberal Political Imaginary," *Rethinking Marxism* 6:1, 1993, 9–23.

11  This was the case with Aid to Families with Dependent Children (AFDC), which was the major means-tested welfare program in the United States. Claimed overwhelmingly by solo-mother families living below the poverty line, AFDC became a lightening rod for racist and sexist anti-welfare sentiments in the 1990s. In 1997, it was "reformed" (aka abolished) in such a way as to eliminate the federal entitlement that had guaranteed (some, inadequate) income support to the poor.

The converse is equally true, however, as feminist claims for recognition impinge on distribution. Proposals to redress androcentric evaluative patterns have economic implications that can work to the detriment of some women. For example, top-down campaigns to suppress female genital mutilation may have negative effects on the economic position of the affected women, rendering them "unmarriageable" while failing to ensure alternative means of support. Likewise, campaigns to suppress prostitution and pornography may have negative effects on the economic position of sex workers. Finally, no-fault divorce reforms in the United States have hurt some divorced women economically, even while enhancing women's legal status.[12] In such cases, reforms aimed at remedying sexist misrecognition have ended up fueling sexist maldistribution. Recognition claims, moreover, are liable to the charge of being "merely symbolic." When pursued in contexts marked by gross disparities in economic position, reforms aimed at affirming distinctiveness tend to devolve into empty gestures; like the sort of recognition that would put women on a pedestal, they mock, rather than redress, serious harms. In such contexts, recognition reforms cannot succeed unless they are joined with struggles for redistribution. In short: *no recognition without redistribution*.

The moral here is the need for bifocal vision in feminist politics. This means looking simultaneously through the two analytically distinct lenses of distribution and recognition. Failure to keep either one of those lenses in view can end up distorting what one sees through the other. Only a perspective that superimposes the two can avoid exacerbating one dimension of sexism in the course of trying to remedy another.

The need, in all cases, is to think integratively, as in campaigns for "comparable worth." Here a claim to redistribute income between men and women was expressly integrated with a claim to change gender-coded patterns of cultural value. The underlying premise was that gender injustices of distribution and recognition are so complexly intertwined that neither can be redressed entirely independently of the other. Thus, efforts to reduce the gender wage gap cannot fully succeed if, remaining wholly "economic," they fail to challenge the gender meanings that code low-paying service occupations as "women's work," largely devoid of intelligence and skill. Likewise, efforts to revalue female-coded traits such as interpersonal sensitivity and nurturance cannot succeed if, remaining wholly "cultural," they

---

12   Lenore Weitzman, *The Divorce Revolution: The Unexpected Social Consequences for Women and Children in America*, New York: Free Press, 1985. The extent of the income losses claimed by Weitzman has been disputed. But there is little doubt that some losses have resulted.

fail to challenge the structural economic conditions that connect those traits with dependency and powerlessness. Only an approach that redresses the cultural devaluation of the "feminine" precisely *within* the economy (and elsewhere) can deliver serious redistribution and genuine recognition.

Elsewhere I have discussed other strategies for integrating a politics of redistribution with a politics of recognition.[13] Here I have argued in general terms that gender justice today requires both redistribution and recognition, that neither alone is sufficient. Thus, I have rebutted arguments that cast the concerns of socialist-feminism as incompatible with those of newer paradigms centered on discourse and culture. Putting aside the usual sectarian blinders, I have proposed conceptions of gender, justice, and recognition that are broad enough to encompass the concerns of both camps. These conceptions are two-dimensional. Spanning both distribution and recognition, they are able to comprehend both the class-like aspects and status aspects of women's subordination.

The concepts proposed here are informed as well by a broader diagnosis of the present conjuncture. On the one hand, I have assumed that gender intersects other axes of subordination in ways that complicate the feminist project. And I have suggested ways of resolving some of the resulting dilemmas—especially for cases in which claims to redress cultural and religious misrecognition seem to threaten to exacerbate sexism. On the other hand, I have situated my approach to feminist politics in relation to the larger shift in the grammar of claims-making "from redistribution to recognition." Where that shift threatens to abet neoliberalism by repressing the problematic of distributive justice, I have proposed a two-dimensional political orientation. This approach keeps alive the insights of Marxism, while also learning from the cultural turn.

In general, then, the approach proposed here provides some conceptual resources for answering what I take to be the key political question of our day: How can feminists develop a coherent programmatic perspective that integrates redistribution and recognition? How can we develop a framework that integrates what remains cogent and unsurpassable in the socialist vision with what is defensible and compelling in the apparently "postsocialist" vision of multiculturalism? If we fail to ask this question, if we cling instead to false antitheses and misleading either/or dichotomies, we will miss the chance to envision social arrangements that can redress both the class-like and status aspects of women's subordination. Only by looking to integrative approaches that unite redistribution and recognition can we meet the requirements of justice for all.

---

13    See especially Fraser, "Social Justice in the Age of Identity Politics."

# 7

# Heterosexism, Misrecognition, and Capitalism: A Response to Judith Butler*

Judith Butler's essay "Merely Cultural" is welcome on several counts.[1] It returns us to deep and important questions in social theory that have gone undiscussed for far too long. And it links a reflection on such questions to a diagnosis of the troubled state of the Left in the current political conjuncture. Most important, however, is Butler's commitment in this essay to identifying, and retrieving, the genuinely valuable aspects of Marxism and the socialist-feminism of the 1970s, which current intellectual and political fashions conspire to repress. Also exemplary is her interest in integrating the best insights of those paradigms with defensible strands of more recent paradigms—including discourse analysis, cultural studies, and poststructuralism—in order to understand contemporary capitalism. These are commitments I wholeheartedly share.

Nevertheless, Butler and I disagree. Our most important disagreements, and the most fruitful for discussion, turn on how precisely to realize this shared project of reclamation and integration. We hold divergent views of what precisely constitutes the enduring legacy of Marxism and the still-relevant insights of socialist-feminism. We also diverge in our respective assessments of the merits of various post-structuralist currents and in our respective views of how these can best inform social theorizing that retains a materialist dimension. Finally, we disagree about the nature of contemporary capitalism.

In order to clear the way for a fruitful discussion of these issues, I want to begin by disposing quickly of what I take to be the red herrings. Butler conjoins her discussion of my book *Justice Interruptus* to a critique of a group of unnamed interlocutors whom she calls "neoconservative

---

* I am grateful for helpful comments from Laura Kipnis and Eli Zaretsky.

1 Judith Butler, "Merely Cultural," in *Adding Insult to Injury: Nancy Fraser Debates Her Critics*, ed. Kevin Olson, London: Verso Books, 2008, 42–56.

Marxists."[2] Whatever the merits of her critique of this group—a question I shall return to later—her strategy of using it to frame a discussion of my work is unfortunate. Despite her disclaimers to the contrary, readers could draw the erroneous conclusion that I share the "neoconservative Marxist" dismissal of the oppression of gays and lesbians as "merely" cultural, hence as secondary, derivative, or even trivial. They might assume that I see sexual oppression as less fundamental, material, and real than class oppression and that I wish to subordinate struggles against heterosexism to struggles against workers' exploitation. Finding me thus lumped together with "sexually conservative orthodox" Marxists, readers could even conclude that I view gay and lesbian movements as unjustified particularisms that have split the Left and on whom I wish forcibly to impose Left unity.

I, of course, believe nothing of the sort. On the contrary, in *Justice Interruptus* I have analyzed the current decoupling of so-called identity politics from class politics—the cultural Left from the social Left—as a constitutive feature of the "postsocialist" condition.[3] Seeking to overcome these splits and to articulate the basis for a united front of the Left, I have proposed a theoretical framework that eschews orthodox distinctions between "base" and "superstructure," "primary" and "secondary" oppressions, and that challenges the primacy of the economic. In the process, I have posited both the conceptual irreducibility of heterosexist oppression and the moral legitimacy of gay and lesbian claims.

Central to my framework is a normative distinction between injustices of distribution and injustices of recognition. Far from derogating the latter as "merely cultural," the point is to conceptualize two equally primary, serious, and real kinds of harm that any morally defensible social order must eradicate. To be misrecognized, in my view, is not simply to be thought ill of, looked down on, or devalued in others' conscious attitudes or mental beliefs. It is rather to be denied the status of a *full partner* in social interaction and prevented from *participating as a peer* in social life—not as a consequence of a distributive inequity (such as failing to receive one's fair share of resources or "primary goods") but rather as a consequence of *institutionalized* patterns of interpretation and evaluation that constitute one as comparatively unworthy of respect or esteem. When such patterns of disrespect and disesteem are institutionalized—for example, in law, social welfare, medicine, and/or popular culture—they impede parity

---

2   Nancy Fraser, *Justice Interruptus: Critical Reflections on the "Postsocialist" Condition*, New York: Routledge 1997.

3   See especially the book's Introduction and Chapter 1, "From Redistribution to Recognition? Dilemmas of Justice in a 'Postsocialist' Age."

of participation, just as surely as do distributive inequities. The result-ing harm is in either case all too real.

In my conception, therefore, misrecognition is an institutionalized social relation, not a psychological state. In essence a status injury, it is analytically distinct from, and conceptually irreducible to, the injus-tice of maldistribution, although it *may* be accompanied by the latter. Whether misrecognition converts into maldistribution, and vice versa, depends on the nature of the social formation in question. In precap-italist, pre-state societies, for example, where status simply *is* the overarching principle of distribution, and where the status order and the class hierarchy are therefore fused, misrecognition simply entails maldistribution. In capitalist societies, in contrast, where the institu-tionalization of specialized economic relations permits the relative uncoupling of economic distribution from structures of prestige, and where status and class can therefore diverge, misrecognition and maldistribution are not fully mutually convertible. Whether and to what extent they coincide today is a question I shall consider below.

Normatively, however, the key point is this: misrecognition consti-tutes a fundamental injustice, whether accompanied by maldistribution or not. And the point has political consequences. It is not necessary to show that a given instance of misrecognition brings with it maldis-tribution in order to certify the claim to redress it as a genuine claim for social justice. The point holds for heterosexist misrecognition, which involves the institutionalization of sexual norms and interpre-tations that deny participatory parity to gays and lesbians. Opponents of heterosexism need not labor to translate claims of sexual status injury into claims of class deprivation in order to vindicate the former. Nor need they show that their struggles threaten capitalism in order to prove they are just.

In my account, then, injustices of misrecognition are as serious as distributive injustices. And they cannot be reduced to the latter. Thus, far from claiming that cultural harms are superstructural reflections of economic harms, I have proposed an analysis in which the two sorts of harms are co-fundamental and conceptually irreducible. From my perspective, therefore, it makes no sense to say that heterosexist misrecognition is "merely" cultural. That locution presupposes the very sort of base-superstructure model, the very sort of economistic monism, that my framework aims to displace.

Butler, in sum, has mistaken what is actually a quasi-Weberian dual-ism of status and class for an orthodox Marxian economistic monism. Erroneously assuming that to distinguish redistribution from recogni-tion is necessarily to devalue recognition, she treats my normative distinction as a "tactic" aimed at derogating gay and lesbian struggles and imposing a new "orthodoxy." Contra Butler, I mean to defend the distinction while disclaiming the tactic. To get at the real issues between us, therefore, requires decoupling two questions that are too closely identified in her discussion. The first is a political question concerning the depth and seriousness of heterosexist oppression; on this, I have argued, we do not disagree. The second is a theoretical question concerning the conceptual status of what Butler misleadingly calls "the material/cultural distinction" as it relates to the analysis of heterosexism and the nature of capitalist society; here lie our real disagreements.[4]

Let me begin unpacking these real disagreements by schematically recapping Butler's critique. As I read it, she offers three principal theoretical arguments against my redistribution/recognition framework. First, she contends that because gays and lesbians suffer material, economic harms, their oppression is not properly categorized as misrecognition. Second, invoking the important 1970s socialist-feminist insight that the family is part of the mode of production, she contends that the heteronormative regulation of sexuality is "central to the functioning of the political economy" and that contemporary

---

4  In what follows I shall leave aside a problem with Butler's rendition of the argument of *Justice Interruptus*. She presents me as arguing categorically that heterosexism is a pure injustice of misrecognition, unalloyed by maldistribution. In fact, I discussed the issue hypothetically in the mode of a thought experiment. Aiming to disclose the distinctive logics of redistribution claims and recognition claims respectively, I invited readers to imagine a conceptual spectrum of oppressed collectivities, ranging from ideal-typical victims of pure maldistribution at one end, to ideal-typical victims of pure misrecognition at the other end, with hybrid or "bivalent" cases in the middle. In this hypothetical spirit, I sketched a conception of a "despised sexuality" as a concrete approximation of the ideal type at the misrecognition end of the spectrum, while explicitly noting that this conception of sexuality was controversial, and leaving open the question of whether and how closely it corresponded to the actually existing homosexual collectivities struggling for justice in the real world. Thus, my "misrecognition" analysis of heterosexism in *Justice Interruptus* is far more qualified than Butler lets on. Recently, moreover, I have argued that for practical purposes, virtually all real-world oppressed collectivities are "bivalent." Virtually all, that is, have both an economic and a status component; virtually all, therefore, suffer both maldistribution and misrecognition *in forms where neither of those injustices is a mere indirect effect of the other but where each has some independent weight*. Nevertheless, not all are bivalent in the same way, nor to the same degree. Some axes of oppression tilt more heavily toward the distribution end of the spectrum, others incline more to the recognition end, while still others cluster closer to the center. On this account, heterosexism, while consisting in part in maldistribution, consists primarily in injustices of misrecognition and is rooted predominantly in a status order that constructs homosexuality as devalued and that institutes it as a despised sexuality. For the original argument, see my "From Redistribution to Recognition?" For the subsequent refinement, see my chapters in Nancy Fraser and Axel Honneth, *Redistribution or Recognition? A Political-Philosophical Exchange*, London: Verso Books, 2003, especially Chapter 1, "Social Justice in the Age of Identity Politics: Redistribution, Recognition, and Participation," 7–109.

struggles against that regulation "threaten the workability" of the capitalist system. Third, after revisiting anthropological accounts of precapitalist exchange, she contends that the distinction between the material and the cultural is "unstable," a "theoretical anachronism" to be eschewed in social theory. None of these arguments is persuasive, in my view, largely because none affords an adequately differentiated and historically situated view of modern capitalist society. Let me consider the three arguments in turn.

Butler's first argument appeals to some indisputable facts about the harms currently suffered by gays and lesbians. Far from being "merely symbolic," these harms include serious economic disadvantages with undeniable material effects. In the United States today, for example, gays and lesbians can be summarily dismissed from civilian employment and military service, are denied a broad range of family-based social-welfare benefits, are disproportionately burdened with medical costs, and are disadvantaged in tax and inheritance law. Equally material are the effects of the fact that homosexuals lack the full range of constitutional rights and protections enjoyed by heterosexuals. In many jurisdictions, they can be prosecuted for consensual sex; and in many more, they can be assaulted with impunity. It follows, claims Butler, from the economic and material character of these liabilities, that the "misrecognition" analysis of heterosexism is mistaken.

Butler's premise is true, of course, but her conclusion does not follow. She assumes that injustices of misrecognition must be immaterial and non-economic. Leaving aside for the moment her conflation of the material with the economic, the assumption is on both counts mistaken.

Consider first the issue of materiality. In my conception, injustices of misrecognition are just as material as injustices of maldistribution. To be sure, the first are rooted in social patterns of interpretation, evaluation, and communication, hence, if you like, in the symbolic order. But this does not mean they are "merely" symbolic. On the contrary, the norms, significations, and constructions of personhood that impede women, racialized peoples, and/or gays and lesbians from parity of participation in social life are materially instantiated—in institutions and social practices, in social action and embodied habitus, and in ideological state apparatuses. Far from occupying some wispy, ethereal realm, they are material in their existence and effects.

From my perspective, therefore, the material harms cited by Butler constitute paradigmatic cases of misrecognition. They reflect the institutionalization of heterosexist meanings, norms, and constructions of personhood in such arenas as constitutional law, medicine, immigration and naturalization policy, federal and state tax codes, social welfare and employment policy, equal opportunity legislation, and the like. What is

institutionalized, moreover, as Butler herself notes, are cultural constructions of entitlement and personhood that produce homosexual subjects as
abjects. This, to repeat, is the essence of misrecognition: the *material*
construction, through the institutionalization of cultural norms, of a class
of devalued persons who are impeded from participatory parity.

If the harms arising from misrecognition can thus be material, can
they also be economic? It is true, as Butler notes, and as I myself expressly
noted in *Justice Interruptus,* that some forms of heterosexism inflict
economic harms on gays and lesbians. The question is how to interpret
them.[5] One possibility is to see these economic harms as direct expressions of the economic structure of society, much like Marxists see the
exploitation of workers. On this interpretation, which Butler appears to
endorse, the economic liabilities of homosexuals would be hard-wired
in the relations of production. To remedy them would require transforming those relations. Another possibility, favored by me, is to see the
economic harms of heterosexism as indirect (mal)distributive consequences of the more fundamental injustice of misrecognition. On this
interpretation, which I defended in *Justice Interruptus,* the roots of
economic heterosexism would be the "relations of recognition": an
institutionalized pattern of interpretation and valuation that constructs
heterosexuality as normative and homosexuality as deviant, thereby
denying participatory parity to gays and lesbians. Change the relations
of recognition and the maldistribution would disappear.

This conflict of interpretations raises deep and difficult questions. Is
it necessary to transform the economic structure of contemporary
capitalism in order to redress the economic liabilities of homosexuals?
What precisely is meant by the "economic structure"? Should one
conceive the heteronormative regulation of sexuality as belonging
directly to the capitalist economy? Or is it better seen as belonging to
a status order that is differentiated from, and complexly related to, the
economic structure? More generally, do the relations of recognition
in late-capitalist society coincide with economic relations? Or do the
institutional differentiations of modern capitalism introduce gaps
between status and class?

To pursue these questions, let us examine Butler's second argument. Here she invokes the 1970s socialist-feminist insight that the
family is part of the mode of production in order to support the thesis
that the heteronormative regulation of sexuality is "central to the
functioning of the political economy." It follows, claims Butler, that

---

5 In general, one should distinguish several questions here: 1) the nature of
the injustices in question; 2) their ultimate causes; 3) the contemporary causal
mechanisms that reproduce them; and 4) their remedies. I am grateful to Erik Olin
Wright for this point (private communication, 1997).

contemporary struggles against that regulation "threaten the worka-bility" of the capitalist system.

Actually, two different variants of the argument are discernible here, one definitional, the other functionalist. According to the first variant, (hetero)sexual regulation belongs by definition to the economic structure. The economic structure simply *is* the entire set of social mechanisms and institutions that (re)produce persons and goods. By definition, then, the family is part of this structure, as the primary site for the reproduction of persons. So, by extension, is the gender order, which standardizes the family's "products" to conform to one of two, and only two, mutually exclusive, seemingly natural kinds of persons: men and women. The gender order, in turn, is held to presuppose a mode of sexual regulation that produces and natural-izes heterosexuality, while simultaneously producing homosexuality as abject. The conclusion drawn by Butler is that the heteronormative regulation of sexuality is a part of the economic structure by defini-tion, *despite the fact that it structures neither the social division of labor nor the mode of exploitation of labor power in capitalist society.*

This definitional argument has an air of Olympian indifference to history. As a result, it risks accomplishing too much. Stipulating that the mode of sexual regulation belongs to the economic structure by definition—even in the absence of any impact on the division of labor or the mode of exploitation—threatens to dehistoricize the idea of the economic structure and drain it of conceptual force. What gets lost is the specificity of capitalist society as a distinctive and highly peculiar form of social organization. This organization creates an order of specialized economic relations that are relatively decoupled from relations of kinship and political authority. Thus, in capitalist society, the link between the mode of sexual regulation, on the one hand, and an order of specialized economic relations whose raison d'être is the accumulation of surplus value, on the other, is attenuated. It is far more attenuated, certainly, than in precapitalist, pre-state soci-eties, where economic relations are largely adumbrated through the mechanisms of kinship and directly imbricated with sexuality. In the late-capitalist society of the twentieth century, moreover, the links between sexuality and surplus value accumulation have been still further attenuated by the rise of what Eli Zaretsky has called "personal life": a space of intimate relations, including sexuality, friendship, and love, that can no longer be identified with the family and that are lived as disconnected from the imperatives of production and repro-duction.[6] In general, then, contemporary capitalist society contains

---

6    Eli Zaretsky, *Capitalism, the Family, and Personal Life*, New York: Harper & Row, 1976.

"gaps": between the economic order and the kinship order; between the family and personal life; between the status order and the class hierarchy. In this sort of highly differentiated society, it does not make sense to me to conceive the mode of sexual regulation as simply a part of the economic structure. Nor to conceive queer demands for the recognition of difference as misplaced demands for redistribution.

In another sense, moreover, the definitional argument accomplishes very little. Butler wants to conclude that struggles over sexuality are economic, but that conclusion has been rendered tautologous. If sexual struggles are economic by definition, then they are not economic in the same sense as are struggles over the rate of exploitation. Simply calling both sorts of struggles "economic" risks collapsing the differences, creating the misleading impression that they will synergize automatically, and blunting our capacity to pose, and answer, hard but pressing political questions as to how they can be *made* to synergize when in fact they diverge or conflict.[7]

This brings me to the functionalist variant of Butler's second argument. Here the claim is that the heteronormative regulation of sexuality is economic, not by definition, but because it is functional to the expansion of surplus value. Capitalism, in other words, "needs" or benefits from compulsory heterosexuality. It follows, according to Butler, that gay and lesbian struggles against heterosexism threaten the "workability" of the capitalist system.

Like all functionalist arguments, this one stands or falls with the empirical relations of cause and effect. Empirically, however, it is highly implausible that gay and lesbian struggles threaten capitalism in its actually existing historical form. That might be the case if homosexuals were constructed as an inferior but useful class of menial laborers whose exploitation was central to the workings of the economy, as African Americans, for example, have been. Then one could say that capital's interests are served by keeping them "in their place." In fact, however, homosexuals are more often constructed as a group whose very existence is an abomination, much like the Nazi construction of Jews; they should have no "place" in society at all. No wonder, then, that the principal opponents of gay and lesbian rights today are not multinational corporations, but religious and

---

7   Thus, the definitional argument simply pushes the need for distinctions to another level. Of course, one *might* say that a political claim can be economic in either of two ways: first, by contesting the production and distribution of economic value, including surplus value; and second, by contesting the production and reproduction of norms, significations, and constructions of personhood, including those concerning sexuality. But I fail to see how this improves on my simpler strategy of restricting the term "economic" to its capitalist meaning and distinguishing claims for recognition from claims for redistribution.

cultural conservatives, whose obsession is status, not profits. In fact, some multinationals, notably American Airlines, Apple Computers, and Disney, have elicited the wrath of such conservatives by instituting gay-friendly policies, such as domestic partnership benefits. They apparently see advantages in accommodating gays, provided they are not subject to boycotts or are big enough to withstand them if they are.

Empirically, therefore, contemporary capitalism seems not to require heterosexism. With its gaps between the economic order and the kinship order, and between the family and personal life, capitalist society now permits significant numbers of individuals to live through wage labor outside of heterosexual families. It could permit many more to do so—provided the relations of recognition were changed. Thus we can now answer a question posed earlier: the economic disabilities of homosexuals are better understood as effects of heterosexism in the relations of recognition than as hard-wired in the structure of capitalism. The good news is that we do not need to overthrow capitalism in order to remedy those disabilities—although we may well need to overthrow it for other reasons. The bad news is that we need to transform the existing status order and restructure the relations of recognition.

With her functionalist argument, Butler has resurrected what is in my view one of the worst aspects of 1970s Marxism and socialist-feminism: the over-totalized view of capitalist society as a monolithic "system" of interlocking structures of oppression that seamlessly reinforce one another. This view misses the "gaps." It has been resoundingly and persuasively critiqued from many directions, including the post-structuralist paradigm that Butler endorses and the Weberian one adapted by me. Functionalist systems theory is one strand of 1970s thought that is better left forgotten.

The question of what should replace functionalism bears on Butler's third argument against my redistribution/recognition framework. This argument is deconstructive. Far from insisting that the roots of heterosexism are economic as opposed to "merely" cultural, its point is to deconstruct the "material/cultural distinction." That distinction, claims Butler, is "unstable." Important currents of neo-Marxian thought, ranging from Raymond Williams to Althusser, have irretrievably thrown it into "crisis." The knock-down argument comes from the anthropologists, however, notably Mauss and Lévi-Strauss. Their respective accounts of "the gift" and "the exchange of women" reveal that "primitive" processes of exchange cannot be assigned to one side or the other of the material/cultural divide. Being both at once, such processes "destabilize" the very distinction. Thus, in invoking the material/cultural distinction today, Butler contends, I have lapsed into a "theoretical anachronism."

This argument is unconvincing for several reasons, the first of which is that it conflates "the economic" with "the material." Butler assumes that my normative distinction between redistribution and recognition rests on an ontological distinction between the material and the cultural. She therefore assumes that to deconstruct the latter distinction is to pull the rug out from under the former. In fact, the assumption does not hold. As I noted earlier, injustices of misrecognition are from my perspective just as material as injustices of maldistribution. Thus, my normative distinction rests on no ground of ontological difference. What it *does* correlate with, in capitalist societies, is a distinction between the economic and the cultural. This, however, is not an ontological distinction but a social-theoretical distinction. The economic/cultural distinction, not the material/cultural distinction, is the real bone of contention between Butler and me, the distinction whose status is at issue.

What, then, is the conceptual status of the economic/cultural distinction? The anthropological arguments do shed light on this matter, in my view, but not in a way that supports Butler's position. As I read them, both Mauss and Lévi-Strauss analyzed processes of exchange in pre-state, precapitalist societies, where the master idiom of social relations was kinship. In their accounts, kinship organized not only marriage and sexual relations, but also the labor process and the distribution of goods; relations of authority, reciprocity, and obligation; and symbolic hierarchies of status and prestige. Neither distinctively economic relations nor distinctively cultural relations existed; hence the economic/cultural distinction was presumably not available to the members of those societies. It does not follow, however, that the distinction is senseless or useless. On the contrary, it can be meaningfully and usefully applied to capitalist societies, which unlike so-called "primitive" societies *do* contain the social-structural differentiations in question.[8] Moreover, it can also be applied *by us* to societies that lack these differentiations in order to indicate how they differ from ours. One can say, for example, as I just did, that in such societies a single order of social relations handles both economic integration and cultural integration, matters that are relatively decoupled in capitalist

---

8    In this brief essay I cannot take up the important but difficult question of how the economic/cultural distinction is best applied to the critical theory of contemporary capitalist society. I discuss this matter at length, however, in "Social Justice in the Age of Identity Politics." Rejecting the view of economy and culture as separate spheres, I propose a critical approach that reveals the hidden connections between them. The point, in other words, is to use the distinction against the grain, making visible, and subject to critique, both the cultural subtexts of apparently economic processes and the economic subtexts of apparently cultural processes. Such a *perspectival dualism*, as I call it, is only possible, of course, once we have the economic/cultural distinction.

society. This, moreover, is precisely the spirit in which I understand Mauss and Lévi-Strauss. Whatever their intentions regarding "the economic" and "the cultural," we gain less from reading them as having "destabilized" the distinction than from reading them as having historicized it. The point, in other words, is to historicize a distinction central to modern capitalism—and with it modern capitalism itself—by situating both in the larger anthropological context and thereby revealing their historical specificity.

Thus, Butler's "destabilization" argument goes astray at two crucial points. First, it illegitimately generalizes to capitalist societies a feature specific to precapitalist societies, namely, the absence of a social-structural economic/cultural differentiation. Second, it erroneously assumes that to historicize a distinction is to render it nugatory and useless in social theory. In fact, historicization does the contrary. Far from rendering distinctions unstable, it renders their usage more precise.

From my perspective, then, historicization represents a better approach to social theory than destabilization or deconstruction.[9] It allows us to appreciate the social-structurally differentiated and historically specific character of contemporary capitalist society. In so doing, it also enables us to locate the anti-functionalist moment, the possibilities for countersystemic "agency" and social change. These appear not in an abstract, transhistorical property of language, such as "resignification" or "performativity," but rather in the actual contradictory character of specific social relations. With a historically specific, differentiated view of contemporary capitalist society, we can locate the gaps, the non-isomorphism of status and class, the multiple contradictory interpellations of social subjects, and the many complex *moral imperatives* that motivate struggles for social justice.

Seen from this perspective, moreover, the current political conjuncture is not adequately grasped by a diagnosis centered on the putative resurgence of orthodox Marxism. It is better grasped, rather, by one that forthrightly acknowledges, and seeks to overcome, splits in the Left between socialist/social-democratic currents oriented to the politics of redistribution, on the one hand, and multiculturalist currents oriented to the politics of recognition, on the other. The

---

9 At another level, however, I mean to endorse deconstruction. It represents an approach to the politics of recognition that is often superior, in my view, to standard identity politics. A deconstructive politics of recognition is transformative, not affirmative, of existing group identities and differentiations. In this respect, it has affinities with socialism, which I understand as a transformative, as opposed to affirmative, approach to the politics of redistribution. (For this argument, see my "From Redistribution to Recognition?") Nevertheless, I do not find deconstruction useful at the level Butler invokes it here, namely, the level of social theory.

indispensable starting point for such an analysis must be a principled acknowledgment that *both sides have legitimate claims*, which must somehow be harmonized programmatically and made to synergize politically. Social justice today, in sum, requires *both* redistribution *and* recognition; neither alone will suffice.

On this last point, I feel certain, Butler and I agree. Despite her reluctance to invoke the language of social justice, and despite our theoretical disagreements, both of us are committed to reclaiming the best elements of socialist politics and to integrating them with the best elements of the politics of the "new social movements." Likewise, we are both committed to retrieving the genuinely valuable strands of the neo-Marxian critique of capitalism and to integrating them with the most insightful strands of post-Marxian critical theorizing. It is the merit of Butler's essay, and I would hope of my own work as well, to have put this project on the agenda once again.

# PART III

Feminism Resurgent?
Confronting Capitalist Crisis in the Neoliberal Era

# 8

# Reframing Justice in a Globalizing World*

Globalization is changing the way we argue about justice. Not so long ago, in the heyday of social democracy, disputes about justice presumed what I shall call a "Keynesian-Westphalian frame." Typically played out within modern territorial states, arguments about justice were assumed to concern relations among fellow citizens, to be subject to debate within national publics, and to contemplate redress by national states. This was true for each of two major families of justice claims— claims for socioeconomic redistribution and claims for legal or cultural recognition. At a time when the Bretton Woods system facilitated Keynesian economic steering at the national level, claims for redistribution usually focused on economic inequities within territorial states. Appealing to national public opinion for a fair share of the national pie, claimants sought intervention by national states in national economies. Likewise, in an era still gripped by a Westphalian political imaginary, which sharply distinguished "domestic" from "international" space, claims for recognition generally concerned internal status hierarchies. Appealing to the national conscience for an end to nationally institutionalized disrespect, claimants pressed national governments to outlaw discrimination and accommodate differences among citizens. In both cases, the Keynesian-Westphalian frame was taken for granted. Whether the matter concerned redistribution or recognition, class differentials or status hierarchies, it went

* This chapter is a revised and expanded version of my second Spinoza Lecture, delivered at the University of Amsterdam, December 2, 2004. The lecture was drafted during my tenure there as Spinoza Professor in spring 2004 and revised during my subsequent fellowship year at the Wissenschaftskolleg zu Berlin, 2004–05. My warmest thanks to both institutions for their generous support of this work. Special thanks to Yolande Jansen and Hilla Dayan for selfless and good-natured assistance in a time of great need and to James Bohman for expert bibliographical advice. Thanks also to Amy Allen, Seyla Benhabib, Bert van den Brink, Alessandro Ferrara, Rainer Forst, Stefan Gosepath, John Judis, Ted Koditschek, Maria Pia Lara, David Peritz, Ann Laura Stoler, and Eli Zaretsky for thoughtful comments on earlier drafts. Thanks, finally, to Kristin Gissberg and Keith Haysom for expert research assistance.

without saying that the unit within which justice applied was the modern territorial state.[1]

To be sure, there were always exceptions. Occasionally, famines and genocides galvanized public opinion across borders. And some cosmopolitans and anti-imperialists sought to promulgate globalist views.[2] But these were exceptions that proved the rule. Relegated to the sphere of "the international," they were subsumed within a problematic that was focused primarily on matters of security, as opposed to justice. The effect was to reinforce, rather than to challenge, the Keynesian-Westphalian frame. That framing of disputes about justice generally prevailed by default from the end of World War II through the 1970s.

Although it went unnoticed at the time, the Keynesian-Westphalian frame gave a distinctive shape to arguments about social justice. Taking for granted the modern territorial state as the appropriate unit, and its citizens as the pertinent subjects, such arguments turned on *what* precisely those citizens owed one another. In the eyes of some, it sufficed that citizens be formally equal before the law; for others, equality of opportunity was also required; for still others, justice demanded that all citizens gain access to the resources and respect they needed in order to be able to participate on a par with others, as full members of the political community. The argument focused, in other words, on *what* should count as a just ordering of social relations within a society. Engrossed in disputing the "what" of

---

1    The phrase "Keynesian-Westphalian frame" is meant to signal the national-territorial underpinnings of justice disputes in the heyday of the postwar democratic welfare state, roughly 1945 through the 1970s. In this period, struggles over distribution in North America and Western Europe were premised on the assumption of state steering of national economies. And national Keynesianism, in turn, was premised on the assumption of an international state system that recognized territorial state sovereignty over domestic affairs, which included responsibility for the citizenry's welfare. Analogous assumptions also governed disputes about recognition in this period. The term "Westphalian" refers to the Treaty of 1648, which established some key features of the international state system in question. However, I am concerned neither with the actual achievements of the Treaty nor with the centuries-long process by which the system it inaugurated evolved. Rather, I invoke "Westphalia" as a political imaginary that mapped the world as a system of mutually recognizing sovereign territorial states. My claim is that this imaginary undergirded the postwar framing of debates about justice in the First World. For the distinction between Westphalia as "event," as "idea/ideal," as "process of evolution," and as "normative scoresheet," see Richard Falk, "Revisiting Westphalia, discovering post-Westphalia," *Journal of Ethics* 6:4, 2002, 311–52.

2    It might be assumed that, from the perspective of the Third World, Westphalian premises would have appeared patently counterfactual. Yet it is worth recalling that the great majority of anti-imperialists sought to achieve independent Westphalian states of their own. In contrast, only a small minority consistently championed justice within a global frame—for reasons that are entirely understandable.

justice, the contestants apparently felt no need to dispute the "who." With the Keynesian-Westphalian frame securely in place, it went without saying that the "who" was the national citizenry.

Today, however, the Keynesian-Westphalian frame is losing its aura of self-evidence. Thanks to heightened awareness of globalization, many observe that the social processes shaping their lives routinely overflow territorial borders. They note, for example, that decisions taken in one territorial state often impact the lives of those outside it, as do the actions of transnational corporations, international currency speculators, and large institutional investors. Many also note the growing salience of supranational and international organizations, both governmental and nongovernmental, and of transnational public opinion, which flows with supreme disregard for borders through global mass media and cybertechnology. The result is a new sense of vulnerability to transnational forces. Faced with global warming, the spread of AIDS, international terrorism, and superpower unilateralism, many believe that their chances for living good lives depend at least as much on processes that trespass the borders of territorial states as on those contained within them.

Under these conditions, the Keynesian-Westphalian frame no longer goes without saying. For many, it has ceased to be axiomatic that the modern territorial state is the appropriate unit for thinking about issues of justice. Nor can it pass by default that the citizens of such states are the pertinent subjects. The effect is to destabilize the previous structure of political claims-making—and therefore to change the way we argue about social justice.

This is true for both major families of justice claims. In today's world, claims for redistribution increasingly eschew the assumption of national economies. Faced with transnationalized production, the outsourcing of jobs, and the associated pressures of the "race to the bottom," once nationally focused labor unions look increasingly for allies abroad. Inspired by the Zapatistas, meanwhile, impoverished peasants and indigenous peoples link their struggles against despotic local and national authorities to critiques of transnational corporate predation and global neoliberalism. Finally, WTO protestors, Occupy movements, and *indignados* directly target the new governance structures of the global economy, which have vastly strengthened the ability of large corporations and investors to escape the regulatory and taxation powers of territorial states.

In the same way, movements struggling for recognition increasingly look beyond the territorial state. Under the slogan "women's rights are human rights," for example, feminists throughout the world are linking struggles against local patriarchal practices to campaigns to reform international law. Meanwhile, religious and ethnic minorities, who face discrimination within territorial states, are reconstituting themselves as diasporas and building transnational publics from which to mobilize international opinion. Finally, transnational coalitions of human-rights activists have worked to build new cosmopolitan institutions, such as the International Criminal Court, which can punish state violations of human dignity.

In such cases, disputes about justice are exploding the Keynesian-Westphalian frame. No longer addressed exclusively to national states or debated exclusively by national publics, claimants no longer focus solely on relations among fellow citizens. Thus, the grammar of argument has altered. Whether the issue is distribution or recognition, disputes that used to focus exclusively on the question of *what* is owed as a matter of justice to community members now turn quickly into disputes about *who* should count as a member and *which* is the relevant community. Not just the "what" but also the "who" is up for grabs.

Today, in other words, arguments about justice assume a double guise. On the one hand, they concern first-order questions of substance, just as before: How much economic inequality does justice permit, how much redistribution is required, and according to which principle of distributive justice? What constitutes equal respect, which kinds of differences merit public recognition, and by which means? But above and beyond such first-order questions, arguments about justice today also concern second-order, meta-level questions: What is the proper frame within which to consider first-order questions of justice? Who are the relevant subjects entitled to a just distribution or reciprocal recognition in the given case? Thus, it is not only the substance of justice, but also the frame, which is in dispute.[3]

The result is a major challenge to our theories of social justice. Preoccupied largely with first-order issues of distribution and/or recognition, these theories have so far failed to develop conceptual resources for reflecting on the meta-issue of the frame. As things stand, therefore, it is by no means clear that they are capable of addressing the double character of problems of justice in a globalizing age.[4]

In this essay, I shall propose a strategy for thinking about the problem of the frame. I shall argue, first, that in order to deal satisfactorily with this problem, the theory of justice must become three-dimensional, incorpo-

---

3   This situation is by no means unprecedented. Even the most cursory reflection discloses historical parallels—for example, the period leading up to the Treaty of Westphalia and the period following World War I. In these moments, too, not just the substance of justice but also the frame was up for grabs.

4   On the elision of the problem of the frame in mainstream theories of justice, see Nancy Fraser, "Democratic Justice in a Globalizing Age: Thematizing the Problem of the Frame," in *Varieties of World-Making: Beyond Globalization*, eds. Nathalie Karagiannis and Peter Wagner, Liverpool: Liverpool University Press, 2006, 193–215.

rating the political dimension of *representation*, alongside the economic dimension of distribution and the cultural dimension of recognition. I shall also argue, second, that the political dimension of representation should itself be understood as encompassing three levels. The combined effect of these two arguments will be to make visible a third question, beyond those of the "what" and the "who," which I shall call the question of the "how." That question, in turn, inaugurates a paradigm shift: what the Keynesian-Westphalian frame casts as the theory of social justice must now become a theory of *post-Westphalian democratic justice*.

## 1. FOR A THREE-DIMENSIONAL THEORY OF JUSTICE: ON THE SPECIFICITY OF THE POLITICAL

Let me begin by explaining what I mean by justice in general and by its political dimension in particular. In my view, the most general meaning of justice is parity of participation. According to this radical-democratic interpretation of the principle of equal moral worth, justice requires social arrangements that permit all to participate as peers in social life. Overcoming injustice means dismantling institutionalized obstacles that prevent some people from participating on a par with others, as full partners in social interaction. Previously, I have analyzed two distinct kinds of obstacles to participatory parity, which correspond to two distinct species of injustice.[5] On the one hand, people can be impeded from full participation by economic structures that deny them the resources they need in order to interact with others as peers; in that case they suffer from distributive injustice or maldistribution. On the other hand, people can also be prevented from interacting on terms of parity by institutionalized hierarchies of cultural value that deny them the requisite standing; in that case they suffer from status inequality or misrecognition.[6] In the first case, the problem is the class structure of society, which corresponds to the economic dimension of justice. In the second case, the problem is the status order, which corresponds to the cultural dimension.[7] In

---

5   See Chapters 6 and 7 of this volume, "Feminist Politics in the Age of Recognition" and "Heterosexism, Misrecognition, and Capitalism." Also, Nancy Fraser, "Social Justice in the Age of Identity Politics: Redistribution, Recognition, and Participation," in Nancy Fraser and Axel Honneth, *Redistribution or Recognition? A Political-Philosophical Exchange*, trans. J. Golb, J. Ingram, and C. Wilke, London: Verso Books, 2003.

6   This *status model* of recognition represents an alternative to the standard identity model. For a critique of the latter and a defense of the former, see Chapter 6 of this volume, "Feminist Politics in the Age of Recognition." See also Nancy Fraser, "Rethinking Recognition: Overcoming Displacement and Reification in Cultural Politics," *New Left Review* 3, 2000, 107–20.

7   Here I assume quasi-Weberian conceptions of class and status. See Max Weber, "Class, Status, Party," in *From Max Weber: Essays in Sociology*, eds. Hans H. Gerth and C. Wright Mills, Oxford: Oxford University Press, 1958.

modern capitalist societies, the class structure and the status order do not neatly mirror each other, although they interact causally. Rather, each has some autonomy vis-à-vis the other. As a result, misrecognition cannot be reduced to a secondary effect of maldistribution, as some economistic theories of distributive justice appear to suppose. Nor, conversely, can maldistribution be reduced to an epiphenomenal expression of misrecognition, as some culturalist theories of recognition tend to assume. Thus, neither recognition theory alone nor distribution theory alone can provide an adequate understanding of justice for capitalist society. Only a two-dimensional theory, encompassing both distribution and recognition, can supply the necessary levels of social-theoretical complexity and moral-philosophical insight.[8]

That, at least, is the view of justice I have defended in the past. And this two-dimensional understanding of justice still seems right to me as far as it goes. But I now believe that it does not go far enough. Distribution and recognition could appear to constitute the sole dimensions of justice only insofar as the Keynesian-Westphalian frame was taken for granted. Once the question of the frame becomes subject to contestation, however, the effect is to make visible a third dimension of justice, which was neglected in my previous work—as well as in the work of many other philosophers.[9]

---

8    For the full argument, see Fraser, "Social Justice in the Age of Identity Politics."

9    The neglect of the political is especially glaring in the case of theorists of justice who subscribe to liberal or communitarian philosophical premises. In contrast, deliberative democrats, agonistic democrats, and republicans have sought to theorize the political. But most of these theorists have had relatively little to say about the relation between democracy and justice; and none has conceptualized the political as one of three dimensions of justice. Deliberative democratic accounts of the political include Jürgen Habermas, *Between Facts and Norms: Contributions to a Discourse Theory of Law and Democracy*, Cambridge, MA: MIT Press, 1996; and Amy Gutmann and Dennis Thompson, *Democracy and Disagreement*, Cambridge: Belknap Press, 1996. Agonistic accounts of the political include William Connolly, *Identity/Difference: Negotiations of Political Paradox*, Ithaca: Cornell University Press, 1991; Bonnie Honig, *Political Theory and the Displacement of Politics*, Ithaca: Cornell University Press, 1993; Chantal Mouffe, *The Return of the Political*, London: Verso Books, 1993; and James Tully, *Strange Multiplicity: Constitutionalism in an Age of Diversity*, Cambridge: Cambridge University Press, 1995. Republican accounts of the political include Quentin Skinner, "The Republican Ideal of Political Liberty," in *Machiavelli and Republicanism*, eds. Gisela Bock, Quentin Skinner, and Maurizio Viroli, Cambridge: Cambridge University Press, 1990; and Philip Pettit, "Freedom as Antipower," *Ethics* 106:3, 1996, 576–604. In contrast to these thinkers, a handful of others have linked the political directly to justice, although not in the way I do here. See, for example, Michael Walzer, *Spheres of Justice*, New York: Basic Books, 1983; Iris Marion Young, *Justice and the Politics of Difference*, Princeton, NJ: Princeton University Press, 1990; Amartya Sen, *Development as Freedom*, New York: Anchor Books, 1999; and Seyla Benhabib, *The Rights of Others: Aliens, Residents, and Citizens*, Cambridge: Cambridge University Press, 2004.

The third dimension of justice is *the political*. Of course, distribution and recognition are themselves political in the sense of being contested and power-laden; and they have usually been seen as requiring adjudication by the state. But I mean political in a more specific, constitutive sense, which concerns the constitution of the state's jurisdiction and the decision rules by which it structures contestation. The political in this sense furnishes the stage on which struggles over distribution and recognition are played out. Establishing criteria of social belonging, and thus determining who counts as a member, the political dimension of justice specifies the reach of those other dimensions: it tells us who is included in, and who excluded from, the circle of those entitled to a just distribution and reciprocal recognition. Establishing decision rules, the political dimension likewise sets the procedures for staging and resolving contests in both the economic and the cultural dimensions: it tells us not only who can make claims for redistribution and recognition, but also how such claims are to be mooted and adjudicated.

Centered on issues of membership and procedure, the political dimension of justice is concerned chiefly with *representation*. At one level, which pertains to the boundary-setting aspect of the political, representation is a matter of social belonging; what is at issue here is inclusion in, or exclusion from, the community of those entitled to make justice claims on one another. At another level, which pertains to the decision-rule aspect, representation concerns the procedures that structure public processes of contestation. At issue here are the terms on which those included in the political community air their claims and adjudicate their disputes.[10] At both levels, the question can arise as to whether the relations of representation are just. One can ask: Do the boundaries of the political community wrongly exclude some who are actually entitled to representation? Do the community's decision rules accord equal voice in public deliberations and fair representation in public decision-making to all members? Such issues of representation are specifically political. Conceptually distinct from both economic and cultural questions, they cannot be reduced to the latter, although, as we shall see, they are inextricably interwoven with them.

To say that the political is a conceptually distinct dimension of justice, not reducible to the economic or the cultural, is also to say that it can give rise to a conceptually distinct species of injustice. Given the view

---

10    Classic works on representation have dealt largely with what I am calling the decision-rule aspect, while ignoring the membership aspect. See, for example, Hannah Fenichel Pitkin, *The Concept of Representation*, Berkeley: University of California Press, 1967; and Bernard Manin, *The Principles of Representative Government*, Cambridge: Cambridge University Press, 1997. Works that do treat the membership aspect include Walzer, *Spheres of Justice*, and Benhabib, *The Rights of Others*. However, both Walzer and Benhabib arrive at conclusions that differ from the ones I draw here.

of justice as participatory parity, this means that there can be distinctively political obstacles to parity, not reducible to maldistribution or misrecognition, although (again) interwoven with them. Such obstacles arise from the political constitution of society, as opposed to the class structure or status order. Grounded in a specifically political mode of social ordering, they can only be adequately grasped through a theory that conceptualizes representation, along with distribution and recognition, as one of three fundamental dimensions of justice.

If representation is the defining issue of the political, then the characteristic political injustice is *misrepresentation*. Misrepresentation occurs when political boundaries and/or decision rules function to wrongly deny some people the possibility of participating on a par with others in social interaction—including, but not only, in political arenas. Far from being reducible to maldistribution or misrecognition, misrepresentation can occur even in the absence of the latter injustices, although it is usually intertwined with them.

We can distinguish at least two different levels of misrepresentation. Insofar as political decision rules wrongly deny some of the included the chance to participate fully, as peers, the injustice is what I call *ordinary-political* misrepresentation. Here, where the issue is intraframe representation, we enter the familiar terrain of political science debates over the relative merits of alternative electoral systems. Do single-member-district, winner-take-all, first-past-the-post systems unjustly deny parity to numerical minorities? And if so, is proportional representation or cumulative voting the appropriate remedy?[11] Likewise, do gender-blind rules, in conjunction with gender-based maldistribution and misrecognition, function to deny parity of political participation to women? And if so, are gender quotas an appropriate remedy?[12] Such questions belong to the sphere of ordinary-political justice, which has usually been played out within the Keynesian-Westphalian frame.

Less obvious, perhaps, is a second level of misrepresentation, which concerns the boundary-setting aspect of the political. Here the injustice arises when the community's boundaries are drawn in such a way as to

11  Lani Guinier, *The Tyranny of the Majority*, New York: Free Press, 1994. Robert Ritchie and Steven Hill, "The Case for Proportional Representation," in *Whose Vote Counts?* eds. Robert Ritchie and Steven Hill, Boston: Beacon Press, 2001, 1–33.

12  Anne Phillips, *The Politics of Presence*, Oxford: Clarendon Press, 1995. Shirin M. Rai, "Political Representation, Democratic Institutions and Women's Empowerment: The Quota Debate in India," in *Rethinking Empowerment: Gender and Development in a Global/Local World*, eds. Jane L. Parpart, Shirin M. Rai, and Kathleen Staudt, New York: Routledge, 2002, 133–45. T. Gray, "Electoral Gender Quotas: Lessons from Argentina and Chile," *Bulletin of Latin American Research* 21:1, 2003, 52–78. Mala Htun, "Is Gender Like Ethnicity? The Political Representation of Identity Groups," *Perspectives on Politics* 2:3, 2004, 439–58.

wrongly exclude some people from the chance to participate *at all* in its authorized contests over justice. In such cases, misrepresentation takes a deeper form, which I shall call *misframing*. The deeper character of misframing is a function of the crucial importance of framing to every question of social justice. Far from being of marginal importance, frame-setting is among the most consequential of political decisions. Constituting both members and nonmembers in a single stroke, this decision effectively excludes the latter from the universe of those entitled to consideration within the community in matters of distribution, recognition, and ordinary-political representation. The result can be a serious injustice. When questions of justice are framed in a way that wrongly excludes some from consideration, the consequence is a special kind of meta-injustice, in which one is denied the chance to press first-order justice claims in a given political community. The injustice remains, moreover, even when those excluded from one political community are included as subjects of justice in another—as long as the effect of the political division is to put some relevant aspects of justice beyond their reach. Still more serious, of course, is the case in which one is excluded from membership in any political community. Akin to the loss of what Hannah Arendt called "the right to have rights," that sort of misframing is a kind of "political death."[13] Those who suffer it may become objects of charity or benevolence. But deprived of the possibility of authoring first-order claims, they become non-persons with respect to justice.

It is the misframing form of misrepresentation that globalization has recently begun to make visible. Earlier, in the heyday of the postwar welfare state, with the Keynesian-Westphalian frame securely in place, the principal concern in thinking about justice was distribution. Later, with the rise of the new social movements and multiculturalism, the center of gravity shifted to recognition. In both cases, the modern territorial state was assumed by default. As a result, the political dimension of justice was relegated to the margins. Where it did emerge, it took the ordinary-political form of contests over the decision rules internal to the polity, whose boundaries were taken for granted. Thus, claims for gender quotas and multicultural rights sought to remove political obstacles to participatory parity for those who were already included in principle in the political community.[14] Taking for granted the Keynesian-Westphalian frame, they did not call into question the assumption that the appropriate unit of justice was the territorial state.

---

13   Hannah Arendt, *The Origins of Totalitarianism*, New York: Harcourt Brace, 1973, 269–84. "Political death" is my phrase, not Arendt's.

14   Among the best accounts of the normative force of these struggles are Will Kymlicka, *Multicultural Citizenship: A Liberal Theory of Minority Rights*, London: Oxford University Press, 1995; and Melissa Williams, *Voice, Trust, and Memory: Marginalized Groups and the Failings of Liberal Representation*, Princeton, NJ: Princeton University Press, 1998.

Today, in contrast, globalization has put the question of the frame squarely on the political agenda. Increasingly subject to contestation, the Keynesian-Westphalian frame is now considered by many to be a major vehicle of injustice, as it partitions political space in ways that block many who are poor and despised from challenging the forces that oppress them. Channeling their claims into the domestic political spaces of relatively powerless, if not wholly failed, states, this frame insulates offshore powers from critique and control.[15] Among those shielded from the reach of justice are more powerful predator states and transnational private powers, including foreign investors and creditors, international currency speculators, and transnational corporations.[16] Also protected are the governance structures of the global economy, which set exploitative terms of interaction and then exempt them from democratic control.[17] Finally, the Keynesian-Westphalian frame is self-insulating; the architecture of the interstate system protects the very partitioning of political space that it institutionalizes, effectively excluding transnational democratic decision-making on issues of justice.[18]

From this perspective, the Keynesian-Westphalian frame is a powerful

---

15   Thomas W. Pogge, "The Influence of the Global Order on the Prospects for Genuine Democracy in the Developing Countries," *Ratio Juris* 14:3, 2001, 326–43, and "Economic Justice and National Borders," *Revision* 22:2, 1999, 27–34. Rainer Forst, "Towards a Critical Theory of Transnational Justice," in *Global Justice*, ed. Thomas Pogge, Oxford: Blackwell Publishers, 2001, 169–87, and "Justice, Morality and Power in the Global Context," in *Real World Justice*, eds. Andreas Follesdal and Thomas Pogge, Dordrecht: Springer, 2005.

16   Richard L. Harris and Melinda J. Seid, *Critical Perspectives on Globalization and Neoliberalism in the Developing Countries*, Boston: Leiden, 2000.

17   Robert W. Cox, "A Perspective on Globalization," in *Globalization: Critical Reflections*, ed. James H. Mittelman, Boulder, CO: Lynne Rienner, 1996, 21–30; and "Democracy in Hard Times: Economic Globalization and the Limits to Liberal Democracy," in *The Transformation of Democracy?* ed. Anthony McGrew, Cambridge: Polity Press, 1997, 49–72. Stephen Gill, "New Constitutionalism, Democratisation and Global Political Economy," *Pacifica Review* 10:1, February 1998, 23–38. Eric Helleiner, "From Bretton Woods to Global Finance: A World Turned Upside Down," in *Political Economy and the Changing Global Order*, eds. Richard Stubbs and Geoffrey R. D. Underhill, New York: St. Martin's Press, 1994, 163–75. Servaes Storm and J. Mohan Rao, "Market-Led Globalization and World Democracy: Can the Twain Ever Meet?" *Development and Change* 35:5, 2004, 567–81. James K. Boyce, "Democratizing Global Economic Governance," *Development and Change* 35:3, 2004, 593–99.

18   John Dryzek, "Transnational Democracy" *Journal of Political Philosophy* 7:1, 1999, 30–51. James Bohman, "International Regimes and Democratic Governance," *International Affairs* 75:3, 1999, 499–513. David Held, "Regulating Globalization?" *International Journal of Sociology* 15:2, 2000, 394–408; *Democracy and the Global Order: From the Modern State to Cosmopolitan Governance*, Cambridge: Polity Press, 1995, 99–140; "The Transformation of Political Community: Rethinking Democracy in the Context of Globalization," in *Democracy's Edges*, eds. Ian Shapiro and Cassiano Hacker-Cordón, Cambridge: Cambridge University Press, 1999, 84–111.

instrument of injustice, which gerrymanders political space at the expense of the poor and despised. For those persons who are denied the chance to press transnational first-order claims, struggles against maldistribution and misrecognition cannot proceed, let alone succeed, unless they are joined with struggles against misframing. It is not surprising, therefore, that some consider misframing the defining injustice of a globalizing age.

Under these conditions of heightened awareness of misframing, the political dimension of justice is hard to ignore. Insofar as globalization is politicizing the question of the frame, it is also making visible an aspect of the grammar of justice that was often neglected in the previous period. It is now apparent that no claim for justice can avoid presupposing some notion of representation, implicit or explicit, insofar as none can avoid assuming a frame. Thus, representation is always already inherent in all claims for redistribution and recognition. The political dimension is implicit in, indeed required by, the grammar of the concept of justice. Thus, no redistribution or recognition without representation.[19]

---

19  I do not mean to suggest that the political is the master dimension of justice, more fundamental than the economic and the cultural. Rather, the three dimensions stand in relations of mutual entwinement and reciprocal influence. Just as the ability to make claims for distribution and recognition depends on relations of representation, so the ability to exercise one's political voice depends on the relations of class and status. In other words, the capacity to influence public debate and authoritative decision-making depends not only on formal decision rules but also on power relations rooted in the economic structure and the status order, a fact that is insufficiently stressed in most theories of deliberative democracy. Thus, maldistribution and misrecognition conspire to subvert the principle of equal political voice for every citizen, even in polities that claim to be democratic. But of course the converse is also true. Those who suffer from misrepresentation are vulnerable to injustices of status and class. Lacking political voice, they are unable to articulate and defend their interests with respect to distribution and recognition, which in turn exacerbates their misrepresentation. In such cases, the result is a vicious circle in which the three orders of injustice reinforce one another, denying some people the chance to participate on a par with others in social life. In general, then, the political is not the master dimension. On the contrary, although they are conceptually distinct and mutually irreducible, the three sorts of obstacles to parity of participation are usually intertwined. It follows that efforts to overcome injustice cannot, except in rare cases, address themselves to one such dimension alone. Rather, struggles against maldistribution and misrecognition cannot succeed unless they are joined with struggles against misrepresentation—and vice-versa. Where one puts the emphasis, of course, is both a tactical and strategic decision. Given the current salience of injustices of misframing, my own preference is for the slogan, "No redistribution or recognition without representation." But even so, the politics of representation appears as one among three interconnected fronts in the struggle for social justice in a globalizing world. For an argument against Rainer Forst's tendency to accord primacy to the political dimension, see Nancy Fraser, "Identity, Exclusion, and Critique: A Response to Four Critics," *European Journal of Political Theory* 6:3, 2007, 305–38; revised and reprinted as "Prioritizing Justice as Participatory Parity: A Rely to Kompridis and Forst," in *Adding Insult to Injury: Nancy Fraser*

In general, then, an adequate theory of justice for our time must be three-dimensional. Encompassing not only redistribution and recognition, but also representation, it must allow us to grasp the question of the frame as a question of justice. Incorporating the economic, cultural, and political dimensions, it must enable us to identify injustices of misframing and to evaluate possible remedies. Above all, it must permit us to pose, and to answer, the key political question of our age: how can we integrate struggles against maldistribution, misrecognition, and misrepresentation within a *post-Westphalian* frame?

## 2. ON THE POLITICS OF FRAMING: FROM STATE-TERRITORIALITY TO SOCIAL EFFECTIVITY?

So far I have been arguing for the irreducible specificity of the political as one of three fundamental dimensions of justice. And I have identified two distinct levels of political injustice: ordinary-political misrepresentation and misframing. Now, I want to examine the politics of framing in a globalizing world. Distinguishing affirmative from transformative approaches, I shall argue that an adequate politics of representation must also address a third level: beyond contesting ordinary-political misrepresentation, on the one hand, and misframing, on the other, such a politics must also aim to democratize the process of frame-setting.

I begin by explaining what I mean by "the politics of framing." Situated at my second level, where distinctions between members and nonmembers are drawn, this politics concerns the boundary-setting aspect of the political. Focused on the issues of who counts as a subject of justice, and what is the appropriate frame, the politics of framing comprises efforts to establish and consolidate, to contest and revise, the authoritative division of political space. Included here are struggles against misframing, which aim to dismantle the obstacles that prevent disadvantaged people from confronting the forces that oppress them with claims of justice. Centered on the setting and contesting of frames, the politics of framing is concerned with the question of the "who."

The politics of framing can take two distinct forms, both of which are now being practiced in our globalizing world.[20] The first approach, which I shall call the *affirmative* politics of framing, contests the boundaries of existing frames while accepting the Westphalian grammar of frame-setting. In this politics, those who claim to suffer injustices of misframing

*Debates Her Critics*, ed. Kevin Olson, London: Verso Books, 2008.

20   In distinguishing "affirmative" from "transformative" approaches, I am adapting terminology I have used in the past with respect to redistribution and recognition. See Nancy Fraser, "From Redistribution to Recognition? Dilemmas of Justice in a 'Postsocialist' Age," *New Left Review* 212, 1995, 68–93, and "Social Justice in the Age of Identity Politics."

seek to redraw the boundaries of existing territorial states or in some cases to create new ones. But they still assume that the territorial state is the appropriate unit within which to pose and resolve disputes about justice. For them, accordingly, injustices of misframing are not a function of the general principle according to which the Westphalian order partitions political space. They arise, rather, as a result of the faulty way in which that principle has been applied. Thus, those who practice the affirmative politics of framing accept that the principle of state-territoriality is the proper basis for constituting the "who" of justice. They agree, in other words, that what makes a given collection of individuals into fellow subjects of justice is their shared residence on the territory of a modern state and/or their shared membership in the political community that corresponds to such a state. Thus, far from challenging the underlying grammar of the Westphalian order, those who practice the affirmative politics of framing accept its state-territorial principle.[21]

Precisely that principle is contested, however, in a second version of the politics of framing, which I shall call the *transformative* approach. For proponents of this approach, the state-territorial principle no longer affords an adequate basis for determining the "who" of justice in every case. They concede, of course, that that principle remains relevant for many purposes; thus, supporters of transformation do not propose to eliminate state-territoriality entirely. But they contend that its grammar is out of sync with the structural causes of many injustices in a globalizing world, which are not territorial in character. Examples include the financial markets, "offshore factories," investment regimes, and governance structures of the global economy, which determine who works for a wage and who does not; the information networks of global media and cybertechnology, which determine who is included in the circuits of communicative power and who is not; and the bio-politics of climate, disease, drugs, weapons, and biotechnology, which determine who will live long and who will die young. In these matters, so fundamental to human well being, the forces that perpetrate injustice belong not to "the space of places," but to "the space of flows."[22] Not locatable within the jurisdiction of any actual or conceivable territorial state, they cannot be made answerable to claims of justice that are framed in terms of the state-territorial principle. In their case, so the argument goes, to invoke

---

21    For the state-territorial principle, see Thomas Baldwin, "The Territorial State," in *Jurisprudence, Cambridge Essays*, eds. H. Gross and T. R. Harrison, Oxford: Clarendon Press, 1992, 207–30. For doubts about the state-territorial principle (among other principles), see Frederick Whelan, "Democratic Theory and the Boundary Problem," in *Nomos XXV: Liberal Democracy*, eds. J. R. Pennock and R. W. Chapman, New York and London: New York University Press, 1983, 13–47.

22    I borrow this terminology from Manuel Castells, *The Rise of the Network Society*, London: Blackwell Publishers, 1996, 440–60.

the state-territorial principle to determine the frame is itself to commit an injustice. By partitioning political space along territorial lines, this principle insulates extra- and non-territorial powers from the reach of justice. In a globalizing world, therefore, it is less likely to serve as a remedy for misframing than as means of inflicting or perpetuating it.

In general, then, the transformative politics of framing aims to change the deep grammar of frame-setting in a globalizing world. This approach seeks to supplement the state-territorial principle of the Westphalian order with one or more *post-Westphalian* principles. The aim is to overcome injustices of misframing by changing not just the boundaries of the "who" of justice, but also the mode of their constitution, hence the way in which they are drawn.[23]

What might a post-Westphalian mode of frame-setting look like? Doubtless it is too early to have a clear view. Nevertheless, the most promising candidate so far is the "all-affected principle." This principle holds that all those affected by a given social structure or institution have moral standing as subjects of justice in relation to it. On this view, what turns a collection of people into fellow subjects of justice is not geographical proximity, but their co-imbrication in a common structural or institutional framework, which sets the ground rules that govern their social interaction, thereby shaping their respective life possibilities, in patterns of advantage and disadvantage.[24]

Until recently, the all-affected principle seemed to coincide in the eyes of many with the state-territorial principle. It was assumed, in keeping with the Westphalian world picture, that the common framework that determined patterns of advantage and disadvantage was precisely the

---

23    I owe the idea of a post-territorial "mode of political differentiation" to John G. Ruggie. See his immensely suggestive essay, "Territoriality and Beyond: Problematizing Modernity in International Relations," *International Organization* 47, 1993, 139–74. Also suggestive in this regard is Raul C. Pangalangan, "Territorial Sovereignty: Command, Title, and Expanding the Claims of the Commons," in *Boundaries and Justice: Diverse Ethical Perspectives*, eds. David Miller and Sohail H. Hashmi, Princeton, NJ: Princeton University Press, 2001, 164–82.

24    Thinking develops in time, often in unanticipated ways. The present chapter, which dates from 2004–5, reflects my view at that time that the all-affected principle was the most promising candidate on offer for a post-Westphalian mode of frame-setting, even though I also register important worries about that principle in note 26 below. Soon thereafter, however, those worries came to seem insurmountable. In later writings, I rejected the all-affected principle in favor of another possibility, not considered here, which refers disputes about the frame to the "all-subjected principle." This "subjection" principle now seems to me to better capture the deep internal connection between the concepts of justice and democracy. But I have elected to forego post hoc revision of this chapter. For the all-subjected principle, see Nancy Fraser, "Abnormal Justice," *Critical Inquiry* 34:3, 2008, 393–422; reprinted in Nancy Fraser, *Sclaes of Justice: Reimagining Political Space in a Globalizing World*, New York: Columbia University Press and Polity Press, 2008.

constitutional order of the modern territorial state. As a result, it seemed that in applying the state-territorial principle, one simultaneously captured the normative force of the all-affected principle. In fact, this was never truly so, as the long history of colonialism and neocolonialism attests. From the perspective of the metropole, however, the conflation of state-territoriality with social effectivity appeared to have an emancipatory thrust, as it served to justify the progressive incorporation, as subjects of justice, of the subordinate classes and status groups who were resident on the territory but excluded from active citizenship.

Today, however, the idea that state-territoriality can serve as a proxy for social effectivity is no longer plausible. Under current conditions, one's chances to live a good life do not depend wholly on the internal political constitution of the territorial state in which one resides. Although the latter remains undeniably relevant, its effects are mediated by other structures, both extra- and non-territorial, whose impact is at least as significant.[25] In general, globalization is driving a widening wedge between state territoriality and social effectivity. As those two principles increasingly diverge, the effect is to reveal the former as an inadequate surrogate for the latter. And so the question arises: is it possible to apply the all-affected principle directly to the framing of justice, without going through the detour of state-territoriality?[26]

---

25  Thomas W. Pogge, *World and Poverty and Human Rights: Cosmopolitan Responsibilities and Reforms*, Cambridge: Polity Press, 2002, especially the sections on "The Causal Role of Global Institutions in the Persistence of Severe Poverty," 112–16, and "Explanatory Nationalism: The Deep Significance of National Borders," 139–44.

26  Everything depends on finding a suitable interpretation of the all-affected principle. The key issue is how to narrow the idea of "affectedness" to the point that it becomes a viable operationalizable standard for assessing the justice of various frames. The problem is that, given the so-called butterfly effect, one can adduce evidence that just about everyone is affected by just about everything. What is needed, therefore, is a way of distinguishing those levels and kinds of effectivity that are sufficient to confer moral standing from those that are not. One proposal, suggested by Carol Gould, is to limit such standing to those whose human rights are violated by a given practice or institution. Another proposal, suggested by David Held, is to accord standing to those whose life expectancy and life chances are significantly affected. My own view is that the all-affected principle is open to a plurality of reasonable interpretations. As a result, its interpretation cannot be determined monologically, by philosophical fiat. Rather, philosophical analyses of affectedness should be understood as contributions to a broader public debate about the principle's meaning. (The same is true for empirical social-scientific accounts of who is affected by given institutions or policies.) In general, the all-affected principle must be interpreted dialogically, through the give-and-take of argument in democratic deliberation. That said, however, one thing is clear. Injustices of misframing can be avoided only if moral standing is not limited to those who are already accredited as official members of a given institution or as authorized participants in a given practice. To avoid such injustices, standing must also be accorded to those non-members and non-participants significantly affected by the institution or practice at issue. Thus, sub-Saharan Africans, who have been involuntarily disconnected from the

This is precisely what some practitioners of transformative politics are attempting to do. Seeking leverage against offshore sources of maldistribution and misrecognition, some globalization activists are appealing directly to the all-affected principle in order to circumvent the state-territorial partitioning of political space. Contesting their exclusion by the Keynesian-Westphalian frame, environmentalists and indigenous peoples are claiming standing as subjects of justice in relation to the extra- and non-territorial powers that impact their lives. Insisting that effectivity trumps state-territoriality, they have joined development activists, international feminists, and others in asserting their right to make claims against the structures that harm them, even when the latter cannot be located in the space of places. Casting off the Westphalian grammar of frame-setting, these claimants are applying the all-affected principle directly to questions of justice in a globalizing world.[27]

In such cases, the transformative politics of framing proceeds simul-taneously in multiple dimensions and on multiple levels.[28] On one level, the social movements that practice this politics aim to redress first-order injustices of maldistribution, misrecognition, and ordinary-political misrepresentation. On a second level, these movements seek to redress meta-level injustices of framing by reconstituting the "who" of justice. In those cases, moreover, where the state-territorial principle serves more to indemnify than to challenge injustice, transformative social movements appeal instead to the all-affected principle. Invoking a post-Westphalian principle, they are seeking to change the very grammar of

---

global economy, count as subjects of justice in relation to it, even if they do not participate officially in it. For the human-rights interpretation, see Carol C. Gould, *Globalizing Democracy and Human Rights*, Cambridge: Cambridge University Press, 2004. For the life expectancy and life-chances interpretation, see David Held, *Global Covenant: The Social Democratic Alternative to the Washington Consensus*, Cambridge: Polity Press, 2004, 99ff. For the dialogical approach, see below, as well as Fraser, "Democratic Justice in a Globalizing Age" and "Abnormal Justice," *Critical Inquiry* 34:3, 2008, 393–422. For the involuntary disconnection of sub-Saharan Africa from the official global economy, see James Ferguson, "Global Disconnect: Abjection and the Aftermath of Modernism," in Ferguson, *Expectations of Modernity: Myths and Meanings of Urban Life on the Zambian Copperbelt*, Berkeley: University of California Press, 1999, 234–54.

27  Manuel Castells, *The Power of Identity*, London: Blackwell Publishers, 1996. John A. Guidry, Michael D. Kennedy, and Mayer N. Zald, *Globalizations and Social Movements*, Ann Arbor: University of Michigan Press, 2000. Sanjeev Khagram, Kathryn Sikkink, and James V. Riker, *Restructuring World Politics: Transnational Social Movements, Networks, and Norms*, Minneapolis: Univeristy of Minnesota Press, 2002. Margaret E. Keck and Kathryn Sikkink, *Activists beyond Borders: Advocacy Networks in International Politics*, Ithaca, NY: Cornell University Press, 1998. Jeffrey St. Clair, "Seattle Diary," December 16, 1999, counterpunch.org.

28  For a useful account, albeit one that differs from the one presented here, see Christine Chin and James H. Mittelman, "Conceptualizing Resistance to Globalisation," *New Political Economy* 2:1, 1997, 25–37.

frame-setting—and thereby to reconstruct the meta-political foundations of justice for a globalizing world.

But the claims of transformative politics go further still. Above and
beyond their other claims, these movements are also claiming a say in
what amounts to a new, post-Westphalian process of frame-setting.
Rejecting the standard view, which deems frame-setting the prerogative
of states and transnational elites, they are effectively aiming to democratize the process by which the frameworks of justice are drawn and
revised. Asserting their right to participate in constituting the "who" of
justice, they are simultaneously transforming the "how"—by which I
mean the accepted procedures for determining the "who."[29] At their
most reflective and ambitious, transformative movements are demanding the creation of new democratic arenas for entertaining arguments
about the frame. In some cases, they are creating such arenas themselves. In the World Social Forum, for example, some practitioners of
transformative politics have fashioned a transnational public sphere
where they can participate on a par with others in airing and resolving
disputes about the frame.[30] In this way, they are prefiguring the possibility of new institutions of *post-Westphalian democratic justice*.[31]

The democratizing dimension of transformative politics points to a
third level of political injustice, above and beyond the two already discussed.
Previously, I distinguished first-order injustices of ordinary-political
misrepresentation from second-order injustices of misframing. Now,
however, we can discern a third-order species of political injustice, which
corresponds to the question of the "how." Exemplified by undemocratic

29   For further discussion of the "how" of justice, see Fraser, "Democratic
Justice in a Globalizing Age" and "Abnormal Justice."

30   James Bohman, "The Globalization of the Public Sphere: Cosmopolitanism,
Publicity and Cultural Pluralism," *Modern Schoolman* 75:2, 1998, 101–17. John A.
Guidry, Michael D. Kennedy, and Mayer N. Zald, *Globalizations and Social Movements*.
Thomas Pomiah, "Democracy vs. Empire: Alternatives to Globalization Presented
at the World Social Forum," *Antipode* 36:1, 2004, 130–33. Maria Pia Lara, "Globalizing
Women's Rights: Building a Public Sphere," in *Recognition, Responsibility, and Rights:
Feminist Ethics and Social Theory. Feminist Reconstructions*, eds. Robin N. Fiore and
Hilde Lindemann Nelson, Totowa, NJ: Rowman & Littlefield, 2003, 181–93.
Nancy Fraser, "Transnationalizing the Public Sphere: On the Legitimacy and
Efficacy of Public Opinion in a Postwestphalian World," *Theory, Culture & Society*
24:4, 2007, 7-30; reprinted in Fraser, *Scales of Justice*.

31   For the time being, efforts to democratize the process of frame-setting are
confined to contestation in transnational civil society. Indispensable as this level is,
it cannot succeed so long as there exist no formal institutions that can translate
transnational public opinion into binding, enforceable decisions. In general, then,
the civil-society track of transnational democratic politics needs to be complemented
by a formal-institutional track. For further discussion of this problem, see Fraser,
"Democratic Justice in a Globalizing Age" and "Abnormal Justice." Also James
Bohman, "International Regimes and Democratic Governance."

processes of frame-setting, this injustice consists in the failure to institutionalize parity of participation at the meta-political level, in deliberations and decisions concerning the "who." Because what is at stake here is the process by which first-order political space is constituted, I shall call this injustice *meta-political misrepresentation*. Meta-political misrepresentation arises when states and transnational elites monopolize the activity of frame-setting, denying voice to those who may be harmed in the process and blocking creation of democratic fora where the latter's claims can be vetted and redressed. The effect is to exclude the overwhelming majority of people from participation in the meta-discourses that determine the authoritative division of political space. Lacking any institutional arenas for such participation, and submitted to an undemocratic approach to the "how," the majority is denied the chance to engage on terms of parity in decision-making about the "who."

In general, then, struggles against misframing are revealing a new kind of democratic deficit. Just as globalization has made visible injustices of misframing, so transformative struggles against neoliberal globalization are making visible the injustice of meta-political misrepresentation. Exposing the lack of institutions where disputes about the "who" can be democratically aired and resolved, these struggles are focusing attention on the "how." By demonstrating that the absence of such institutions impedes efforts to overcome injustice, they are revealing the deep internal connections between democracy and justice. The effect is to bring to light a structural feature of the current conjuncture: struggles for justice in a globalizing world cannot succeed unless they go hand in hand with struggles for *meta-political democracy*. At this level too, then, no redistribution or recognition without representation.

### 3. PARADIGM SHIFT: POST-WESTPHALIAN DEMOCRATIC JUSTICE

I have been arguing that what distinguishes the current conjuncture is intensified contestation concerning both the "who" and the "how" of justice. Under these conditions, the theory of justice is undergoing a paradigm shift. Earlier, when the Keynesian-Westphalian frame was in place, most philosophers neglected the political dimension. Treating the territorial state as a given, they endeavored to ascertain the requirements of justice theoretically, in a monological fashion. Thus, they did not envision any role in determining those requirements for those who would be subject to them, let alone for those who would be excluded by the national frame. Neglecting to reflect on the question of the frame, these philosophers never imagined that those whose fates would be so decisively shaped by framing decisions might be entitled to participate in making them. Disavowing any need for a dialogical democratic moment, they were content to produce mono-logical theories of social justice.

Today, however, monological theories of social justice are becom-ing increasingly implausible. As we have seen, globalization cannot help but problematize the question of the "how," as it politicizes the question of the "who." The process goes something like this: as the circle of those claiming a say in frame-setting expands, decisions about the "who" are increasingly viewed as political matters, which should be handled democratically, rather than as technical matters, which can be left to experts and elites. The effect is to shift the burden of argu-ment, requiring defenders of expert privilege to make their case. No longer able to hold themselves above the fray, they are necessarily embroiled in disputes about the "how." As a result, they must contend with demands for meta-political democratization.

An analogous shift is currently making itself felt in normative philoso-phy. Just as some activists are seeking to transfer elite frame-setting prerogatives to democratic publics, so some theorists of justice are propos-ing to rethink the classic division of labor between theorist and *demos*. No longer content to ascertain the requirements of justice in a monological fashion, these theorists are looking increasingly to dialogical approaches, which treat important aspects of justice as matters for collective decision-making, to be determined by the citizens themselves, through democratic deliberation. For them, accordingly, the grammar of the theory of justice is being transformed. What could once be called the "theory of social justice" now appears as the "theory of *democratic justice*."[32]

In its current form, however, the theory of democratic justice remains incomplete. To complete the shift from a monological to dialogical theory requires a further step, beyond those envisioned by most proponents of the dialogical turn.[33] Henceforth, democratic processes of determination must be applied not only to the "what" of justice, but also to the "who" and the "how." In that case, by adopting a democratic approach to the "how," the theory of justice assumes a guise appropriate to a globalizing world. Dialogical at *every* level, meta-political as well as ordinary-political, it becomes a theory of *post-Westphalian democratic justice*.

The view of justice as participatory parity lends itself easily to such an

---

32   The phrase comes from Ian Shapiro, *Democratic Justice*, New Haven: Yale University Press, 1999. But the idea can also be found in Jürgen Habermas, *Between Facts and Norms*; Seyla Benhabib, *The Rights of Others*; and Rainer Forst, *Contexts of Justice: Political Philosophy Beyond Liberalism and Communitarianism*, trans. J. M. M. Farrell, Berkeley: University of California Press, 2002.

33   None of the theorists cited in the previous note has attempted to apply the "democratic justice" approach to the problem of the frame. The thinker who comes closest is Rainer Forst, as he appreciates the importance of framing. But even Forst does not envision democratic processes of frame-setting.

approach. This principle has a double quality that expresses the reflexive character of democratic justice. On the one hand, the principle of participatory parity is an outcome notion, which specifies a substantive principle of justice by which we may evaluate social arrangements: the latter are just if and only if they permit all the relevant social actors to participate as peers in social life. On the other hand, participatory parity is also a process notion, which specifies a procedural standard by which we may evaluate the democratic legitimacy of norms: the latter are legitimate if and only if they can command the assent of all concerned in fair and open processes of deliberation, in which all can participate as peers. By virtue of this double quality, the view of justice as participatory parity has an inherent reflexivity. Able to problematize both substance and procedure, it renders visible the mutual entwinement of those two aspects of social arrangements. Thus, this approach can expose both the unjust background conditions that skew putatively democratic decision-making and the undemocratic procedures that generate substantively unequal outcomes. As a result, it enables us to shift levels easily, moving back and forth as necessary between first-order and meta-level questions. Making manifest the co-implication of democracy and justice, the view of justice as participatory parity supplies just the sort of reflexivity that is needed in a globalizing world.

Let me conclude by recalling the principal features of the theory of justice that I have sketched here. An account of post-Westphalian democratic justice, this theory encompasses three fundamental dimensions: economic, cultural, and political. As a result, it renders visible, and criticizable, the mutual entwinement of maldistribution, misrecognition, and misrepresentation. In addition, this theory's account of political injustice encompasses three levels. Addressing not only ordinary-political misrepresentation, but also misframing and meta-political misrepresentation, it allows us to grasp the problem of the frame as a matter of justice. Focused not only on the "what" of justice, but also on the "who" and the "how," it enables us to evaluate the justice of alternative principles and alternative processes of frame-setting. Above all, as I noted before, the theory of post-Westphalian democratic justice encourages us to pose, and hopefully to answer, the key political question of our time: how can we integrate struggles against maldistribution, misrecognition, and misrepresentation within a post-Westphalian frame?

# 9

# Feminism, Capitalism, and the Cunning of History[*]

I would like here to take a broad, sweeping look at second-wave feminism. Not at this or that activist current, nor at this or that strand of feminist theorizing; not at this or that geographical slice of the movement, nor at this or that sociological stratum of women. I want, rather, to try to see second-wave feminism whole, as an epochal social phenomenon. Looking back at nearly forty years of feminist activism, I want to venture an assessment of the movement's overall trajectory and historical significance. In looking back, however, I hope also to help us look forward. By reconstructing the path we have traveled, I hope to shed light on the challenges we face today—in a time of massive economic crisis, social uncertainty, and political realignment.

I am going to tell a story, then, about the broad contours and overall meaning of second-wave feminism. Equal parts historical narrative and social-theoretical analysis, my story is plotted around three points in time, each of which places second-wave feminism in relation to a specific moment in the history of capitalism. The first point refers to the movement's beginnings in the context of what I will call "state-organized capitalism." Here I propose to chart the emergence of second-wave feminism from out of the anti-imperialist New Left as a radical challenge to the pervasive androcentrism of state-led capitalist societies in the postwar era. Conceptualizing this phase, I shall

---

 * This chapter originated as a keynote lecture presented at the Cortona Colloquium on "Gender and Citizenship: New and Old Dilemmas, Between Equality and Difference," Cortona, Italy, November 7–9, 2008. Thanks to the Giangiacomo Feltrinelli Foundation and to the French State, the Île-de-France region, and the École des hautes études en sciences sociales, which supported this work through the framework of the Blaise Pascal International Research Chairs. For helpful comments, I thank the Cortona participants, especially Bianca Beccalli, Jane Mansbridge, Ruth Milkman, and Eli Zaretsky, and the participants in an EHESS seminar at the Groupe de sociologie politique et morale, especially Luc Boltanski, Estelle Ferrarese, Sandra Laugier, Patricia Paperman, and Laurent Thévenot.

identify the movement's fundamental emancipatory promise with its expanded sense of injustice and its structural critique of society. The second point refers to the process of feminism's evolution in the dramatically changed social context of rising neoliberalism. Here, I propose to chart not only the movement's extraordinary successes but also the disturbing convergence of some of its ideals with the demands of an emerging new form of capitalism—post-Fordist, "disorganized," transnational. Conceptualizing this phase, I shall ask whether second-wave feminism has unwittingly supplied a key ingredient of what Luc Boltanski and Eve Chiapello call "the new spirit of capitalism." The third point refers to a possible reorientation of feminism in the present context of capitalist crisis and political realignment, which could mark the beginnings of a shift from neoliberalism to a new form of social organization. Here, I propose to examine the prospects for reactivating feminism's emancipatory promise in a world that has been rocked by the twin crises of finance capital and US hegemony.

In general, then, I propose to situate the trajectory of second-wave feminism in relation to the recent history of capitalism. In this way, I hope to help revive the sort of socialist-feminist theorizing that first inspired me decades ago and that still seems to me to offer our best hope for clarifying the prospects for gender justice in the present period. My aim, however, is not to recycle outmoded dual-systems theories, but rather to integrate the best of recent feminist theorizing with the best of recent critical theorizing about capitalism.

To clarify the rationale behind my approach, let me explain my dissatisfaction with what is perhaps the most widely held view of second-wave feminism. It is often said that the movement's relative success in transforming culture stands in sharp contrast with its relative failure to transform institutions. This assessment is double-edged: on the one hand, feminist ideals of gender equality, so contentious in the preceding decades, now sit squarely in the social mainstream; on the other hand, they have yet to be realized in practice. Thus, feminist critiques of, for example, sexual harassment, sexual trafficking, and unequal pay, which appeared incendiary not so long ago, are widely espoused today; yet this sea-change at the level of attitudes has by no means eliminated those practices. And so, it is frequently said: second-wave feminism has wrought an epochal cultural revolution, but the vast change in *mentalitées* has not (yet) translated into structural, institutional change.

There is something to be said for this view, which rightly notes the widespread acceptance today of feminist ideas. But the thesis of cultural success-cum-institutional failure does not go very far in illuminating the historical significance and future prospects of second-wave feminism. Positing that institutions have lagged behind culture, as if one could change while the other did not, it suggests that we need only make the former catch up with the latter in order to realize feminist hopes. The effect is to obscure a more complex, disturbing possibility: that the diffusion of cultural attitudes born out of the second wave has been part and parcel of another social transformation, unanticipated and unintended by feminist activists—a transformation in the social organization of postwar capitalism. This possibility can be formulated more sharply: the cultural changes jump-started by the second wave, salutary in themselves, have served to legitimate a structural transformation of capitalist society that runs directly counter to feminist visions of a just society.

In this chapter, I aim to explore this disturbing possibility. My hypothesis can be stated thus: What was truly new about the second wave was the way it wove together in a critique of androcentric, state-organized capitalism what we can understand today as three analytically distinct dimensions of gender injustice: economic, cultural, and political. Subjecting state-organized capitalism to wide-ranging, multifaceted scrutiny, in which those three perspectives intermingled freely, feminists generated a critique that was simultaneously ramified and systematic. In the ensuing decades, however, the three dimensions of injustice became separated, both from one another and from the critique of capitalism. With the fragmentation of the feminist critique came the selective incorporation and partial recuperation of some of its strands. Split off from one another and from the societal critique that had integrated them, second-wave hopes were conscripted in the service of a project that was deeply at odds with our larger, holistic vision of a just society. In a fine instance of the cunning of history, utopian desires found a second life as feeling currents that legitimated the transition to a new form of capitalism: post-Fordist, transnational, neoliberal.[1]

In what follows, I propose to elaborate this hypothesis in three steps, which correspond to the three plot points mentioned earlier. In a first step, I shall reconstruct the second-wave feminist critique of androcentric, state-organized capitalism as integrating concerns we associate today with three perspectives on justice—redistribution, recognition, and representation. In a second step, I shall sketch the coming apart of that constellation and the selective enlistment of some of its strands to legitimate neoliberal capitalism. In a third step, I shall weigh the prospects for recovering feminism's emancipatory promise in the present moment of economic crisis and political opening.

---

1   In this essay, I am drawing on, but also updating and complicating, my previous account of these matters in "Mapping the Feminist Imagination: From Redistribution to Recognition to Representation," *Constellations: An International Journal of Critical and Democratic Theory* 13:3, September 2005, 295–307; reprinted in Nancy Fraser, *Scales of Justice: Reimagining Political Space in a Globalizing World*, New York: Columbia University Press and Polity Press, 2008.

## 1. FEMINISM AND STATE-ORGANIZED CAPITALISM

Let me begin by situating the emergence of second-wave feminism in the context of state-organized capitalism. By "state-organized capitalism," I mean the hegemonic social formation in the postwar era, a social formation in which states played an active role in steering their national economies.[2] We are most familiar with the form taken by state-organized capitalism in the welfare states of what was then called the First World, which used Keynesian tools to soften the boom-bust cycles endemic to capitalism. Drawing on experiences of depression and war-time planning, these states implemented various forms of *dirigisme*, including infrastructure investment, industrial policy, redistributive taxation, social provision, business regulation, nationalization of some key industries, and decommodification of public goods. Certainly, it was the most wealthy and powerful OECD states that were able to "organize" capitalism most successfully in the decades following World War II. But a variant of state-organized capitalism could also be found in what was then called the Third World. In impoverished postcolonies, newly independent "developmental states" sought to use their more limited capacities to jump-start national economic development by means of import substitution policies, infrastructural investment, nationalization of key industries, and public spending on education.[3]

In general, then, I use the expression "state-organized capitalism" to refer to the OECD welfare states and the postcolonial developmental states of the postwar period. It was in these countries, after all, that second-wave feminism first erupted in the early 1970s. To explain what exactly provoked the eruption, let me note four defining characteristics of the political culture of state-organized capitalism.

1) *Economism*: By definition, as I already noted, state-organized capitalism involved the use of public political power to regulate (and in some cases, to replace) economic markets. This was largely a matter of crisis management in the interest of capital. Nevertheless, the states in question derived much of their political legitimacy from their

---

2    For a discussion of this term, see Frederick Pollock, "State Capitalism: Its Possibilities and Limitations," in *The Essential Frankfurt School Reader*, eds. Andrew Arato and Eike Gebhardt, London: Continuum, 1982/95, 71–94.

3    Then, too, economic life in the communist world was notoriously state-organized, and there are those who would still insist on calling it state-organized capitalism. Although there may well be some truth in that view, I will follow the more conventional path of excluding the communist world from this first moment of my story, in part because it was not until after 1989 that second-wave feminism emerged as political force in what were by then ex-communist countries.

claims to promote inclusion, social equality, and cross-class solidarity. Yet these ideals were interpreted in an economistic and class-centric way. In the political culture of state-organized capitalism, social questions were framed chiefly in distributive terms, as matters concerning the equitable allocation of divisible goods, especially income and jobs, while social divisions were viewed primarily through the prism of class. Thus, the quintessential social injustice was unfair economic distribution, and its paradigm expression was class inequality. The effect of this class-centric, economistic imaginary was to marginalize, if not wholly to obscure, other dimensions, sites, and axes of injustice.

2) *Androcentrism*: It followed that the political culture of state-organized capitalism envisioned the ideal-typical citizen as an ethnic-majority male worker—a breadwinner and a family man. It was widely assumed, too, that this worker's wage should be the principal, if not the sole, economic support of his family, while any wages earned by his wife should be merely supplemental. Deeply gendered, this "family wage" construct served both as a social ideal, connoting modernity and upward mobility, and as the basis for state policy—in matters of employment, welfare, and development. Granted, the ideal eluded most families, as a man's wage was rarely by itself sufficient to support children and a non-employed wife. And granted, too, the Fordist industry to which the ideal was linked was soon to be dwarfed by a burgeoning low-wage service sector. But in the 1950s and 1960s, the family-wage ideal still served to define gender norms and to discipline those who would contravene them, reinforcing men's authority in households and channeling aspirations into privatized domestic consumption. Equally important, by valorizing waged work, the political culture of state-organized capitalism obscured the social importance of unwaged care work and reproductive labor. Institutionalizing androcentric understandings of family and work, it naturalized injustices of gender and removed them from political contestation.

3) *Étatism*: State-organized capitalism was étatist, suffused with a technocratic, managerial ethos. Relying on professional experts to design policies, and on bureaucratic organizations to implement them, welfare and developmental states treated those whom they ostensibly served more as clients, consumers, and taxpayers than as active citizens. The result was a depoliticized culture, which treated questions of justice as technical matters, to be settled by expert calculation or corporatist bargaining. Far from being empowered to interpret their needs democratically, via political deliberation and contestation, ordinary citizens were positioned (at best) as passive recipients of satisfactions defined and dispensed from on high.

4) *Westphalianism*: Finally, state-organized capitalism was, by definition, a national formation, aimed at mobilizing the capacities of

national states to support national economic development in the name—if not always in the interest—of the national citizenry. Made possible by the Bretton Woods regulatory framework, this formation rested on a division of political space into territorially bounded polities. As a result, the political culture of state-organized capitalism institutionalized the "Westphalian" view that binding obligations of justice apply only among fellow citizens. Subtending the lion's share of social struggle in the postwar era, this view channeled claims for justice into the domestic political arenas of territorial states. The effect, notwithstanding lip-service to international human rights and to anti-imperialist solidarity, was to truncate the scope of justice, marginalizing, if not wholly obscuring, cross-border injustices.[4]

In general, then, the political culture of state-organized capitalism was economistic, androcentric, étatist, and Westphalian—all characteristics that came under attack in the late 1960s and 1970s. In those years of explosive radicalism, second-wave feminists joined their New Left and anti-imperialist counterparts in challenging the economism, the étatism, and (to a lesser degree) the Westphalianism of state-organized capitalism, while also contesting the latter's androcentrism—and with it, the sexism of their comrades and allies. Let us consider these points one by one.

1) *Second-wave feminism contra economism*: Rejecting the exclusive identification of injustice with class maldistribution, second-wave feminists joined other emancipatory movements to burst open the restrictive, economistic imaginary of state-organized capitalism. Politicizing "the personal," they expanded the meaning of justice, reinterpreting as injustices social inequalities that had been overlooked, tolerated, or rationalized since time immemorial. Rejecting both Marxism's exclusive focus on political economy and liberalism's exclusive focus on law, they unveiled injustices located elsewhere—in the family and in cultural traditions, in civil society and in everyday life. In addition, second-wave feminists expanded the number of axes that could harbor injustice. Rejecting the primacy of class, socialist-feminists, black-feminists, and anti-imperialist feminists also opposed radical-feminist efforts to install gender in that same position of categorial privilege. Focusing not only on gender, but also on class, "race," sexuality, and nationality, they pioneered an "intersectionist" alternative that is widely accepted today. Finally, second-wave feminists extended the purview of justice to take in such previously private matters as sexuality, housework, reproduction, and violence against

---

4  For a fuller account of the "Westphalian political imaginary" and its effects in truncating the scope of justice, see Chapter 8 of this volume, "Reframing Justice in a Globalizing World."

women. In so doing, they effectively broadened the concept of injustice to encompass not only economic inequalities but also hierarchies of status and asymmetries of political power. With the benefit of hindsight, we can say that they replaced a monistic economistic view of justice with a broader, three-dimensional understanding encompassing economy, culture, and politics.

The result was no mere laundry list of single issues. On the contrary, what connected the plethora of newly discovered injustices was the notion that women's subordination was systemic, grounded in the deep structures of society. Second-wave feminists argued, of course, about how best to characterize the social totality—whether as "patriarchy," as a "dual-systems" amalgam of capitalism and patriarchy, as an imperialist world system, or, in my own preferred view, as a historically specific, androcentric form of state-organized capitalist society, structured by three interpenetrating orders of subordination: (mal)distribution, (mis)recognition, and (mis)representation. But despite such differences, most second-wave feminists (with the notable exception of liberal-feminists) concurred that overcoming women's subordination required radical transformation of the deep structures of the social totality. This shared commitment to systemic transformation bespoke the movement's origins in the broader emancipatory ferment of the times.

2) *Second-wave feminism contra androcentrism*: If second-wave feminism partook of the general aura of sixties radicalism, it nevertheless stood in a tense relation with other emancipatory movements. Its chief target, after all, was the *gender* injustice of state-organized capitalism, hardly a priority for non-feminist anti-imperialists and New Leftists. In subjecting state-organized capitalism's androcentrism to critique, moreover, second-wave feminists had also to confront sexism within the Left. For liberal and radical feminists, this posed no special problem; they could simply turn separatist and exit the Left. For socialist-feminists, anti-imperialist feminists, and feminists of color, in contrast, the difficulty was to confront sexism within the Left while remaining part of it.

For a time, at least, socialist-feminists succeeded in maintaining that difficult balance. They located the core of androcentrism in a gender division of labor that systematically devalued activities, both paid and unpaid, that were performed by or associated with women. Applying this analysis to state-organized capitalism, they uncovered the deep-structural connections between women's responsibility for the lion's share of unpaid caregiving, their subordination in marriage and personal life, the gender segmentation of labor markets, men's domination of the political system, and the androcentrism of welfare provision, industrial policy, and development schemes. In effect, they exposed the family wage as the point where gender maldistribution, misrecognition, and misrepresentation converged. The result was a critique that integrated economy, culture, and politics in a systematic account of women's subordination in state-organized capitalism. Far from aiming simply to promote women's full incorporation as wage-earners in capitalist society, socialist-feminists sought to transform the system's deep structures and animating values—in part by decentering wage work and valorizing unwaged activities, especially the socially necessary carework performed by women.

3) *Second-wave feminism contra étatism*: But feminists' objections to state-organized capitalism were as much concerned with process as with substance. Like their New Left allies, they rejected the bureau-cratic-managerial ethos of state-organized capitalism. To the widespread 1960s critique of Fordist organization, they added a gender analysis, interpreting the culture of large-scale, top-down institutions as expressing the modernized masculinity of the professional-manage-rial stratum of state-organized capitalism. Developing a horizontal counter-ethos of sisterly connection, second-wave feminists created the entirely new organizational practice of consciousness-raising. Seeking to bridge the sharp étatist divide between theory and prac-tice, they styled themselves as a countercultural democratizing movement—anti-hierarchical, participatory, and demotic. In an era when the acronym "NGO" did not yet exist, feminist academics, lawyers, and social workers identified more with the grassroots than with the reigning professional ethos of depoliticized expertise.

But unlike some of their countercultural comrades, most feminists did not reject state institutions *simpliciter*. Seeking, rather, to infuse the latter with feminist values, they envisioned a participatory-democratic state that empowered its citizens. Effectively reimagining the relation between state and society, they sought to transform those positioned as passive objects of welfare and development policy into active subjects, empowered to participate in democratic processes of need interpretation. The goal, accordingly, was less to dismantle state insti-tutions than to transform them into agencies that would promote, and indeed express, gender justice.

4) *Second-wave feminism contra and pro Westphalianism*: More ambiva-lent, perhaps, was second-wave feminism's relation to the Westphalian dimension of state-organized capitalism. Given its origins in the global anti–Vietnam War ferment of the time, the movement was clearly disposed to be sensitive to transborder injustices. This was especially the case for feminists in the developing world, whose gender critique was interwoven with a critique of imperialism. But there, as elsewhere, most feminists viewed their respective states as the principal addressees of their demands. Thus, second-wave feminists tended to reinscribe the Westphalian frame at the level of practice, even when they criticized it at the level of theory. That frame, which divided the world into bounded

territorial polities, remained the default option in an era when states still seemed to possess the requisite capacities for social steering and when the technology enabling real-time transnational networking was not yet available. In the context of state-organized capitalism, then, the slogan "sisterhood is global" (itself already contested as imperializing) functioned more as an abstract gesture than as a post-Westphalian political project that could be practically pursued.

In general, then, second-wave feminism remained ambivalently Westphalian, even as it rejected the economism, androcentrism, and étatism of state-organized capitalism. On all those issues, however, it manifested considerable nuance. In rejecting economism, the feminists of this period never doubted the centrality of distributive justice and the critique of political economy to the project of women's emancipation. Far from wanting to minimize the economic dimension of gender injustice, they sought, rather, to deepen it, by clarifying its relation with the two additional dimensions of culture and politics. Likewise, in rejecting the androcentrism of the family wage, second-wave feminists never sought simply to replace it with the two-earner family. For them, rather, overcoming gender injustice required ending the systematic devaluation of caregiving and the gender division of labor, both paid and unpaid. Finally, in rejecting the étatism of state-organized capitalism, second-wave feminists never doubted the need for strong political institutions capable of organizing economic life in the service of justice. Far from wanting to free markets from state control, they sought rather to democratize state power, to maximize citizen participation, to strengthen accountability, and to increase communicative flows between state and society.

All told, second-wave feminism espoused a transformative political project, premised on an expanded understanding of injustice and a systemic critique of capitalist society. The movement's most advanced currents saw their struggles as multidimensional, aimed simultaneously against economic exploitation, status hierarchy, and political subjection. To them, moreover, feminism appeared as part of a broader emancipatory project, in which struggles against gender injustices were necessarily linked to struggles against racism, imperialism, homophobia, and class domination, all of which required transformation of the deep structures of capitalist society.

## 2. FEMINISM AS THE "NEW SPIRIT OF CAPITALISM": NEOLIBERAL RESIGNIFICATIONS

As it turned out, that project remained largely stillborn, a casualty of deeper historical forces, which were not well understood at the time. With the benefit of hindsight, we can now see that the rise of second-wave feminism coincided with a historical shift in the character of capitalism, from the state-organized variant just discussed to neoliberalism. Reversing the previous formula, which sought to "use politics to tame markets," proponents of this new form of capitalism proposed to use markets to tame politics. Dismantling key elements of the Bretton Woods framework, they eliminated the capital controls that had enabled Keynesian steering of national economies. In place of *dirigisme*, they promoted privatization and deregulation; in place of public provision and social citizenship, "trickle-down" and "personal responsibility"; in place of the welfare and developmental states, the lean, mean "competition state." Road-tested in Latin America, this approach served to guide much of the transition to capitalism in East/Central Europe. Although publicly championed by Thatcher and Reagan, it was applied only gradually and unevenly in the First World. In the Third, by contrast, neoliberalization was imposed at the gunpoint of debt, as an enforced program of "structural adjustment," which overturned all the central tenets of developmentalism and compelled postcolonial states to divest their assets, open their markets, and slash social spending.

Interestingly, second-wave feminism thrived in these new conditions. What had begun in the context of state-organized capitalism as a radical anti-systemic movement was now *en route* to becoming a broad-based mass social phenomenon. Attracting adherents of every class, ethnicity, nationality, and political ideology, feminist ideas found their way into every nook and cranny of social life and transformed the self-understandings of all whom they touched. The effect was not only vastly to expand the ranks of activists but also to reshape commonsense views of family, work, and dignity.

Was it mere coincidence that second-wave feminism and neoliberalism prospered in tandem? Or was there some perverse, subterranean elective affinity between them? That second possibility is heretical, to be sure, but we fail to investigate it at our own peril. Certainly, the rise of neoliberalism dramatically changed the terrain on which second-wave feminism operated. The effect, I shall argue here, was to resignify feminist ideals. Aspirations that had a clear emancipatory thrust in the context of state-organized capitalism assumed a far more ambiguous meaning in the neoliberal era. With welfare and developmental states under attack from free-marketeers, feminist critiques of economism, androcentrism, étatism, and Westphalianism took on a new valence. Let me clarify this dynamic of resignification by revisiting those four foci of feminist critique.[5]

---

5  I borrow the term "resignification" from Judith Butler, "Contingent Foundations," in Seyla Benhabib, Judith Butler, Drucilla Cornell, and Nancy Fraser, *Feminist Contentions: A Philosophical Exchange*, New York: Routledge, 1994.

1) *Feminist anti-economism resignified*: Neoliberalism's rise coincided with a major alteration in the political culture of capitalist societies. In this period, claims for justice were increasingly couched as claims for the recognition of identity and difference.[6] With this shift "from redistribution to recognition" came powerful pressures to transform second-wave feminism into a variant of identity politics. A progressive variant, to be sure, but one that tended nevertheless to overextend the critique of culture, while downplaying the critique of political economy. In practice, the tendency was to subordinate social-economic struggles to struggles for recognition, while in the academy, feminist cultural theory began to eclipse feminist social theory. What had begun as a needed corrective to economism devolved in time into an equally one-sided culturalism. Thus, instead of arriving at a broader, richer paradigm that could encompass both redistribution and recognition, second-wave feminists effectively traded one truncated paradigm for another.

The timing, moreover, could not have been worse. The turn to recognition dovetailed all too neatly with a rising neoliberalism that wanted nothing more than to repress all memory of social egalitarianism. Thus, feminists absolutized the critique of culture at precisely the moment when circumstances required redoubled attention to the critique of political economy.[7] As the critique splintered, moreover, the cultural strand became decoupled not only from the economic strand, but also from the critique of capitalism that had previously integrated them. Unmoored from the critique of capitalism and made available for alternative articulations, these strands could be drawn into what Hester Eisenstein has called "a dangerous liaison" with neoliberalism.[8]

2) *Feminist anti-androcentrism resignified*: It was only a matter of time, therefore, before neoliberalism resignified the feminist critique of androcentrism. To explain how, I propose to adapt an argument made by Luc Boltanski and Eve Chiapello. In their important book *The New Spirit of Capitalism*, they contend that capitalism periodically remakes itself in moments of historical rupture, in part by recuperating strands of critique directed against it. In such moments, elements of anti-capitalist critique are resignified to legitimate an emergent new form of capitalism, which thereby becomes endowed with the higher, moral significance needed to motivate new generations to

---

6   For this shift in the grammar of political claims-making, see Nancy Fraser, "From Redistribution to Recognition? Dilemmas of Justice in a 'Postsocialist' Age," *New Left Review* 212, July/August 1995, 68–93; reprinted in Nancy Fraser, *Justice Interruptus: Critical Reflections on the "Postsocialist" Condition*, New York: Routledge, 1997.

7   For a fuller argument, see Fraser, "Mapping the Feminist Imagination."

8   Hester Eisenstein, "A Dangerous Liaison? Feminism and Corporate Globalization," *Science and Society* 69:3, 2005, 487–518.

shoulder the inherently meaningless work of endless accumulation. For Boltanski and Chiapello, the "new spirit" that has served to legitimate the flexible neoliberal capitalism of our time was fashioned from the New Left's "artistic" critique of state-organized capitalism, which denounced the grey conformism of corporate culture. It was in the accents of May '68, they claim, that neoliberal management theorists propounded a new "connexionist," "project" capitalism, in which rigid organizational hierarchies would give way to horizontal teams and flexible networks, thereby liberating individual creativity.[9] The result was a new romance of capitalism with real-world effects—a romance that enveloped the tech start-ups of Silicon Valley and that today finds its purest expression in the ethos of Google.

Boltanski and Chiapello's argument is original and profound. Yet, because it is gender-blind, it fails to grasp the full character of the spirit of neoliberal capitalism. To be sure, that spirit includes (what I would call) a masculinist romance of the free, unencumbered, self-fashioning individual, which they aptly describe. But neoliberal capitalism has as much to do with Walmart, *maquiladoras*, and microcredit as with Silicon Valley and Google. And its indispensable workers are disproportionately women, not only young single women, but also married women and women with children; not only racialized women, but women of virtually all nationalities and ethnicities. As such women have poured into labor markets around the globe, the effect has been to undercut once and for all state-organized capitalism's ideal of the family wage. In disorganized neoliberal capitalism, that ideal has been replaced by the newer, more modern norm of the two-earner family. Nevermind that the reality that underlies the new ideal is depressed wage levels, decreased job security, declining living standards, a steep rise in the number of hours worked for wages per household, exacerbation of the double shift—now often a triple or quadruple shift—and a rise in female-headed households. Disorganized capitalism turns a sow's ear into a silk purse by elaborating a new romance of female advancement and gender justice.

Disturbing as it may sound, I am suggesting that second-wave feminism has unwittingly provided a key ingredient of the new spirit of neoliberalism. Our critique of the family wage now supplies a good part of the romance that invests flexible capitalism with a higher meaning and a moral point. Endowing their daily struggles with an

---

9  Luc Boltanski and Eve Chiapello, *The New Spirit of Capitalism*, trans. Geoffrey Elliott, London: Verso Books, 2005. For an interpretation of psychoanalysis as the spirit of "the second industrial revolution," which concludes by positing feminism as the spirit of the "third," see Eli Zaretsky's important essay, "Psychoanalysis and the Spirit of Capitalism," *Constellations: An International Journal of Critical and Democratic Theory* 15:3, 2008, 366–81.

ethical meaning, the feminist romance attracts women at both ends of the social spectrum: at one end, the female cadres of the professional middle classes, determined to crack the glass ceiling; at the other end, the female temps, part-timers, low-wage service workers, domestics, sex workers, migrants, EPZ workers, and micro-credit borrowers, seeking not only income and material security, but also dignity, self-betterment, and liberation from traditional authority. At both ends, the dream of women's emancipation is harnessed to the engine of capitalist accumulation. Thus, second-wave feminism's critique of the family wage has enjoyed a perverse afterlife. Once the centerpiece of a radical critique of androcentrism, it serves today to intensify capitalism's valorization of waged labor.

3) *Feminist anti-étatism resignified*: Neoliberalism has also resignified the anti-étatism of the previous period, making it grist for schemes aimed at reducing state action *tout court*. In the new climate, it seemed but a short step from second-wave feminism's critique of welfare-state paternalism to Margaret Thatcher's critique of the nanny state. That was certainly the experience in the United States, where feminists watched helplessly as Bill Clinton triangulated their nuanced critique of a sexist and stigmatizing system of poor relief into a plan to "end welfare as we know it," which abolished the federal entitlement to income support.[10] In the postcolonies, meanwhile, the critique of the developmental state's androcentrism morphed into enthusiasm for NGOs, which emerged everywhere to fill the space vacated by shrinking states. Certainly, the best of these organizations provided urgently needed material aid to populations bereft of public services. Yet the effect was often to depoliticize the grassroots and to skew the agendas of local groups in directions favored by First-World funders. By its very stopgap nature, moreover, NGO action did little to challenge the receding tide of public provision or to build political support for responsive state action.[11]

The explosion of micro-credit illustrates the dilemma. Counterposing feminist values of empowerment and participation from below to the passivity-inducing red tape of top-down étatism, the architects of these projects have crafted an innovative synthesis of individual

---

10  Nancy Fraser, "Clintonism, Welfare, and the Antisocial Wage: The Emergence of a Neoliberal Political Imaginary," *Rethinking Marxism* 6:1, 1993, 9–23; Nancy Fraser with Kate Bedford, "Social Rights and Gender Justice in the Neoliberal Moment: A Conversation about Gender, Welfare, and Transnational Politics. An Interview with Nancy Fraser," *Feminist Theory* 9:2, 2008, 225–46.

11  Sonia Alvarez, "Advocating Feminism: The Latin American Feminist NGO 'Boom,'" *International Feminist Journal of Politics*, 1:2, 1999, 181–209; Carol Barton, "Global Women's Movements at a Crossroads: Seeking Definition, New Alliances and Greater Impact," *Socialism and Democracy* 18:1, 2009, 151–84.

self-help and community networking, NGO oversight and market mechanisms—all aimed at combating women's poverty and gender subjection. The results so far include an impressive record of loan repayments and anecdotal evidence of lives transformed. What has been concealed, however, in the feminist hoopla surrounding these projects, is a disturbing coincidence: micro-credit has burgeoned just as states have abandoned macro-structural efforts to fight poverty, efforts that small-scale lending cannot possibly replace.[12] In this case too, then, the feminist critique of bureaucratic paternalism has been recuperated by neoliberalism. A perspective aimed originally at transforming state power into a vehicle of citizen empowerment and social justice is now used to legitimate marketization and state retrenchment.

4) *Feminist contra and pro Westphalianism resignified*: Finally, neoliberalism altered for better and for worse second-wave feminism's ambivalent relation to the Westphalian frame. In the new context of "globalization," it no longer goes without saying that the bounded territorial state is the sole legitimate container for obligations of, and struggles for, justice. Thus, feminists have joined environmentalists, human-rights activists, and critics of the WTO in challenging that view. Operationalizing post-Westphalian intuitions that had remained un-actionable in state-organized capitalism, they have targeted transborder injustices that had been marginalized or neglected in the previous era. Utilizing new communications technologies to establish transnational networks, feminists have pioneered innovative strategies like the "boomerang effect," which mobilizes global public opinion to spotlight local abuses and to shame the states that condone them.[13] The result was a promising new form of feminist activism—transnational, multi-scalar, post-Westphalian.

But the transnational turn brought difficulties too. Often stymied at the level of the state, many feminists directed their energies to the "international" arena, especially to a succession of UN-related conferences, from Nairobi to Vienna to Beijing and beyond. Building a presence in "global civil society" from which to engage new regimes of global governance, they became entangled in some of the problems I have already noted. For example, campaigns for women's human rights focused overwhelmingly on issues of violence and reproduction,

---

12   Uma Narayan, "Informal Sector Work, Micro-credit, and Third World Women's 'Empowerment': A Critical Perspective," paper presented at the XXII World Congress of Philosophy of Law and Social Philosophy, May 24–29, 2005, Granada, Spain. See also Carol Barton, "Global Women's Movements at a Crossroads," and Hester Eisenstein, "A Dangerous Liaison? Feminism and Corporate Globalization."

13   Margaret Keck and Kathryn Sikkink, *Activists beyond Borders: Advocacy Networks in International Politics*, Ithaca, NY: Cornell University Press, 1998.

as opposed, for example, to poverty. Ratifying the Cold War split between civil and political rights, on the one hand, and social and economic rights, on the other, these efforts, too, have privileged recognition over redistribution.[14] In addition, these campaigns intensified the NGO-ification of feminist politics, widening the gap between professionals and the grassroots, while according disproportionate voice to English-speaking elites. Analogous dynamics have been operating, too, in the feminist engagement with the policy apparatus of the European Union—especially given the absence of genuinely transnational, Europe-wide grassroots movements. Thus, the feminist critique of Westphalianism has proved ambivalent in the era of neoliberalism. What began as a salutary attempt to expand the scope of justice beyond the nation-state has ended up dovetailing in some respects with the administrative needs of a new form of capitalism.

In general, then, the fate of feminism in the neoliberal era presents a paradox. On the one hand, the relatively small countercultural movement of the previous period has expanded exponentially, successfully disseminating its ideas across the globe. On the other hand, feminist ideas have undergone a subtle shift in valence in the altered context. Unambiguously emancipatory in the era of state-organized capitalism, critiques of economism, androcentrism, étatism, and Westphalianism now appear fraught with ambiguity, susceptible to serving the legitimation needs of a new form of capitalism. After all, this capitalism would much prefer to confront claims for recognition over claims for redistribution, as it builds a new regime of accumulation on the cornerstone of women's waged labor and seeks to disembed markets from democratic political regulation in order to operate all the more freely on a global scale.

### 3. FEMINISM AGAINST NEOLIBERALISM?

Today, however, this capitalism is itself at a critical crossroads. The global financial crisis may mark the beginning of neoliberalism's end as an economic regime. Meanwhile, the associated political crisis (of the Westphalian state, of Europe, of US hegemony) may herald the dissolution of the order of governance in which neoliberalism thrived. Finally, the revival of anti-systemic protest (even if so far fragmented, ephemeral, and devoid of programmatic content) may signal the early stirrings of a new wave of mobilization aimed at articulating an alternative. Perhaps, accordingly, we stand poised at the brink of yet another "great transformation," as massive and profound as the one I have just described.

---

14    Carol Barton, "Global Women's Movements at a Crossroads."

If so, then the shape of the successor society will be the object of intense contestation in the coming period. And feminism will feature importantly in such contestation—in two different senses and at two different levels: first, as a social movement whose fortunes I have traced here, which will seek to ensure that the successor regime institutionalizes a commitment to gender justice; but also, second, as a general discursive construct that feminists in the first sense no longer own and do not control—an empty signifier of the good (akin, perhaps, to "democracy"), which can and will be invoked to legitimate a variety of different scenarios, not all of which promote gender justice. An offspring of feminism in the first, social-movement sense, this second, discursive sense of "feminism" has gone rogue. As the discourse becomes independent of the movement, the latter is increasingly confronted with a strange shadowy version of itself, an uncanny double that it can neither simply embrace nor wholly disavow.[15]

In this chapter, I have mapped the disconcerting dance of these two feminisms in the shift from state-organized capitalism to neoliberalism. What should we conclude from my story? Certainly not that second-wave feminism has failed *simpliciter*. Nor that it is to blame for the triumph of neoliberalism. Surely not that feminist ideals are inherently problematic; nor that they are always already doomed to be resignified for capitalist purposes. I conclude, rather, that we for whom feminism is above all a movement for gender justice need to become more historically self-aware as we operate on a terrain that is also populated by our uncanny double.

To that end, let us return to the question: What, if anything, explains our "dangerous liaison" with neoliberalism? Are we the victims of an unfortunate coincidence, who happened to be in the wrong place at the wrong time and so fell prey to the most opportunistic of seducers, a capitalism so indiscriminately promiscuous that it would instrumentalize any perspective whatever, even one inherently foreign to it? Or is there some subterranean elective affinity between feminism and neoliberalism? If any such affinity does exist, it lies, I suggest, in the critique of traditional authority.[16] Such authority is a longstanding target of feminist activism, which has sought at least since Mary Wollstonecraft to emancipate women from personalized subjection to men, be they fathers, brothers, priests, elders, or husbands. But traditional authority also appears in some periods as an

---

15  This formula of "feminism and its doubles" could be elaborated to good effect with respect to the 2008 US presidential election, where the uncanny doubles included both Hillary Clinton and Sarah Palin.

16  I owe this point to Eli Zaretsky (personal communication). Cf. Hester Eisenstein, "A Dangerous Liaison? Feminism and Corporate Globalization."

obstacle to capitalist expansion, part of the surrounding social substance in which markets have historically been embedded and which has served to confine economic rationality within a limited sphere.[17] In the current moment, these two critiques of traditional authority, the one feminist, the other neoliberal, appear to converge.

Where feminism and neoliberalism diverge, in contrast, is over post-traditional forms of gender subordination—constraints on women's lives that do not take the form of personalized subjection, but arise from structural or systemic processes in which the actions of many people are abstractly or impersonally mediated. A paradigm case is what Susan Okin has characterized as "a cycle of socially caused and distinctly asymmetric vulnerability by marriage," in which women's traditional responsibility for childrearing helps shape labor markets that disadvantage women, resulting in unequal power in the economic marketplace, which in turn reinforces, and exacerbates, unequal power in the family.[18] Such market-mediated processes of subordination are the very lifeblood of neoliberal capitalism. Today, accordingly, they should become a major focus of feminist critique, as we seek to distinguish ourselves from, and to avoid resignification by, neoliberalism. The point, of course, is not to drop the struggle against traditional male authority, which remains a necessary moment of feminist critique. It is, rather, to disrupt the easy passage from such critique to its neoliberal double—above all by reconnecting struggles against personalized subjection to the critique of a capitalist system that, while promising liberation, actually imposes a new mode of domination.

In hopes of advancing this agenda, I would like to conclude by revisiting one last time my four foci of feminist critique.

For an *anti-neoliberal anti-economism*: The crisis of neoliberalism offers the opportunity to reactivate the emancipatory promise of second-wave feminism. Adopting a fully three-dimensional account of injustice, we might now integrate in a more balanced way the dimensions of redistribution, recognition, and representation that splintered in the previous era. Grounding those indispensable aspects of feminist critique in a robust, updated sense of the social totality, we should reconnect feminist critique to the critique of capitalism—and thereby reposition feminism squarely on the Left.

For an *anti-neoliberal anti-androcentrism*: Likewise, the crisis of neoliberalism offers the chance to break the spurious link between our

---

17    In some periods, but not always. In many contexts, capitalism is more apt to adapt than to challenge traditional authority. For the embedding of markets, see Karl Polanyi, *The Great Transformation*, 2$^{nd}$ ed., Boston: Beacon, 1944 [2001]. For a feminist critique of Polanyi, see Chapter 10 of this volume, "Between Marketization and Social Protection."

18    Susan Moller Okin, *Justice, Gender, and the Family*, New York: Basic Books, 138.

critique of the family wage and flexible capitalism. Reclaiming our critique of androcentrism, feminists might militate for a form of life that decenters waged work and valorizes uncommodified activities, including, but not only, carework. Now performed largely by women, such activities should become valued components of a good life for everyone.

For an *anti-neoliberal anti-étatism*: The crisis of neoliberalism also offers the chance to break the spurious link between our critique of étatism and marketization. Reclaiming the mantel of participatory democracy, feminists might militate now for a new organization of political power, one that subordinates bureaucratic managerialism to citizen empowerment. The point, however, is not to dissipate but to strengthen public power. Thus, the democracy we seek today is one that fosters equal participation, while using politics to tame markets and to steer society in the interest of justice.

For an *anti-neoliberal post-Westphalianism*: Finally, the crisis of neoliberalism offers the chance to resolve, in a productive way, our longstanding ambivalence about the Westphalian frame. Given capital's transnational reach, the public capacities needed today cannot be lodged solely in the territorial state. Here, accordingly, the task is to break the exclusive identification of democracy with the bounded political community. Joining other progressive forces, feminists might militate now for a new, post-Westphalian political order—a multi-scalar order, democratic at every level and dedicated to overcoming injustice in every dimension, along every axis and on every scale.[19]

I am suggesting, then, that this is a moment in which feminists should think big. Having watched the neoliberal onslaught instrumentalize our best ideas, we have an opening now in which to reclaim them. In seizing this moment, we might just bend the arc of the impending great transformation in the direction of justice—and not only with respect to gender.

---

19   Fraser, *Scales of Justice*.

# 10

# Between Marketization and Social Protection: Resolving the Feminist Ambivalence

The current crisis of neoliberal capitalism is altering the landscape of feminist theory. During the last two decades, most theorists kept their distance from the sort of large-scale social theorizing associated with Marxism. Apparently accepting the necessity of academic specialization, they settled on one or another branch of disciplinary inquiry, conceived as a freestanding enterprise. Whether the focus was jurisprudence or moral philosophy, democratic theory or cultural criticism, the work proceeded in relative disconnection from fundamental questions of social theory. The critique of capitalist society—pivotal for earlier generations—all but vanished from the agenda of feminist theory. Critique centered on capitalist crisis was pronounced reductive, deterministic, and dépassé.

Today, however, such verities lie in tatters. With the global financial system teetering, worldwide production and employment in freefall, and the looming prospect of a prolonged recession, capitalist crisis supplies the inescapable backdrop for every serious attempt at critical theory. Henceforth, feminist theorists cannot avoid the question of capitalist society. Large-scale social theory, aimed at clarifying the nature and roots of crisis, as well as the prospects for an emancipatory resolution, promises to regain its place in feminist thought.

Yet how exactly should feminist theorists approach these matters? How to overcome the deficits of discredited economistic approaches, which focus exclusively on the "systemic logic" of the capitalist economy? How to develop an expanded, non-economistic understanding of capitalist society, which incorporates the insights of feminism, ecology, multiculturalism, and postcolonialism? How to conceptualize crisis as a *social* process in which economics is mediated by history, culture, geography, politics, ecology, and law? How to comprehend the full range of social struggles in the current conjuncture, and how assess the potential for emancipatory social transformation?

The thought of Karl Polanyi affords a promising starting point for such theorizing. His 1944 classic *The Great Transformation* elaborates an account of capitalist crisis as a multifaceted historical process that began with the industrial revolution in Britain and proceeded, over the course of more than a century, to envelop the entire world, entraining imperial subjection, periodic depressions, and cataclysmic wars.[1] For Polanyi, moreover, capitalist crisis was less about economic breakdown in the narrow sense than about disintegrated communities, ruptured solidarities, and despoiled nature. Its roots lay less in intra-economic contradictions, such as the tendency of the rate of profit to fall, than in a momentous shift in the place of economy vis-à-vis society. Overturning the heretofore universal relation, in which markets were embedded in social institutions and subject to moral and ethical norms, proponents of the "self-regulating market" sought to build a world in which society, morals, and ethics were subordinated to, indeed modeled on, markets. Conceiving labor, land, and money as "factors of production," they treated those fundamental bases of social life as if they were ordinary commodities and subjected them to market exchange. The effects of this "fictitious commodification," as Polanyi called it, were so destructive of habitats, livelihoods, and communities as to spark an ongoing counter-movement for the "protection of society." The result was a distinctive pattern of social conflict, which he called "the double movement": a spiraling conflict between free-marketeers, on the one hand, and social protectionists, on the other, which led to political stalemate and, ultimately, to fascism and World War II.

Here, then, is an account of capitalist crisis that transcends the cramped confines of economistic thinking. Masterful, capacious, and encompassing action at multiple scales, *The Great Transformation* weaves together local protest, national politics, international affairs, and global financial regimes in a powerful historical synthesis.

Of special interest to feminists, moreover, is the centrality of social reproduction in Polanyi's account. Granted, he does not himself use that expression. But the disintegration of social bonds is no less pivotal to his view of crisis than is the destruction of economic values—indeed those two manifestations are inextricably inter-twined. And capitalist crisis is in large part a *social* crisis, as untrammeled marketization endangers the fund of human capacities available to create and maintain social bonds. Because it foregrounds this social reproductive strand of capitalist crisis, Polanyi's thought resonates with recent feminist work on "social depletion" and the

---

1    Karl Polanyi, *The Great Transformation*, 2ⁿᵈ ed., Boston: Beacon Press, 1944 [2001].

"crisis of care."[2] His framework is capable, at least in principle, of embracing many feminist concerns.

These points alone would qualify Polanyi as a promising resource for feminists seeking to understand the travails of twenty-first-century capitalist society. But there are other, more specific reasons for turning to him today. The story told in *The Great Transformation* has strong echoes in current developments. Certainly, there is a *prima facie* case for the view that the present crisis has its roots in recent efforts to disencumber markets from the regulatory regimes (both national and international) established in the aftermath of World War II. What we today call "neoliberalism" is nothing but the second coming of the very same nineteenth-century faith in the "self-regulating market" that unleashed the capitalist crisis Polanyi chronicled. Now, as then, attempts to implement that creed are spurring efforts to commodify nature, labor, and money: witness the burgeoning markets in carbon emissions and biotechnology; in child-care, schooling, and the care of the old; and in financial derivatives. Now, as then, the effect is to despoil nature, rupture communities, and destroy livelihoods. Today, moreover, as in Polanyi's time, counter-movements are mobilizing to protect society and nature from the ravages of the market. Now, as then, struggles over nature, social reproduction, and global finance constitute the central nodes and flashpoints of crisis. On its face, then, today's crisis is plausibly viewed as a second great transformation, a "great transformation" redux.

For many reasons, Polanyi's perspective holds considerable promise for theorizing today. Yet feminists should not rush to embrace it uncritically. Even as it overcomes economism, *The Great Transformation* turns out, on closer inspection, to be deeply flawed. Focused single-mindedly on harms emanating from disembedded markets, the book overlooks harms originating elsewhere, in the surrounding "society." Occulting non-market-based forms of injustice, it also tends to whitewash forms of social protection that are at the same time vehicles of domination. Focused overwhelmingly on struggles against market-based depredations, the book neglects struggles against injustices rooted in "society" and encoded in social protections.

Thus, feminist theorists should not embrace Polanyi's framework in

---

2  Recent feminist accounts of social reproduction, "social depletion," and the "crisis of care" include *Power, Production, and Social Reproduction: Human In/Security in the Global Political Economy*, eds. Isabella Bakker and Steven Gill, New York: Palgrave MacMillan, 2003; Arlie Hochschild, *The Commercialization of Intimate Life: Notes from Home and Work*, Berkeley, CA: University of California Press, 2003; Shirin Rai, Catherine Hoskyns, and Dania Thomas, "Depletion and Social Reproduction," CSGR Working Paper 274/11, Warwick University: Centre for the Study of Globalisation and Regionalisation, available at www2.warwick.ac.uk; and Silvia Federici, *Revolution at Point Zero: Housework, Reproduction, and Feminist Struggle*, New York: PM Press, 2012.

the form in which appears in *The Great Transformation*. What is needed, rather, is a revision of that framework. The goal should be a new, quasi-Polanyian conception of capitalist crisis that not only avoids reductive economism but also avoids romanticizing "society."

That is my aim in the present chapter. Seeking to develop a critique that comprehends "society" as well as "economy," I propose to broaden Polanyi's problematic to encompass a third historical project of social struggle that crosscuts his central conflict between marketization and social protection. This third project, which I shall call "emancipation," aims to overcome forms of subjection rooted in "society." Central to both iterations of the great transformation, the one analyzed by Polanyi and the one we are living through now, struggles for emancipation constitute the missing third that mediates every conflict between marketization and social protection. The effect of introducing this missing third will be to transform the double movement into a *triple movement*, encompassing marketization, social protection, and emancipation.

The triple movement will form the core of a new, quasi-Polanyian perspective that can clarify the stakes for feminists in the present capitalist crisis. After elaborating this new perspective in sections one through four of this chapter, I will use it in sections five through seven to analyze the *ambivalence* of feminist politics.

## 1. POLANYI'S KEY CONCEPTS: DISEMBEDDED MARKETS, SOCIAL PROTECTION, AND THE DOUBLE MOVEMENT

I begin by recalling Polanyi's distinction between embedded and disembedded markets. Integral to *The Great Transformation*, this distinction carries strong evaluative connotations, which need to be subject to feminist scrutiny.

Famously, Polanyi distinguished two different relations in which markets can stand to society. On the one hand, markets can be "embedded," enmeshed in non-economic institutions and subject to non-economic norms, such as "the just price" and "the fair wage." On the other hand, markets can be "disembedded," freed from extra-economic controls and governed immanently, by supply and demand. The first possibility, claims Polanyi, represents the historical norm; throughout most of history, in otherwise disparate civilizations and in widely separated locales, markets have been subject to non-economic controls, which limit what can be bought and sold, by whom, and on what terms. The second possibility is historically anomalous; a nineteenth-century British invention, the "self-regulating market" was an utterly novel idea whose deployment, Polanyi contends, threatens the very fabric of human society.

For Polanyi, markets can never in fact be fully disembedded from the larger society. The attempt to make them so must inexorably fail.

For one thing, markets can function properly only against a non-economic background of cultural understandings and solidary relations; attempts to disembed them destroy that background. For another, the attempt to establish "self-regulating markets" proves destructive of the fabric of society, provoking widespread demands for their social regulation. Far from enhancing social cooperation, then, the project of disembedding markets inevitably triggers social crisis.

It is in these terms that *The Great Transformation* recounts a capitalist crisis that stretched from the industrial revolution to World War II. For Polanyi, moreover, the crisis encompassed not only the efforts of commercial interests to disembed markets, but also the combined counter-efforts of rural landowners, urban workers, and other strata to defend "society" against "economy." For Polanyi, finally, it was the sharpening struggle between these two camps, the marketizers and the protectionists, that lent the distinctive shape of a "double movement" to the crisis. If the first prong of that movement took us from a mercantilist phase, in which markets were socially and politically embedded, to a laisser-faire phase, in which they became (relatively) disembedded, the second prong should carry us, so Polanyi hoped, to a new phase, in which markets would be re-embedded in democratic welfare states. The effect would be to return the economy to its proper place in society.

In general, then, the distinction between embedded and disembedded markets is integral to all of Polanyi's central concepts, including society, protection, crisis, and the double movement. Equally important, the distinction is strongly evaluative. Embedded markets are associated with social protection, figured as shelter from the harsh elements. Disembedded markets are associated with exposure, with being left to swim naked in "the icy waters of egotistical calculation."[3] These inflections—embedded markets are good, disembedded markets bad—carry over to the double movement. The first, exposing movement, signifies danger; the second, protective movement, connotes safe haven.

What should feminists make of these ideas? On its face, the distinction between embedded and disembedded markets has much to offer to feminist theorizing. For one thing, it points beyond economism, to an expansive understanding of capitalist crisis as a multifaceted historical process, as much social, political, and ecological as economic. For another, it points beyond functionalism, grasping crisis, not as an objective "system breakdown," but as an *intersubjective* process that includes the responses of social actors to perceived shifts in their

---

3  Karl Marx and Friedrich Engels, "The Communist Manifesto" (1848), in *The Marx-Engels Reader*, 2nd edition, ed. Robert C. Tucker, New York: W.W. Norton & Company, 1978, 475.

situation and to one another. Then, too, Polanyi's distinction makes possible a crisis critique that does not reject markets as such, but only the dangerous, disembedded, variety. Consequently, the concept of an embedded market affords the prospect of a progressive alternative both to the wanton disembedding promoted by neoliberals and to the wholesale suppression of markets traditionally favored by communists.

Nevertheless, the evaluative subtext of Polanyi's categories is problematic. On the one hand, his account of embedded markets and social protections is far too rosy. Romanticizing "society," it occults the fact that the communities in which markets have historically been embedded have also been the locus of domination. Conversely, Polanyi's account of disembedding is far too dark. Having idealized society, it occludes the fact that, whatever their other effects, processes that disembed markets from oppressive protections contain an emancipatory moment.

Thus, present-day feminist theorists must revise this framework. Avoiding both wholesale condemnation of disembedding and wholesale approbation of (re-)embedding, we must open *both* prongs of the double movement to critical scrutiny. Exposing the normative deficits of "society," as well as those of "economy," we must validate struggles against domination *wherever* it roots.

To this end, I propose to draw on a resource not utilized by Polanyi, namely, the insights of feminist movements. Unmasking power asymmetries occluded by him, these movements exposed the predatory underside of the embedded markets he tended to idealize. Protesting protections that were also oppressions, they raised claims for emancipation. Exploiting their insights, and drawing on the benefits of hindsight, I propose to rethink the double movement in relation to feminist struggles for *emancipation*.

## 2. EMANCIPATION: THE MISSING "THIRD"

To speak of emancipation is to introduce a category that does not appear in *The Great Transformation*. But the idea, and indeed the word, figured importantly throughout the period Polanyi chronicled. One need only mention epochal struggles to abolish slavery, liberate women, and free non-European peoples from colonial subjection—all waged in the name of "emancipation." It is surely odd that these struggles should be absent from a work purporting to chart the rise and fall of what it calls "nineteenth-century civilization." But my point is not simply to flag an omission. It is rather to note that struggles for emancipation directly challenged oppressive forms of social protection, while neither wholly condemning nor simply celebrating marketization. Had they been included, these movements would have destabilized the dualistic narrative schema of *The Great Transformation*. The effect would have been to explode the double movement.

To see why, consider that emancipation differs importantly from Polanyi's chief positive category, social protection. Whereas protection is opposed to exposure, emancipation is opposed to domination. While protection aims to shield "society" from the disintegrative effects of unregulated markets, emancipation aims to expose relations of domination wherever they root, in society as well as in economy. While the thrust of protection is to subject market exchange to non-economic norms, that of emancipation is to subject both market exchange and non-market norms to critical scrutiny. Finally, whereas protection's highest values are social security, stability, and solidarity, emancipation's priority is non-domination.

It would be wrong, however, to conclude that emancipation is always allied with marketization. If emancipation opposes domination, marketization opposes the extra-economic regulation of production and exchange, whether such regulation is meant to protect or to liberate. While marketization defends the supposed autonomy of the economy, understood formally as a demarcated sphere of instrumental action, emancipation ranges across the boundaries that demarcate spheres, seeking to root out domination from *every* "sphere."[4] While the thrust of marketization is to liberate buying and selling from moral and ethical norms, that of emancipation is to scrutinize *all* types of norms from the standpoint of justice. Finally, whereas marketization claims efficiency, individual choice, and the negative liberty of non-interference as its highest values, emancipation's priority, as I said, is non-domination.

It follows that struggles for emancipation do not map neatly onto either prong of Polanyi's double movement. Granted, such struggles appear on occasion to converge with marketization—as, for example, when they condemn as oppressive the very social protections that free-marketeers are seeking to eradicate. On other occasions, however, they converge with protectionist projects—as, for example, when they denounce the oppressive effects of marketization. On still other occasions, struggles for emancipation diverge from both prongs of the double movement—as, for example, when they aim neither to dismantle nor to defend existing protections, but rather to transform the mode of protection. Thus, convergences, where they exist, are conjunctural and contingent. Aligned consistently neither with protection nor marketization, struggles for emancipation represent a

---

4   For an account of the official economic realm as both institutionally demarcated from and suffused with lifeworld norms, see Chapter 1 of this volume, "What's Critical About Critical Theory?"

third force that disrupts Polanyi's dualistic schema. To give such struggles their due requires us to revise his framework—by transforming its
double movement into a triple movement.[5]

## 3. EMANCIPATION FROM HIERARCHICAL PROTECTIONS

To see why, consider feminist claims for emancipation. These claims
explode the double movement by disclosing a specific way in which
social protections can be oppressive: namely, in virtue of entrenching
status hierarchies. Such protections deny some who are included in principle as members of society the social preconditions for full participation
in social interaction.[6] The classic example is gender hierarchy, which
assigns women a lesser status, often akin to that of a male child, and
thereby prevents them from participating fully, on a par with men, in
social interaction. But one could also cite caste hierarchies, including
those premised on racialist ideologies. In all such cases, social protections
work to the advantage of those at the top of the status hierarchy, affording
lesser (if any) benefit to those at the bottom. What they protect, accordingly, is less society *per se* than social hierarchy. No wonder, then, that
feminist, anti-racist, and anti-caste movements have mobilized against
such hierarchies, rejecting the protections they purport to offer. Insisting
on full membership in society, they have sought to dismantle arrangements that deny them the social prerequisites of participatory parity.[7]

---

5    For a fuller account of "emancipation" as a third pole of social aspiration, not
reducible to protection or marketization, see Nancy Fraser, "Marketization, Social
Protection, Emancipation: Toward a Neo-Polanyian Conception of Capitalist Crisis,"
in *Business as Usual: The Roots of the Global Financial Meltdown*, eds. Craig Calhoun and
Georgi Derlugian, New York: New York University Press, 2011, 137–58.

6    Hierarchy is not the only way in which social protections can be oppressive.
The arrangements that embed markets can also be oppressive in a second way: in
virtue of being "misframed." *Misframing* is a neologism I have coined for mismatches
of scale—in this case between the scale at which markets are embedded, which is
usually national, and that at which they expose people to danger, which is often
transnational. The oppression of misframing arises when protective arrangements
externalize the negative effects of markets onto "outsiders," wrongly excluding
some of those exposed, while saddling them with the costs of protecting others. For
the general concept of misframing, see "Reframing Justice," Chapter 8 of this
volume. For an account of colonialism and its neo-imperial successor regimes as
paradigmatic cases of misframed protections, and indeed as protection rackets, see
Nancy Fraser, "Marketization, Social Protection, Emancipation."

7    For an account of participatory parity as a principle of justice, see "Feminist
Politics in the Age of Recognition," Chapter 6 of this volume. For a fuller defense
of this principle, see Nancy Fraser, "Social Justice in the Age of Identity Politics:
Redistribution, Recognition, and Participation," in Nancy Fraser and Axel
Honneth, *Redistribution or Recognition? A Political-Philosophical Exchange*, trans. Joel
Golb, James Ingram, and Christiane Wilke, London: Verso Books, 2003.

The feminist critique of hierarchical protection runs through every stage of Polanyi's history, although it is never mentioned by him. During the mercantilist era, feminists like Mary Wollstonecraft criticized the traditional social arrangements that embedded markets. Condemning gender hierarchies entrenched in family, religion, law, and social custom, they demanded such fundamental prerequisites of participatory parity as an independent legal personality, religious freedom, education, the right to refuse sex, rights of custody in children, and the right to speak in public and to vote. During the laisser-faire period, feminists demanded equal access to the market. Exposing the latter's instrumentalization of sexist norms, they opposed protections that denied them the right to own property, sign contracts, control wages, practice professions, work the same hours and receive the same pay as men, all prerequisites of full participation in social life. During the post-WWII era, "second-wave" feminists targeted the "public patriarchy" instituted by welfare states. Condemning social protections premised on "the family wage," they demanded equal pay for work of comparable worth, parity for caregiving and wage-earning in social entitlements, and an end to the gender division of labor, both paid and unpaid.[8]

In each of these epochs, feminists raised claims for emancipation, aimed at overcoming domination. At some moments, they targeted traditional community structures that *embedded* markets; at others, they aimed their fire at the forces that were *dis*embedding markets; at still others, their principal foes were those who were *re*-embedding markets in oppressive ways. Thus, feminist claims did not align consistently with either pole of Polanyi's double movement. On the contrary, their struggles for emancipation constituted a third prong of social movement, which cut across the other two. What Polanyi called a double movement was actually a triple movement.

## 4. CONCEPTUALIZING THE TRIPLE MOVEMENT

But what exactly does it mean to speak of a "triple movement"? This figure conceptualizes capitalist crisis as a three-sided conflict among forces of marketization, social protection, and emancipation. It understands each of these three terms as conceptually irreducible, normatively ambivalent, and inextricably entangled with the other two. We have already seen, contra Polanyi, that social protection is often ambivalent, affording relief from the disintegrative effects of marketization, while simultaneously entrenching domination. But, as we shall see, the same is true of the other two terms. The disembedding of markets does indeed have the

---

8  For the second-wave feminist critique of "public patriarchy" and the family wage, see Chapters 2, 3, and 4 of this volume.

negative effects Polanyi stressed, but it can also beget positive effects to the extent that the protections it disintegrates are oppressive. Nor is emancipation immune to ambivalence, as it produces not only liberation but also strains in the fabric of existing solidarities; even as it dismantles domination, emancipation can also dissolve the solidary ethical basis of social protection, thereby clearing the way for marketization.

Seen this way, each term has both a *telos* of its own and a potential for ambivalence that unfolds through its interaction with the other two terms. None of the three can be adequately grasped in isolation from the others. Nor can the social field be adequately grasped by focusing on only two terms. It is only when all three are considered together that we begin to get an adequate view of the grammar of social struggle in capitalist crisis.

Here, then, is the core premise of the triple movement: the relation between any two sides of the three-sided conflict must be mediated by the third. Thus, as I have just argued, the conflict between marketization and social protection must be mediated by emancipation. Equally, however, as I will argue next, conflicts between protection and emancipation must be mediated by marketization. In both cases, the dyad must be mediated by the third. To neglect the third is to distort the logic of capitalist crisis and of social movement.[9]

## 5. THE TABLES TURNED: EMANCIPATION'S AMBIVALENCE IN THE NEW GREAT TRANSFORMATION

So far, I have been using the triple movement to explore the ambivalence of social protection. Now, however, I want to turn the tables and use the triple movement to explore the ambivalences of emancipation. Thus, having just stressed the need to view conflicts between marketization and social protection as mediated by emancipation, a mediation Polanyi neglected, I want now to stress the need to view conflicts between protection and emancipation as mediated by marketization, a mediation that I believe has been neglected by important currents of the feminist movement.

Here, accordingly, I shift the focus to the "great transformation" of our own time. To understand this transformation, we must begin with the "Embedded Liberalism" that was established in the aftermath of World War II.[10] Underpinned by the international regulatory frame-

---

9  For a fuller discussion of the triple movement, see Fraser, "Marketization, Social Protection, Emancipation."

10  I borrow the phrase "Embedded Liberalism," as well as the concept, from John G. Ruggie, "International Regimes, Transactions, and Change: Embedded Liberalism in the Postwar Economic Order," *International Organization* 36:2, 1982, 379–415.

work known as Bretton Woods, Embedded Liberalism encompassed the Keynesian welfare states of the First World and the developmental states of the Third. Since the 1980s, however, those arrangements have come under pressure from neoliberalism, which has promoted the renewed disembedding of markets, thereby provoking the most severe capitalist crisis since the Great Depression.

Let us then analyze the current crisis by means of the figure of the triple movement, just as Polanyi used the double movement to understand the previous crisis. For us, as for him, the point is to clarify prospects for a new wave of democratic re-embedding, stabilized by a global regime of political-economic regulation. For us, however, social protection must be re-envisioned in the light of emancipation. Thus, our task is to envision arrangements for re-embedding markets that simultaneously serve to overcome domination.

I begin by noting that, in our time, each prong of the triple movement has zealous exponents. Marketization is fervently championed by neoliberals. Social protection commands support in various forms, some savory, some unsavory—from nationally oriented social democrats and trade-unionists to anti-immigrant populist movements, from neotraditional religious movements to anti-globalization activists, from environmentalists to indigenous peoples. Emancipation fires the passions of various successors to the new social movements, including multiculturalists, international feminists, gay and lesbian liberationists, cosmopolitan democrats, human-rights activists, and proponents of global justice. It is the complex relations among these three types of projects that impress the shape of a triple movement on the present crisis of capitalist society.

Consider, now, the role of emancipatory projects within this constellation. Since at least the 1960s, such movements have challenged oppressive aspects of social protection in Embedded Liberalism. Earlier, New Leftists exposed the oppressive character of bureaucratically organized welfare regimes, which disempower their ostensible beneficiaries. Likewise, anti-imperialists unmasked the oppressive character of First World social protections that were financed through unequal exchange, on the backs of ex-colonial peoples. More recently, multiculturalists have disclosed the oppressive character of social protections premised on majority religious or majority ethnocultural self-understandings, which penalize members of minority groups. Finally, and most important for my purposes here, second-wave feminists have exposed the oppressive character of social protections premised on gender hierarchies.

In each case, the movement disclosed a type of domination and raised a corresponding claim for emancipation. In each case, too, however, the movement's claims for emancipation were ambivalent—they could line up in principle either with marketization or with social protection. In the first case, where emancipation aligned with

marketization, it would serve to erode not just the oppressive dimension, but social protection *simpliciter*. In the second case, where
emancipation aligned with social protection, it would serve not to
erode, but rather to transform, the mode of protection.

This argument holds, I claim, for all the emancipatory movements
I just mentioned. Here, however, I focus on second-wave feminism's
critique of an oppressive dimension of social protection in Embedded
Liberalism. Too often, I argue, this movement saw itself as locked in a
two-sided struggle. Focused on opposing oppressive protections, it
was not always sufficiently aware of the triple movement's third prong,
namely, efforts to extend and autonomize markets. Neglecting the
rise of neoliberalism, many second-wave feminists misunderstood
their situation and misjudged the likely consequences of their actions.
The result of their failure to mediate the conflict between emancipation and social protection with reference to marketization is even now
shaping the course of capitalist crisis in the twenty-first century.[11]

## 6. FEMINIST AMBIVALENCES

Recall that second-wave feminism targeted the gender-hierarchical
character of social protections in the postwar welfare state. In the US,
this meant exposing the gender subtext of a system divided into stigmatized poor relief for women and children, on the one hand, and
respectable social insurance for those constructed as "workers," on the
other. In Europe, it meant disclosing a related androcentric hierarchy
in the division between mothers' pensions and social entitlements tied
to waged work. In both cases, feminists discerned traces of an older
schema, inherited from before the War, known as "the family wage."
That schema envisioned the ideal-typical citizen as a breadwinner and
a family man, whose wage was the principal, if not the sole, economic
support of his family, and whose wife's wages, if any, were supplemental. Deeply gendered, this "family wage" ideal supplied a central
portion of the ethical substance on which postwar welfare states drew
to re-embed markets. Normalizing women's dependency, the resulting system of social protection compromised women's chances to
participate fully, on a par with men, in social life. Institutionalizing
androcentric understandings of family and work, it naturalized gender
hierarchy and removed it from political contestation. Equally important, by valorizing waged work, Embedded Liberalism's mode of
protection obscured the social importance of unwaged carework.[12]

---

11  See "Feminism, Capitalism, and the Cunning of History," Chapter 9 of this
volume.

12  See "A Genealogy of 'Dependency': Tracing a Keyword of the US Welfare

Such was the feminist critique of Embedded Liberalism. Politically and intellectually powerful, this critique was nonetheless ambivalent, capable of leading in either of two directions. Taken one way, the feminist critique of the family wage would aim to secure women's full access to employment and to employment-linked entitlements on a par with men. In that case, it would tend to valorize wage labor and the androcentric ideal of individual independence, effectively devaluing unwaged carework, interdependence, and solidarity.[13] Targeting the traditional gender ethos that was still serving to embed markets, a feminism of this sort could end up furthering their disembedding. Intentional or not, the effect could be to align the struggle against gender hierarchy with marketization.

In principle, however, the feminist critique of oppressive protection could develop in another way. Differently articulated, the feminist struggle for emancipation could align with the other pole of the triple movement, the pole of social protection. In this second scenario, the thrust of feminist critique would be to reject androcentric valuations, especially the overvaluation of waged labor and the undervaluation of unwaged carework. Casting carework as a matter of public importance, the movement's thrust would be to re-envision social arrangements in a way that enabled everyone—male or female—to perform both sets of activities, without the strains that beset all such efforts today. Rejecting, too, the gender-coded opposition between dependence and independence, a pro-protectionist feminism would serve to break the spurious link between social hierarchy and the dependency that is a universal feature of the human condition.[14] Valorizing solidarity and interdependence, the critique would work not to dissolve, but to transform social protections.

As a matter of fact, second-wave feminism encompassed both orientations. For the most part, so-called liberal and radical feminists gravitated in the direction of marketization, while socialist-feminists and feminists of color were more likely to align with forces for social protection. In the first case, the alignment was not always intended. Not all liberal and radical feminists consciously aimed to replace the family wage with the two-earner family. But by failing to situate their struggle for emancipation in the context of the triple movement, they could end up unwittingly abetting the forces seeking to disembed and deregulate markets. In the other case, by contrast, the alignment was

---

State," Chapter 3 of this volume.

13   This approach resembles the Universal Breadwinner model I criticized in "After the Family Wage," Chapter 4 of this volume.

14   This approach resembles the Universal Caregiver model I advocated in "After the Family Wage," Chapter 4 of this volume.

relatively conscious. Feminists whose concerns dovetailed with protectionist forces tended to have an intuitive grasp of the logic of the triple movement. They were often aware that their struggle for emancipation intersected with another struggle, between protection and deregulation. Positioning themselves in a three-sided game, they sought to avoid abetting the forces of marketization, even while vigorously opposing oppressive protections.

Arguably, feminist ambivalence has been resolved in recent years in favor of marketization. Insufficiently attuned to the rise of free-market fundamentalism, mainstream feminists have ended up supplying the rationale for a new mode of capital accumulation, heavily dependent on women's wage labor. As women have streamed into labor markets across the globe, the ideal of the family wage is losing ground to the newer, more modern norm of the two-earner family. Certainly, the reality that underlies the new ideal is catastrophic for many: depressed wage levels, decreased job security, declining living standards, a steep rise in the number of hours worked for wages per household, and exacerbation of the double shift—now often a triple or quadruple shift. But neoliberalism cloaks its depredations beneath an enchanting, charismatic veil: invoking the feminist critique of the family wage, it promises liberation through waged labor in the service of capital. Clearly, feminist ideas suffuse the experience of the female cadres of the professional middle classes, determined to crack the glass ceiling. Equally, however, they lend a higher meaning and moral point to the daily struggles of millions of female temps, part-timers, low-wage service workers, domestics, sex workers, migrants, EPZ workers, and micro-credit borrowers, who seek not only income and security, but also dignity, self-betterment, and liberation from traditional authority. In both cases, the dream of women's emancipation is harnessed to the engine of capital accumulation. Thus, feminism's critique of the family wage has assumed a marketizing valence. Once capable of aligning with social protection, it serves increasingly today to intensify neoliberalism's valorization of waged labor.[15]

## 7. FOR A NEW ALLIANCE OF EMANCIPATION WITH SOCIAL PROTECTION

What should we conclude from this account? Certainly not that second-wave feminism has failed *simpliciter*. Nor that it is to blame for the triumph of neoliberalism. Surely not that struggles for emancipation are inherently problematic, always already doomed to be

---

15   For the argument that feminism has ended up supplying a portion of the "new spirit of capitalism," see "Feminism, Capitalism, and the Cunning of History," Chapter 9 of this volume.

recuperated for marketizing projects. I conclude, rather, that we who aim to emancipate women from gender hierarchy need to become more aware that we operate on a terrain that is also populated by marketizing forces. Above all, we need to reckon with emancipation's inherent ambivalence, its capacity to go in either of two directions—to ally either with the forces of marketization or with those promoting social protection. Only by appreciating this ambivalence, and by anticipating its potential unintended effects, can we undertake collective political reflection on how we might best resolve it.

Let me return to the larger questions that have inspired this chapter. Reflecting on the great transformation we are living through now, I have effectively rewritten Polanyi's project. By theorizing the double movement, he portrayed the conflicts of his time as an epochal battle for the soul of the market: Will nature, labor, and money be stripped of all ethical meaning, sliced, diced, and traded like widgets, and to hell with the consequences? Or will markets in those fundamental bases of human society be subject to ethically and morally informed political regulation? That battle remains as pressing as ever in the twenty-first century. But the triple movement casts it in a sharper light, as crosscut by two other major battles of epochal significance. One is a battle for the soul of social protection. Will the arrangements that re-embed markets in the post-neoliberal era be oppressive or emancipatory, hierarchical or egalitarian—and we might add, misframed or well-framed, difference-hostile or difference-friendly, bureaucratic or participatory? That battle, too, is as pressing as ever. But it is crosscut by yet another epochal battle—in this case for the soul of emancipation. Will the emancipatory struggles of the twenty-first century serve to advance the disembedding and deregulation of markets? Or will they serve to extend and democratize social protections and to make them more just?

These questions suggest a project for those of us who remain committed to emancipation. We might resolve to break off our dangerous liaison with marketization and forge a principled new alliance with social protection.[16] In realigning the poles of the triple movement, we could integrate our longstanding interest in non-domination with legitimate interests in solidarity and social security, without neglecting the importance of negative liberty. Embracing a broader understanding of social justice, such a project would serve at once to honor Polanyi's insights and remedy his blindspots.

---

16  I borrow the phrase "dangerous liaison" from Hester Eisenstein, "A Dangerous Liaison? Feminism and Corporate Globalization," *Science and Society* 69:3, 2005, 487–518.

# INDEX

abortion 58
action contexts 24–30
African-Americans: AFDC claimants 75, 78–79, 104; dependency 103–4
Aid to Families with Dependent Children (AFDC) 75, 78–79, 86, 97, 104, 106, 171n
American Psychiatric Association 102–3
American Revolution, the 95
androcentrism 2, 14, 120–21, 128, 132, 133, 134, 162, 172, 213; capitalist 211, 213, 215–16, 217, 219–21; Marxist 23n; neoliberal 219–21, 225–26
apolitical countercultural activity 49
Arendt, Hannah 64, 66, 197

Bakhtin, Mikhail 58n
Beck, Ulrich 13
bodies, social construction of 48
Boltanski, Luc 14, 210, 219–20
Bourdieu, Pierre 59n
Braybrooke, David 56n
Bretton Woods system 189, 214, 218, 237
Brown, Carol 44
Butler, Judith 153–54; achievements 175; analysis of heterosexism 178–83; destabilization argument 185; economic/cultural distinction 184–85; material harms cited by 179–80; "Merely Cultural" 11–12, 175; rebuttal of 11–12, 175–86

Cameron, Deborah 147
capitalism 1, 3; androcentrism 211, 213, 215–16, 217, 219–21; classical 40; crisis of 5, 16, 227–28, 231, 235–36, 236–38; economism 212–13, 214–15, 217, 219; étatism 213, 216, 217, 221–22; and the family 29; feminist critique 211, 212–17; industrial 89–95, 109; inter-institutional relations in classical 32–39; moral-cultural dimension 26; neoliberal 211,

223–26; postindustrial 112–13; regulation of sexuality 180–83; rise of 12; rise of neoliberalism 217–23; second-wave feminism and 14–15, 209–26; state-organized 212–17, 220, 224; welfare-state 33, 51; Westphalianism 213–14, 216–17, 222–23
capitalist economy 26–27
capitalist paid work 22–23
Caregiver Parity model 9, 114, 128–32, 133
carework 121, 124–25, 128–32, 133–35, 215–16, 238, 239
Chiapello, Eve 14, 210, 219–20
child abuse 74
childrearing 21–22, 23–24, 31, 32, 36, 39, 50, 128
citizenship 36–39, 50, 90
civil society 64n, 120, 133
class compromise 3
Clinton, Bill 124n, 221
Cloward, Richard A. 78–79
codependency 102
colonial native dependency 92–93
communication 30, 48, 49, 72–73
communicative action 24n
communicative ethics 80n
communicatively achieved action 29–30
Communism, fall of 4
comparable worth 125, 126, 172–73
consumer role, the 35–36, 40, 43–44
consumption 35–36
crisis-management 43
Critical Theory 1–2, 6–7, 19–51; action contexts 24–30; definition 19–20; Habermas's society model 27–32; legal 81–82; public-private separation 32–39; socialist-feminist 51n, 53–82; social-theoretical categorical framework 21–32; and welfare-state capitalism 40–50
cultural feminism 9, 160